Bush base: forest farm

The relationship between humans and their natural surroundings is a paradoxical one. Humans impose their knowledge and will on the world around them, yet at the same time subscribe to myths and beliefs which portray them and their natural surroundings as inseparable, with neither more powerful than the other. This paradox is explored in the essays in *Bush Base: Forest Farm*, which uses an anthropological perspective to direct new light on development and environmental studies.

The contributors, all anthropologists who have had practical experience of development programmes, present case studies drawn from Africa and Asia, and reflect upon their theoretical implications. They reject the traditional sharp dichotomies of human settlement and external natural environment – farm or camp on the one hand, and forest or bush on the other – and suggest instead that the people, their indigenous knowledge and their forest or bush exist within each other. They argue that although the concept of sustainable development takes greater cognisance of the environment, there is still a need to place at their centre an appreciation of people's cosmologies and cultural understandings.

Combining practical experience and theoretical rigour, the book looks critically at a number of key approaches to third world development. It will be essential reading for students, teachers and policy makers in anthropology, development studies and environment studies.

Elisabeth Croll and **David Parkin** are members of the Department of Anthropology at the School of Oriental and African Studies, University of London.

EIDOS (European Inter-University Development Opportunities Study Group) was founded in 1985 and brought together British, Dutch and German anthropologists actively engaged in the study of development. The broad purpose of EIDOS workshops has been to assess critically the dissemination and specialization of anthropological and sociological knowledge in different European centres and to further the understanding of the ways in which that knowledge has directly influenced development.

Bush base: forest farm

Culture, environment and development

Edited by Elisabeth Croll and David Parkin

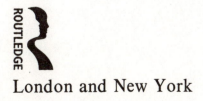

London and New York

First published 1992
by Routledge
11 New Fetter Lane, London EC4P 4EE

Simultaneously published in the USA and Canada
by Routledge
a division of Routledge, Chapman and Hall, Inc.
29 West 35th Street, New York, NY 10001

Reprinted in 1997

Printed and bound in Great Britain by
Mackays of Chatham PLC, Chatham, Kent

British Library Cataloguing in Publication Data
A catalogue record for this book is available from the British Library.

Library of Congress Cataloguing in Publication Data
A catalogue record for this book is available from the Library of Congress.

ISBN 0–415–06656–5 (hbk)
ISBN 0–415–06657–3 (pbk)

Contents

Figures and tables

FIGURES

TABLES

Contributors

Pieteke M. Banga: the State University of Utrecht, Department of Social Anthropology, Utrecht, The Netherlands.

Elisabeth Croll: Departmeent of Anthropology at the School of Oriental and African Studies, London.

Carol A. Drijver: the PED, Leiden, The Netherlands.

Michael Drinkwater: the Department of Rural Sociology, The Agricultural University, Wageningen, The Netherlands.

Tim Ingold: the Department of Social Anthropology, University of Manchester, Manchester.

Igor Krupnik: the Scott Polar Research Institute, University of Cambridge, Cambridge.

Melissa Leach: the Institute of Development Studies, University of Sussex, Brighton.

Augustin Nkundabashaka: Faculté de Sciences Economique, Sociales et de Gestion, Université Nationale du Rwanda.

David Parkin: Department of Anthropology at the School of Oriental and African Studies, London.

Gerard Persoon: CML, Leiden, The Netherlands.

Johan Pottier: the School of Oriental and African Studies, London.

Günther Schlee: the Sociology of Development Research Centre, Universität Bielefeld, Bielefeld, Germany.

Rosalind Shaw: the Department of Sociology and Anthropology, Tufts University, Massachusetts, USA.

Walter E. A. van Beek: the State University of Utrecht, Department of Social Anthropology, Utrecht, The Netherlands.

Jan P. M. van den Breemer: the Institute of Cultural and Social Studies, Leiden University, Leiden, The Netherlands.

Piers Vitebsky: the Scott Polar Research Institute, University of Cambridge, Cambridge.

Preface

The chapters in this collection were first presented at a workshop at the School of Oriental and African Studies, University of London in June 1989. It was organized under the auspices of EIDOS (European Inter-University Development Opportunities Study-Group), which was founded in 1985 and brought together British, Dutch and German anthropologists studying development discourse. Currently, the main participating institutions are the Department of Anthropology and Sociology, School of Oriental and African Studies, University of London; the Institute of Cultural Anthropology/Non-Western Sociology, the Free University, Amsterdam; the Department of Rural Sociology, the Agricultural University, Wageningen; and the Sociology of Development Research Centre, University of Bielefeld, West Germany. EIDOS also has a wide network of participating social anthropologists and sociologists from other European institutes.

EIDOS's aim is to critically assess the dissemination and specialization of anthropological and sociological knowledge and development studies in different European centres by arranging student exchanges and by providing support for a series of workshops. The purpose of EIDOS workshops is to further understanding of how anthropological and sociological debates inform meanings and concepts of development, development priorities, patterns and projects, and the socio-cultural inputs to and consequences of new development programmes. The workshops examine new approaches to a number of the more specific and intractable problems of social and economic development including practice and policy transformation in development; indigenous knowledge and the generation of ignorance; the analysis of power relations and resource distribution between interest groups, actors and institutions; and organizational linkages and the 'translation' of meaning and policy. Volumes on these topics will include: *Practising Development*; *The Growth of Ignorance*; *Policy and Practice*; *The Traders' Dilemma*; *African Languages, Development and the State*.

To provide a pertinent focus relevant to the interests of both anthropologists and development specialists, the workshop held in June 1989 took as its central theme the environment, defined in terms of its practical and symbolic utilization, including the cultural perceptions surrounding its deployment to the advantage of local populations. For example, the workshop examined beliefs and attitudes about land and water, the allocation of their space, be it directional, axial or concentric, their compatibility with varying economic activities including divisions between and combinations of crops, cash and subsistence, animal husbandry and residence and migratory patterns. Two important areas of particular interest to the participants were: the environment as a source of food in relation to food preferences, food taboos, values attributed to food differences and famine foods; and the degeneration of the environment particularly in relation to land and water use and non-use including over-cropping, over-grazing and beliefs concerning their avoidance.

The authors wish to thank the following: the Economic and Science Research Council, the ERASMUS Bureau of the European Economic Commission, the Nuffield Foundation and the School of Oriental and African Studies, University of London for providing funding for the workshop; and Sharon Lewis of the Department of Anthropology at SOAS for her organizational help.

Elisabeth Croll
David Parkin

Part I

Bush base: forest farm

1 Anthropology, the environment and development

Elisabeth Croll and David Parkin

As concepts, the environment and development together presuppose an interest in the management of natural resources. Anthropology adds to this a concern with the ways in which peoples bring their cultural imaginations to bear on the utility of such resources. Here, the relationship between humans and their natural surroundings often appears paradoxical. Humans create and exercise understanding and agency on their world around them, yet operate within a web of perceptions, beliefs and myths which portray persons and their environments as constituted in each other, with neither permanently privileged over the other. This anthropological vista thus links an earlier interest in indigenous classification of the ecological and economic with the interpretive construction by people of themselves in their environment.

Whether with regard to questions of immediate subsistence or in the name of development, anthropological approaches suggest that environmental transformations can no longer be seen as problems of human activity in relation to non-human physical surroundings. Instead anthropologists question the conventional oppositions between human and non-human agency, or between person and environment, with the result that persons and their changing environments are regarded as part of each other, and as reciprocally inscribed in cosmological ideas and cultural understanding. Overall, this study attacks the sharp dichotomy of human settlement (base or farm) and external 'natural' environment (bush, forest), arguing from African and Asian case studies that most peoples do ascribe a sometimes capricious agency to their environment which they are obliged to interpret and negotiate, and that they commonly regard themselves as inseparably part of it: the forest is the people, in the same way that the ancestors are, in a sense, extensions of the living.

The anthropological emphasis on people's local knowledge and use of their environments, based often on years of painstaking observation carried out in the people's language, provides a perspective that few other disciplines can match. Ethnographies abound in latticed descriptions and analyses of the management of local resources. The anthropological perspective, however, may not seem at first to be addressing environmental issues at all. These are approached, as it were, from the shadows: through ritual, beliefs in spirits and holy sites, ideas of human birth and regeneration, the common origins of mankind and animals, the consubstantiality of human and plant life, the characterization of 'natural' hazards as the wages of sin or the work of malicious non-human forces, or of rain and fertility as the reward of just behaviour or divine beneficence. Anthropologists, then, are not just concerned with technical or ecological questions, but with the construction of knowledge and the power and pressures behind choices and decisions regarding peoples' cultural and physical environments, and with the ways in which these environments 'speak back' either through people or independently. Currently, the increasing interest in the environment generally and also in the specificity of local environments has created and highlighted the potential contributions of anthropologists to our understanding of environment and development issues.

During the past decade, growing awareness and concern with the natural environment has led to the view that environmental issues, choices and problems are popular, political and academic issues of worldwide import. The United Nations has published several seminal reports and convened a series of international meetings on the environment. The World Bank now has an environmental unit; the media have environmental pages or weeks, and universities new and proposed centres for the study of the environment. Much of this concern has focused on the unprecedented demands on land, water, forest and other natural resources. Particular attention has been directed towards the repercussions for the natural resources and the environment of such activities as: the clearing of bush and forest lands, farming marginal lands, intensifying cultivation or herding in the interests of productivity, the effects of irrigation systems and the construction of reservoirs and the redistribution of populations and creation of new settlements, and pollution and the depletion of firewood and other fuels. Most countries face serious economic pressures, both international and domestic, to over-exploit their environmental resource base, and already this is a source of political unrest and international tension. The dimensions of the problem are now considered so acute that it is fashionable to refer to environmental stress, an environmental crisis or even environmental survival.

The environmental stresses or crises were exacerbated by the economic trends of the early 1980s when falling commodity prices, debilitating burdens of debt, high interest rates and declining financial flows and reductions in aid were all seen to force poor countries to produce more raw materials (minerals, woods crops) to expand the production of agricultural goods and generally overtax the environment. No country it seems is exempt from the problems of depletion, degradation and deterioration, but the developing countries are most at risk as they continue to over-exploit their soils, over-graze fragile grasslands and cut dwindling forest stocks to export more in order to service debts and finance the inputs needed for recovery. Overusing environmental resources in order to survive, the poor further deplete their environment, in turn further exacerbating the difficulties of managing an impoverished resource base. The cycles and downward spirals set in motion by economic factors focus sharply the inseparable links between environmental issues and development.

The term 'development' has been in use for many decades, evoking powerful images signifying progress, aspirations, ideals, promises or plans which in common addressed a desire for social, political and economic betterment. So all-embracing were the meanings attributed to the term that there was and is little common agreement as to its specific meaning. Over the past few decades the changes in definition might be summarized by the following sequence: as economic growth, as modernization, as distributive justice and as socio-economic transformation. In more recent years development has been further redefined to take account of its erosion of environmental resources. Like the environment, development, too, can now be said to have its own downward spiral, i.e. the very resources on which it is based are increasingly at risk from the existing management practices and environmental exploitation presently undertaken in its name.

Agriculture, forestry, energy production and mining generate at least half of the gross national product of many developing countries and the capacities of their natural resources very much underlie the maintenance and growth of these economies. They now face enormous pressure to over-exploit their resource base both for continuing growth and development and for sustenance and survival. However, previous concern centred mainly on the negative repercussions of the process of development for the environment. Now it is increasingly recognized that, in turn, environmental deterioration can undermine economic development. Today there is equal concern about the ways in which environmental degradation can slow, halt or reverse economic development. In many regions investigation and documentation reveals how environmental degradation is eroding the resource base of the potential for further development. Presently, much of development aid aims at replenishing the resource base rather than or as a prerequisite to generating new economic activities. That is, the very process of development itself cannot subsist upon a deteriorating environmental resource base; the environment cannot be protected when development ignores the costs of environment destruction and the necessity of replenishment and enhancement.

These increasingly explicit links between economic development and environmental stress prompted the United Nations General Assembly in 1983 to appoint a World Commission on Environment and Development. Its aim was to re-examine the critical environment and development issues and to propose long-term strategies for achieving sustainable development that takes account of the inter-relationships between people, resources, environment and development. The resulting Brundtland Report was important in that it officially acknowledged and expanded on the linkages between development and the environment and provided international legitimacy and popular currency for the term 'sustainability'. The Report focused on one central theme: that the failure to manage the environment and sustain development threatened both. Many present development trends degrade the environment and leave more persons poor and vulnerable to its vicissitudes. It also highlighted the linkages between poverty, inequality and ecological degradation and thus in the interests of both the environment and the poor advocated and popularized the term sustainable development.

Sustainable development is both economic and ecological in focus. It does not reject the notion of economic growth but advocates that is based on policies that sustain and expand the environmental resource base. Economies, it is argued, may grow, but should remain firmly attached to their ecological roots, which should be continuously nurtured, protected and replenished so that they support future long-term growth. Within this context, the Brundtland Report, which assumes the condition of economic growth and the possibility that production processes would constantly be modernized, has been the subject of a number of critiques (Court 1990). These critiques are primarily directed at its conception of development based on economic growth, itself based on the exploitation of limited capital tied up in natural resources, and it is this very conception which causes environmental destruction. In this primary sense 'sustainability' may not only be endangered by ecologically unwise agricultural practices but also by all agriculture. It follows that production must not degrade resources beyond the point of renewal.

A second important critique is that local populations should share fully in available power and be permitted uncontrolled access to their own natural resources while continuing to live within their own cultural and social contexts. As Chambers pointed out 'the environment and development are means, not ends in themselves. The environment and development are for people, not people for environment and development' (1986:7). He argued for an emphasis on 'sustainable livelihood' which enabled causal connections to be made between development and livelihood and between environment and livelihood. The new interest in the way that environmental issues are constructed socially both before and during development had increasingly highlighted the relevance of the experiences of indigenous peoples in 'managing their environment'. Thus, there has been an increasingly important body of work which draws attention to the management of ecosystems, especially agro-ecosystems, by those immediately dependent on their environmental resources – and the disregard, devaluation or ignorance of this experience and local knowledge by those practising environmental management in the name of development. These chapters take cognisance of a number of these studies.

Many of the post-Brundtland Report studies have also focused on two major, relevant areas frequently omitted in the debates about environment and development. The first is the relevance of the framework of global economic relations for the study of and protection of the environment. For instance, Redclift (1984; 1987) has argued that the investigation of the international economic and political forces behind unsustainable practices has received little attention. That is, the very linkage between development and global politics and economics is detrimental to the environment: 'the problems of initiating sustainable development alternatives are frequently undermined by the pursuit of illusory, and detrimental policies, whose origin lies in the North and in the relationship that is maintained between North and South' (1987: 22).

Second is the relation between person and environment which rejects the previous ways in which the 'environment' was usually regarded as located outside ourselves, as a space inhabited. It was the bounded quality of the environment wich was seen as its defining characteristic. Radical ecologists are among those who have taken a renewed interest in people's relation with nature, and for them the solution lies in rejecting previous codes for reading nature, instead pursuing a more spiritual version of ecology, a kind of pantheism in which moral and practical cues are taken from the environment. Such views do not appear to have gained wide currency, but as Redclift (1987) has argued, they are potentially elements in a new discourse which is more holistic and incorporates a cross-cultural approach. Examining another culture's concept of the environment and sustainability is a logical consequence of considering development and the environment as an integrated process based upon conceptual integration. In a social and cultural construction of the environment, it is not only a part of nature but also a part of culture which by implication argues for a recognition of cultural diversity.

If anthropologists (beginning with Daryll Ford who intriguingly invited speculation on the material and cosmic worlds as each informing the other in *African Worlds* (1954) have long argued that the environment and cosmos are inseparable, they have been much slower to incorporate the phenomenon of development into their analytical frameworks. In retrospect, what would Forde and his colleagues have made of this addition? It is one thing to describe statically or cyclically the role of myth, rite and belief in the shaping of land use and understanding but quite another to include also the influence of a new epistemology premissed on changing society through the role and methods of outside specialists. In the modern world, however, it can be argued that development has joined religion as an ideological force of global significance. It does not just refer to methods and plans about how to get things done, but entails moral prescriptions, various collective enthusiasms, different and competing hierarchies of adherents and an overriding assumption that human betterment is society's primary essence, that for which it exists and by which it justifies itself. The Durkheimian parallel can be elaborated indefinitely. The analogy at least serves to remind anthropologists that, to some degree, development is as much a fact of everyday life for most peoples of the world as the other kinds of overarching frameworks of assumption and action. It is not peripheral, to be interrogated by those not carried along by the mainstream (a false idea in itself), but is intertwined with the many other discourses which pattern the anthropological object.

The concept of sustainable development not only provides a framework for the integration of environmental policies and development strategies, but is also a new opportunity for anthropologists to contribute their skills and insights. The concept also embraces and is premissed on many core assumptions of anthropological interest and analysis such as order, agency, time, space, classification and the deployment of power and knowledge (Fardon 1985). The very notion of sustainability is predicated on perceptions of time, aiming to meet the needs of the present without compromising those of future generations. Moreover, conceptions of such needs are perceived to be socially and culturally determined. In deploying the broadest possible definitions of development, the concept of sustainable development incorporates both the material and non-material into a new and holistic conceptual ordering, simultaneously recognizing that there can be no fixed or single order. The Brundtland Report stresses that it is perceived as a process of change in which the 'utilisation of resources, the direction of investment, the orientation of technical development and institutional change are all in harmony' but also emphasizes that harmony is not perceived as a fixed state, but rather a process of change punctuated by the unplanned, unforeseen and unexpected. Moreover, there can be no single order or blueprint for sustainable development, given the wide cultural variations in ecological, economic and social perceptions and practices.

Finally, international, national and popular bodies increasingly recognized that the achievement of sustainable development rests on the exercise of political agency or will. The Brundtland Report argues that it is the distribution of power and influence which lies 'at the heart of most environmental and development challenges'. Indeed, it reiterated that many problems of resource depletion and environmental stress arise from disparities in economic and political power so that sustainable development is conceived not so much to be about natural resources of the physical environment as about issues of control, power, participation and self-determination. Today, it is not so much that environmental difficulties are new, but that previous conceptions of development tended to simplify ecological systems, reduce the diversity of species and strategies and ignore cultural variations in ecological conditions, perception and concepts. These are only beginning to be understood in their complexity and diversity. At the centre lies the difficult, negotiable and contested relationship between person and environment, and crucially, anthropological perspectives on cultural understandings of the environment.

REFERENCES

Brundtland, G. *et al.* (1987) *Our Common Future: World Commission on Environment and Development*, Oxford: Oxford University Press.
Chambers, R. (1986) *Sustainable Livelihoods*, Mimeo, University of Sussex, Institute of Development Studies.

de la Court, T. (1990) *Beyond Brundtland, Green Development in the 1990s,* London: Zed Press.

Fardon, R. (1985) *Power and Knowledge, Anthropological and Sociological Approaches,* Edinburgh: Scottish Academic Press.

Forde, D. (ed.) (1954) *African Worlds: Studies in the Cosmological Ideas and Social Values of African Peoples,* London: Oxford University Press, reprinted 1984.

Redclift, M. (1984) *Development and the Environmental Crisis: Red or Green Alternatives,* London: Methuen.

—— (1987) *Sustainable Development, Exploring the Contradictions,* London: Routledge.

2 Cultural understandings of the environment

Elisabeth Croll and David Parkin

A WORKING ENVIRONMENT

An old man weaving mats and baskets in front of his house in Giriama country in Kenya dismissed the idea that this was work. This and similar activities, such as growing tobacco, keeping goats, and trapping small animals, he regarded as spare-time activities fitted in with more important tasks such as attending meetings, advising younger people and tending ancestral shrines. Real work, for him (as for everyone else), was urban salaried work or entrepreneurial farming, and then subsistence farming. An elderly Chinese grandmother modestly described herself as too old to work now 'only able to do her bit by cooking the meals, taking care of the grandsons and raising two pigs and chickens'. What she neglected to add was that her non-work contribution, selling pigs, chickens and eggs, provided just under half the household's total annual cash income. A salaried worker in a southwest France village casually referred to the many hours he spent tending his fields of maize, sunflowers or planting fruit trees, as merely a pleasant distraction (*pour m'amuser*) and looked forward to his retirement so that he could devote more time to this.

In all three cases, each individual earned more from such apparently agreeable sidelines than from any accessible salaried employment. The subsistence and domestic work of Giriama women is similarly regarded as non-work compared to wage-employment and intensive, commercial farming, though not, however, as a form of leisure pursuit. Here, too, women's contributions far outweigh what they or men could ever earn in the formal labour market (Parkin 1979). In China, where a skilled woman's annual income from farming and handicrafts could far exceed the wages of an able-bodied male, an important issue has been whether domestic sidelines are considered as formal income-generating activities or 'work' deserving of legislation and protection, or whether they are to remain informally indistinguishable from domestic labour (Croll 1983).

These kinds of work are undervalued in such comparisons by the workers themselves because they have been taught or have learned that 'work', as a terminologically distinct concept, refers to tasks itemized, organized and controlled by a social hierarchy of employers or state officials. It does not refer to work carried out on one's own initiative which merges with other everyday tasks. The Giriama old man and the Chinese grandmother are also fully aware of the back-breaking work involved in men's clearing new ground, and in the planting, weeding and harvesting undertaken mainly by women. But they distinguish between such regularly vital activities and their own, what they regard as inessential ones.

Here is a labour hierarchy in which materially productive activities are only given differential value in relation to an idea of the absolute worth of a salaried or commercial living. The old people's contribution dovetails so importantly into the wider mosaic of productivity that boundaries between essential and inessential labour become meaningless, for if the elderly did not earn money in this way, then someone else in the homestead would have to make up the shortfall.

Such so-called lesser kinds of work do not necessarily depend, as does factory or office work and some forms of intensive, commercialized farming, on an ideal of standardized rules of procedure, timed measurement of tasks and precise expectations of results. They constitute instead a kind of productive *bricolage*, in which tasks are carried out according to available materials, weather conditions, availability of land, and the health, skills and disposition of the producer. They expand and contract according to need and desire and are intertwined with other activities but neither strictly prescribe nor are prescribed by them.

In fact, all work is a form of productive *bricolage* from the worker's viewpoint. Salaried employment and commercial farming may be based on ideals of rules, regularity and precisely determined results, but the reality of fluctuating levels of employment and cash-crop prices, and agricultural failures, oblige people to resort to coping strategies and constantly to re-assess what are their own resources and assets and how much these are part of what they themselves are as persons and how much are external to them. It seems worthwhile, however, retaining the term, productive *bricolage*, to refer relatively to tasks over which agents see themselves as having some control, as distinct from work controlled by others outside the home.

Productive *bricolage* is not utopian: too many droughts, excessive floods, epidemics and famines testify to its inadequacy. It is, however, an unorthodox starting-point for transcending the perennial dichotomies between work and non-work, between the environment and its exploitation by people within it, and between culture as a system of strategies and meanings and the external, surrounding landscape on which these are brought to bear.

This idea of the exteriority of the environment has an epistemological consequence. It presupposes that ultimately persons are passive in the face of environmental menace. Here the environment is a capricious or intentionally controlling agent and the human the object, who may nevertheless seek mastery over it. Similarly, the privileging of salaried work and commercial farming over clusters of smaller tasks is based on the idea of some people being subject to the power and will of others (employers, the state) and of non-human agents (weather, the soil, opportunities, luck, land and sea spirits and so on).

The distinction between people and things as environmental agents is indeed best rendered as that between the human and non-human components of the cosmologies of many peoples. In this sense environment is never a neutrally acting force, innocently shaping or interacting with human interests. This is obviously the case when westerners speak metaphorically of a human political or economic environment influencing human events, or of the environment as geographically comprising physical terrains of forest, mountain, savannah or bush, acting upon populations. As numerous chapters in this volume indicate, such habitats are chosen by or forced upon people and become ontologically part of them as a result of such choices or pressures. People identify, give names to, and thank or blame their habitat for their prosperity or misfortune, often personifying it in their own deeds and misdeeds.

The most prevalent example of such identification is drawn from people's distinction between village or settlement and bush or forest. In personifying the latter they create overlap and ambiguity between categories which in the hands of outsiders sharply separate culture and environment and types of knowledge about them.

A FALSE DICHOTOMY: CULTURE AND ENVIRONMENT

Ellen (1982: 277) urges us to resist a discourse of such oppositions as 'man' and 'nature' or 'society' and 'nature': human ecology *is* human society. Ingold (Chapter 3) similarly criticizes that between 'culture' and 'environment': the idea that culture imposes meaning on an empty *tabula rasa* of an environment is only to say that people read into things what they want and so makes unnecessary the very idea of environment. Environmental determinism reverses this priority and makes humanity its *tabula rasa* so denying both culture and human volition an initiatory role in shaping events. Neither this nor its opposite, cultural determinism, are much found in current literature except in modified, 'soft' forms. So-called possibilism, the idea that environments do not determine people's activities and cultures but only limit them to within a sometimes wide range of possible constraints, is the prime soft candidate. Yet, as Ellen argues (1982: 50–1), this, too, appeals to ultimate limits and so is in the end deterministic.

These points refer to a voluminous literature on ecological anthropology over the last half century and need not be reiterated. The central epistemological problem seems to rest on the use of such dichotomies as culture and environment, man and nature, society and habitat, as prescribing subsequent argument. Such an analytical contrast locks one into proving or disproving it but perhaps never reaching the conclusion that it may be a false assumption.

Others also suffer such impasses. As, for example, Richards (1985: 54) points out: agricultural experts in Africa may 'package' types of farming practice and discriminate between those thought suitable and unsuitable for particular areas and peoples, failing to realize that African farmers have, for generations, developed experimentation skills according to changing conditions and needs. If, in the twentieth century, they still practise shifting cultivation, this is not because they have no knowledge about crop rotation or other intensive-farming techniques. On the contrary, there is some evidence that they have long been aware of such alternatives but have found them wanting: much of Africa has, and has had, sparsely populated areas where there is a labour shortage for intensive farming. It differs from many Asian regions in which a high-density population has often favoured, for instance, terraced agriculture or rotational cropping. Shifting cultivation in sparsely populated areas enables farmers to keep forest or wilderness at bay through the slash-and-burn method, but enables them to move into other areas when new soil is needed so leaving the previous area to long-term fallow. Into this mosaic of shifting plots is fitted an indigenous system of intercropping of diverse plant species, which variously benefit from the different stages of regenerative growth in the return from cleared settlement to bush. Neither fixed settlements nor mono-cropping in ordered lines would be an improvement on the indigenous method (see Pottier and Nkundabashaka, Chapter 9, this volume).

Richards' approach is culturally and environmentally non-deterministic: environment and culture are neither reified nor do they interact with each other in a game of alternating dominance and concession. Rather, the farmers themselves are the principal agents in shaping their own destiny. Of course critics will impute 'sentimentality' and the 'Myth of Merrie Africa' to this populist approach. But it is not here argued that hazards beyond human control do not cause utter blight and misery. Alternatively, we can reject the extreme argument that takes such 'natural' misfortunes as evidence of farmers' impotence and out-dated techniques. No-one can wholly predict and control hazards, but, now and for generations past, peasant farmers have created diverse skills which cannot be ranged in a scale of evolutionary development: just as some hunters and gatherers may be aware of settled agriculture but find it irrelevant to their needs, so farmers may find shifting cultivation and intercropping more efficient than intensive methods of food production.

With regard to Africa, Richards (1985) not only urges outsiders to recognize traditional skills, but claims for them the status of an indigenous science, from which western agricultural and development specialists can learn. Numerous chapters in the current volume (not just those from West Africa where this is emphasized) justify this appeal to reverse the learning process, for instance the notion of coping has become increasingly a key word in describing indigenous science.

The title of a recent work is *Coping with Uncertainty in Food Supply* (de Garine and Harrison 1988), while that of another of Richards' books is *Coping with Hunger* (1986). Similarly, Shaw (Chapter 12, this volume) talks of farmers' 'coping strategies'. This concept connotes the flexible methods of interpretation and experimentation typical of ecologies which have not come under the rule of textbook theories and admonitions. The metaphor is born of a more general movement in the natural and, especially, social sciences towards methodological reflexivity, in which facts are no longer simply tested against theories, but are, together with the theories, investigated for their rhetorical effect. This represents a trend towards a politico-semantic appreciation of theories and their findings: of how theories and data are used in power struggles to achieve particular ends and not just to advance neutral areas of knowledge.

Analogously, Ingold (Chapter 3) attacks the classical ecological claim that organisms fit and test themselves against and within environmental niches, as if the latter exist prior to the organism, which has only to find them. An organism not only makes sense of possible niches, it imaginatively creates them out of spaces and situations, competing with other organisms, therefore, not just for already existing refuges but for imaginative supremacy.

People likewise do not just adapt to environments, they make them, shaping them from both materials and the possibilities they see in the habitat and surrounding life forms. What is interesting here is the way in which peoples classify their environment, sometimes including and sometimes excluding themselves. Yet, while much of the foregoing has stressed the experimental and often provisional nature of peoples' coping strategies and their changing interpretations of what constitutes work or resources, it is also evident that when people do classify they can only proceed step by step on the basis of distinctions of some sort. We do not need to debate whether thought is necessarily fundamentally binary to accept the role of oppositional or contrastive thinking in human cosmology, however much such distinctions may constantly be dissolved, reconvened and recombined.

The peoples discussed in this volume do indeed often start an explanation of their ecology from a key distinction, such as that between village and bush. We may then encounter a conundrum: peoples cope and experiment by flexibly transcending set ideas; simultaneously they commonly resort to seemingly timeless cosmological dichotomies when explaining to themselves and each other how they live, work, thrive and survive.

What is the relationship between this apparent flux and fixity of environmental understanding? How do such folk distinctions differ from those made by, for example, development advisers and central governments in their evaluations of modern and traditional methods of cultivation, herding and land and forest usage? Is the way 'experts' distinguish between modern and traditional methods paradigmatic of the ways peoples themselves separate domesticated settlements from wild bush? And if so, why do outside specialists and local folk so often disagree as to what is relevant in the management of such distinctions? In the latter, what kind of negotiations and renegotiations take place with regard to the meanings of, say, bush and farm, cleared and uncleared, cultivated and uncultivated or the wild and the tame?

Crucially, negotiation involves a hierarchy of power of things over people, of people over people and some people over things. Control and therefore power is thus central to discussions of the environment and its relations to culture and human endeavour. Here the implications for power and control that such folk and external distinctions carry will be examined, beginning not with those voiced by specialists but those inhering in people's own cosmologies.

AN IMAGINATIVE DICHOTOMY: BUSH AND BASE

Others have established recognition of the diversity of indigenous knowledge or sciences and the need to learn from them. Here we try to understand the cosmological premisses of such diverse forms of reasoning, which, while experimental, do also turn upon common oppositions, that between village and bush being perhaps the most prevalent, figuring especially in the chapters on West Africa and elsewhere, too. Oppositions can, of course, be set up by a people and then transcended, for example, that between village and bush: having been established they may then be merged, portrayed as antagonistic or, conversely, as life-nurturing, or provide people with alternate modes of identification.

The identification of persons with the surrounding bush and forest is most marked in the Dogon example described by van Beek and Banga (Chapter 4). In fact it is more a merging of human and non-human existence than an identification, for the bush or forest actually become human beings over time: trees and plants are a life force which nourishes humans. Without the bush, humans and their villages stagnate, cannot progress and eventually die. The authors even say that the Dogon do not see themselves as agents of their own reproduction, thus, humans cannot themselves replenish the bush, for they are not its masters. Nor need they do so, for the bush is regarded by the Dogon as *sui generis* inexhaustible.

This seems to preclude outsiders' attempts to get the Dogon to protect the bush and forest from degradation through overuse: if they see themselves as subject to the omnipotence of wild trees and their habitat, then how can anything they do save or increase vegetation? But this is mistakenly to conclude that the forest or bush is a potential adversary *vis-à-vis* humans, and that it rigidly controls human destiny. True, there is a hierarchy of forest over humans, but this is based not on an unreflecting use of power by trees but on the expectation of respect from humans. The Dogon must both respect the bush and work on its endless transformation into humanity. They work not *on* or *against* the environment (the typical western way), but respectfully *with* it. Freedman (1969) drew this distinction, describing the Chinese geomancer's view of the environment of buildings and landscape as ideally to be integrated harmoniously with the lives of people, as distinct from the once-typical western perspective, to see the environment as an outside force or field to be attacked, conquered and domesticated by establishing towns and buildings. Undoubtedly, this view underlies most forms of colonial domination.

The Dogon sense of themselves and their bush is hierarchical not colonial: the bush is central to human life but does not dominate it. Bush and village together make up a spiritual and moral entity, exemplified in the punitive entry of masks from the bush into the village. These masks are worn by men, chastising the women's lack of respect in using certain trees favoured by men. Clearly, male concerns are served by this drama which further elaborates the hierarchy as being that of forest over men, and men over women, but with respect for wild vegetation as fundamental. Where forest degradation does occur, it cannot be said to be due to Dogon indifference or unconcern. If deterioration of the bush is to be reversed, it has to take account of the Dogon veneration of their forest and of their view of it as the life force which makes possible their own existence as village-based humans. Village and bush, human and forest, are complementary and part of each other and by no means opposed.

The situation described by Leach (Chapter 5) for the Mende of Sierra Leone is a contrasting case of the forest being regarded as opposing humankind and an obstacle to human progress, for the Mende believe that the bush contains innumerable dangers including evil spirits, and that it constantly threatens farms cleared from the forest. Men echo earlier warrior values in their attack upon trees when they hack them away for farming.

Yet, although humans and forest are antagonistically poised in their relationship with each other, particular strands of association indicate the precarious balance and ambiguity which obtains. Thus, forest spirits can be malign but can also lead a man to unexpected riches; the bush harbours dangers but is also a source of potency and regeneration – secret society initiations take place there; the forest is resisted in its threat to reclaim the space which has been cleared for an upland rice farm, but then welcomed when the farm is left subsequently to fallow. The upland farm itself is intermediary between town and bush, partaking of the forest and the human settlement. Finally, the spaces occupied by farm, forest or town are, through their transformations one into the other, subject to fluctuations of identity.

This ambiguity favours metaphorical play in the relationship between human settlement and forest and between men and women. In carving out forest space, men claim that they make farms for the women, which seems to denote the virgin forest as male, and the cultivable space as female. Yet the fact that some husbandless, female household heads themselves clear bush, while some low-status men cultivate in women's spaces, and that the relationships of some women to each other (e.g. senior and junior co-wives) become more like those of men to women, render such clear associations untenable.

In their warrior mode, men *are* like the forest, while women as domestic sustainers of cleared farmland connote the human security of the village. But not all men and women assume such modes and it is precisely the metaphorical room for renegotiations of identity that the ambiguous, triangular opposition of forest, farm and town affords. It is these kinds of 'affordances' (see Ingold in Chapter 3) that human potentialities exploit. Thus, while the Dogon experience forest and village as ontologically part of each other, the one being the life force for the other's continuing existence, the Mende situation is neither straight-forward nor hierarchical: Do humans or the forest control creativity? Do men in fact dominate women? These are matters to be negotiated.

What does come across as a fundamental distinction is that between abrupt, one-off acts of transformation (e.g. men's vigorous conversion of forest into women's farming space, or men's immediate disinterest in a farm after the harvest) and the gradual changes that characterize farm life and its slow reversion to bush, during which women harvest at different times as a result of intercropping. We have an image of male bursts of energy that open and close pathways in the environment, while female is the power that first sustains and then slowly seals off such pathways. But this is an archetypal image which informs cosmological understanding but does not prescribe social roles and actions, which, throughout, are defined through negotiating the meanings of cleared and uncleared spaces.

This picture of negotiable and creative uncertainty is, however, threatened by a recent shift from upland to swamp rice farming, and to cocoa and coffee cultivation and vegetable gardens. Women clear and cultivate swamp farms and gardens themselves unlike in the upland farms where men clear for women. Conversely, men alone own tree crops. Whether swamp or tree-crop cultivation, the plots are perma-nent, just as men's and women's tasks are sharply distinct and not complementary. Marital relations have also deteriorated. The environ-mental ambiguity associated with upland rice farming in forest spaces has given way to more predictable control of swamp and tree-crop farming but to greater uncertainty in gender relations. The meta-phorical association of forest and farm with men and women has been reduced in the face of socio-agricultural changes which are becoming more common in other parts of Africa and Asia.

Echoing perhaps the western search for balanced ecosystems, academics commonly emphasize the wisdom of indigenous cos-mologies which treat tree, plant, animal and human interactions as a single spiritual, moral and regenerative system. In their different ways, the Dogon and Mende attitudes to their forests and bush sustain the view that such cosmologies are often well, if imperfectly, suited to traditional or pre-cash-cropping conditions.

Van den Breemer (Chapter 6) raises the question of how is it that a people's wise, conservationist understanding of their forests can nevertheless be abandoned in favour of growing new crops that will inevitably ruin them. The Aouan of the Ivory Coast fervently observed their earth goddess's prohibition on cultivating rice and the cola tree and keeping goats. No explanation is given, yet they appear to be logically consistent with other aspects of social life and with environmental preservation. Van den Breemer argues that, with an increasing population and more individualistic and permanent farming plots, rice cultivation is harmful long term to the forest, because it needs sunlight and therefore extensive clearing of forest, which under modern conditions has less chance of regrowth. The goat harms vegetation more than sheep, for it has sharper hooves, stronger and broader jaws and can climb to greater heights. An unintended consequence of the bans on rice and goats is that the ecological balance is more easily maintained.

This is reinforced by powerful beliefs insisting on separating the bush and village by a neutral zone and by a system of rest days when neither the forest nor village can be worked. The Aouan explicitly affirm that the bush, like social life, needs to be restored regularly if it is to fulfil its function of replenishing human needs and resources. In maintaining a separation between bush and village, the Aouan see themselves as conserving both themselves and their environment.

Their beliefs are similar to those of the Dogon, but traditionally lack the ambiguity of the Mende relationship between settlement and forest. A kind of ambiguity has been thrust upon them, for, recently, increasing conversion to Christianity and Islam, and government encouragement to plant rice in the forest, has obliged them to defy the divine prohibition. Eventually as former non-Aouan slaves and dependants began to do so, the Aouan finally followed suit, so eliminating the conservational effect of their cosmology.

The Aouan have not, then, completely abandoned their belief in the bans but have found practical reasons for ignoring them with regard to rice cultivation. But this exception may be enough to transform their environment radically. Meanwhile, the cosmology has sufficient sway in its present form to advance in effect a folk theory of environmental conservation, which may be a valuable asset to outside agricultural officers.

Schlee (Chapter 7) also illustrates environmental conservationism as inherent in indigenous beliefs in and restrictions on the use of landscapes in describing the remote Gabbra camel herders and neighbouring peoples of the Kenyan/Ethiopian borderlands, but focuses on the fundamental ontology of their identification with the territory and mountains in their region. The Gabbra nomads make pilgrimages to a variety of holy sacrificial sites at times determined by solar and lunar cycles, culminating in great age-set transitions. Each Gabbra subgroup has its own holy site and follows a specific route to it, resulting in routes of different groups converging, diverging and cross-cutting each other, each journey being part of the sacred attachment to the destination. The routes are made up of distinctive landmarks that are given meaning by the Gabbra and figure in origin myths.

Thus, a group may re-enact its origins and formation on the route to its site. Groups do not claim exclusive rights over particular areas, either to the holy site itself or parts covered by the journey. The various groups recognize landscapes and the history that each represents from their own particular perspectives, acknowledging that, while for one group a mountain is the sacred endpoint of their journey, for another it is part of a chain that reaches its own endpoint.

These cross-cutting routes broadly follow a south–north direction towards the holy sites, each moving in a precise direction. Schlee calls this patterning in space one-dimensional: the various landmarks (points) on a route are connected to each other as if by lines. The holy sites he calls zero-dimensional. Together, these two types of spatial imagining constitute the Gabbra view of their landscape as a continuing personal history and ontology. What is of special significance is the absence of territorial boundaries.

Schlee notes that the Gabbra are perfectly aware of the pragmatic importance of boundaries in other respects and will defend them like any other people. But as pastoralists they appropriate space more like hunters and gatherers than agriculturalists and nation states. The latter divide land up into delimited surface areas, i.e. two-dimensionally. Pastoralists, however, move from one relevant feature of the landscape to another, turning and following an alternative route if necessary, depending on available pasture. Bounded areas would thus be incompatible with nomadism, which is not to suggest that nomads wander into pasturelands totally at will: they negotiate with others, based on the shared understanding of land as one- rather than two-dimensional. The pilgrimage routes can, therefore, be seen as reiterating information about the landscape and providing a distinctive Gabbra identity, which will also at times overlap with that of other pastoralist groups in the region. The holy sites are best viewed as ontological reference points, to and from which lines are attached.

Schlee presents us with a complicated, fascinating ecocosmology that does not really fit any folk dichotomy: the distinction between holy sites as zero- and pilgrimage and pastoralist routes as one-dimensional, is hardly one expressed by the Gabbra themselves. And where, as in other parts of East Africa, farmers and pastoral nomads compete for diminishing land, both dimensions are evident, and the situation becomes even more complicated. In trying to order such apparent complexity, development projects often place, say, cattle pastoralists into demarcated group ranches similarly to organizing farmers into settlement schemes. But order for one agent is disorder to another. How much longer will the Gabbra pilgrimages, which are constitutive of their pastoral livelihoods, remain unaffected by such issues?

OUTSIDE ADVICE AND INSIDE WISDOM

The threat to such ecocosmologies does seem, in all the cases in this volume, to derive from market and political pressures to grow cash crops, resettle, farm or herd in new, formally defined ways. However, so-called traditional ecocosmologies do not always harmoniously integrate persons with their environment. Perhaps such cosmologies satisfactorily explain to people disasters and misfortunes over which they have no control, such as incessant drought, floods, disease and war. Like witchcraft, they explain the problem as aberrant but specific, so making it manageably credible, and allowing personal adjustment to change.

Such 'self-mystification' needs no special commendation and clearly can divert people from confronting recurring dangers, but like productive *bricolage*, it is a sometimes successful coping strategy whose rationale is not always understood when changes are proposed from outside. The experimental nature of such strategy blurs set differences, contrasting starkly with the firm distinctions often made by outside specialists between 'traditional' and 'modern' farming, herding and land and forest use.

A distorting feature of any applied dichotomy of this kind is that it is already hierarchical, the external view tending towards the status of an absolute, scientific truth, and the local one having provisional and relative standing, sometimes approved but more often denounced. When a people no longer believes in its indigenous ecocosmology (if an alternative is rhetorically substituted by a higher authority), they may lose their experimental adaptability. It may be dismissed as mere trial-and-error and as inferior to so-called scientifically based prescriptions.

Drijver (Chapter 8) shows how a series of 'lessons' can be learned through analysing development projects which have failed and succeeded. As with anthropological typology-making, the number of lessons can increase indefinitely as more and more projects are examined. Alternatively, if the lessons are seen as having both a local significance drawn from a particular case and as only possibly relevant to other cases, then they avoid the danger of becoming posited as universally significant. The fact that it is necessary to read all the cases Drijver presents to appreciate the findings of any single one, makes generalization beyond them especially difficult.

For instance, Drijver convincingly shows that a development or conservation project is more likely to succeed provided the local people are both consulted and take central decisions in its implementation, a participatory approach that can lead to unexpected changes in the original aims and interests. He includes an Indian project which was particularly successful after sufficient reallocation of land had been made among all households and each had a share of irrigable land and so, thereafter, co-operated in making the irrigation system work.

What might have happened in a community with sharp, entrenched divisions between large and small landowners? Would the former agree to reallocation? Under a political regime favourable to them, it is unlikely. Are not Drijver's lessons applicable only within relatively egalitarian societies, as his four cases suggest, and is his approach not in fact a kind of useful though limited form of social (rather than environmental) possibilism? The chapter is additionally interesting for raising this question of the ultimate power interests at work in the distribution of environmental changes and directions.

While the division between rich and poor landowners, or stock owners, is an obvious example of such unequal participation and decision-making, there still remains that between a community and an outside agent, who does not modify his specialist knowledge by incorporating local ideas.

Participation has to be seen in the light of power differences which include some members of a society but exclude others lacking influence. Pottier and Nkundabashaka (Chapter 9) describe how farming extension workers in Rwanda encourage mono-cropping and the use of fertilizer and scorn the traditional self-fertilizing system of intercropping. A housing estate in Butare town accommodates salaried workers who, identifying with the educated extension workers and their appeal to modern, scientific methods, grow the recommended crops in neat, straight lines and use chemical fertilizers and pesticides. They do not plant either bananas or sorghum which the extension workers regard as unproductive, taking too long to grow. In a different part of town, traditional intercropping occurs constantly resulting in humus-rich soil. Bananas and sorghum are grown, the former sometimes alone and sometimes providing shade for other crops. Weeds interspersed with sorghum, and using only the flat, top soil, allows the land effectively to fallow. Farmers experiment with the numerous possibilities of shade and sunlight that such intercropping affords, discovering and developing, for instance, different bean strains. The long-term productivity and soil quality exceeds that of the modern plots, but does not meet the rule-based requirements of the extension workers. Folk wisdom challenges their textbook knowledge.

Cosmology here once again enters into the thinking of farmers and extension workers. The banana grove, central in the organization of traditional intercropping, nevertheless is a dark area associated with buried ancestors who, if angered, are feared for the madness they may induce in people. It is both male and female and so, like a persistent religious cult, called Ryangombe, which also merges male and female, threatens notions of fixed structure and hierarchy. Extension workers distrust it and sense its decentring and destabilizing connotations, just as they and government distrust the Ryangombe cult. Their cosmological unease with the banana grove supports or perhaps is supported by their agricultural definition of the banana as a plant to be rejected.

The authors point out the problem of how the extension workers might listen to and learn from the traditional farmers, the most important of whom are women, about their agricultural knowledge and techniques. Dialogue is not helped by the fact that the Ryangombe cult is a vehicle more of protest than debate, as the farmers' co-operative has also become.

However, women have been given equality in these spheres. Given that most traditional farmers are women, then it may be through women's partial control over the co-operative that men, including the extension workers, will have to listen to women. As the main authors of intercropping in and around banana groves, women are associated with its fertility.

A main problem of both the co-operative and the radical, anti-establishment Ryangombe cult is that members tend to want to replace old ideas and practices wholesale with new ones, rather than gradually changing. However, in representing the fertility and environmental creativity that comes from intercropping, women may be able to advocate a gentle mix of old and modern methods and an environmental approach which encourages flexibility and negotiability (as among the Mende). Such women will then have transcended the absolutist stance of the extension workers.

Drinkwater (Chapter 10) discusses programmatic and inflexible government land-use policy with reference to cattle herding in Zimbabwe. His analysis seeks to provoke outside range-management specialists into understanding the cattle herders' own viewpoint, but does not claim that it is always superior. Indeed, more unanswered questions are raised than the case began with, which he sees as opening up interpretive possibilities rather than solutions.

The Zimbabwe government has always rigidly adopted the same policy of restricting the number of cattle to the carrying capacity of the land, through rotational grazing between permanent paddocks. The environment is here envisaged as existing in a fixed, external relationship to humans and cattle. Drinkwater observes that farmers use a number of herding strategies which vary according to the time of year, and the availability of different forage and of labour. He actually favours the 'opportunistic' strategy employed by herders who reduce or increase their herds, and even the size of their beasts, depending on available grass or other nutrition rather than the 'conservative' government strategy based on fixed notions of the land's carrying capacity. This is again an appeal to recognize the variability of practice, skill and opportunity in indigenous farming management as against the fixed textbook assumptions.

The inevitable protest from outside advisers is that allowing unrestrained grazing will lead, and has led, to overgrazing and soil erosion. This is said to be especially so in societies where cattle numbers are a status index and increased as much as possible regardless of consequences, along with a general rise in the human population.

Drinkwater does not ask whether there really are such societies which apparently engage 'irrationally' in the destruction of the habitat on which they depend, or whether they do so in ignorance, or whether their documentation is a myth to support outside agents' dominant theoretical premisses. It does appear in the Zimbabwe case, that farmers are extremely sensitive to the fragile relationship between man, beast and pasture availability and try to manage the sizes of their herds accordingly.

He seeks to question the official assumptions about the savannah land in which much grazing occurs, and supports the views of some ecologists that this form of tropical vegetation actually has a much broader cycle of environmental decline and regeneration than is commonly supposed. What sometimes appears as degradation of land through overgrazing may in fact be the lower end of the cycle, at which point cattle are withdrawn to other areas, allowing subsequent regrowth of pasture.

Folk wisdom may well be right in most such cases, but it is alarming that in other African regions, e.g. the Sahara and Sahel fringes, not even local expertise has been of help in cattle devastation. However, Drinkwater is not arguing for the inevitable supremacy and correctness of indigenous approaches to communal cattle-keeping. Rather, he seeks to convince advisers that local herders have a flexible and adaptable knowledge of their circumstances and see gains as presupposing risks and tactics. He advocates a forum in which outsiders' and farmers' theories are jointly evaluated rather than ranked.

Like Drijver, Drinkwater is clearly uninterested in the people's cosmology, or in the dilemmas of belief, desire and practice reported elsewhere. Is there no equivalent to the Rwandan extension workers' distrust of the banana grove because of the ancestral wrath and dangers that it harbours? Is the Zimbabwean official view so devoid of such allegorical judgement, which notions of pure reason cannot capture? It may of course be that the Zimbabweans described are themselves this pragmatic, though other ethnographies might suggest otherwise (e.g. Schoffeleers 1979).

However, we are challenged in Drijver's and Drinkwater's chapters on how to justify such excursions into conceptual otherness. The justification is surely that what westerners call economic efficiency and environmental preservation omits consideration (often deliberately) of the extent to which peoples identify personally with their habitat and with its produce. In Zimbabwe where cattle have been central in the use of bridewealth to make family alliances, and spirit mediums have figured prominently in the recent organization of national politics and armed struggle (Lan 1985), the identification with the land and its produce is crucial.

The Mentaiwan of Siberut island in Indonesia described by Persoon (Chapter 11) express their identification with their forest environment through their belief that all things have souls, even immaterial concepts. There must be complete harmony between them and any disharmony is repaired through ritual prescriptions and taboos. As among the Aouan, there is a system of rest days to allow regeneration of the forest. The Mentaiwan traditionally grow fruit trees in a small forest area which has been cleared but allowed to redevelop around the fruit trees, which are themselves nourished by the humus of felled vegetation left to decompose rather than be burned.

The sago tree partakes of this inseparable identification of human and forest. It is never cultivated but is sufficiently abundant in the wild that it may be sought out for sago flour when wanted. To process one tree takes about a month but provides a household with food for about 4 months. The Mentaiwan most nearly approach Sahlins' description of affluent foragers (1974: 1–39), able to eat well, with sago as their reliable staple, and able to satisfy the need for a range of food and other products directly from their habitat. The sago also plays a central role in brideprice, other exchanges and the payment of fines.

Why then are the Mentaiwan being obliged by the Indonesian central government to switch to producing rice? An overarching reason is that rice is regarded generally in Indonesia as a socially more acceptable and dignified food, more befitting a civilized people. As a so-called tribal people who have had minimal contact with central Indonesian values until recently, the Mentaiwan are thus urged to join the mainstream of Indonesian culture.

Persoon shows that in all respects rice is more damaging to this particular environment, for similar reasons to the Aouan case. Although rice intrinsically is more nutritional than sago, the latter is always supplemented with vegetables, fish, etc., whereas rice is eaten as a main food without such supplements. Again, women cultivate rice, resulting in an increased workload. Men assume ownership of the trees producing copra, cloves and coffee planted in and alongside the permanent rice fields.

A subsidiary reason for the shift from sago to rice is the central government's reluctance to condone a form of subsistence which does not involve constantly intensive labour. A common criticism is that sago is a 'lazy man's food'. Thus governmental discourse also includes a moral evaluation of the Mentaiwan people. This evaluation reflects the view, associated with western thinking, that the environment is a protagonist to be attacked, tamed and worked upon, a colonial view of the environment, in which a material non-human other is exploited by centred and expansionary humans. This view may well become more prevalent in Africa and Asia, as central governments ruling over large polities, comprising many, often small and culturally heterogeneous peoples, attempt to standardize not only forms of education, language, and administration, but also what and how people should farm and eat, setting peoples apart from and polarizing their relationship with their environment.

CATEGORIES OF MISUNDERSTANDING

We are here back to the 'western' idea of environment not as onto-logically part of a people who give and draw sustenance from it, but as resting on the distinction between dominating and subordinating agents: with humans sometimes exploiting it, sometimes being controlled by it, or humans exploiting each other by means of available resources. This language of predation and exploitation is only one variant of the many possible cultural understandings of peoples' relationship to their environ-ment. It still guides much thinking in development and aid projects, although often less explicitly than previously.

The appeal of such rigid distinctions separating, for instance, an environment from the human agents working on it is both their simplicity and their facility for privileging one view over another as its determinant (as in the so-called environmentalist and possibilist approaches already discussed).

We have tried to show that, in starting from peoples' own dichotomies, a highly varied picture emerges of the relationship of humans to their habitats. Distinctions may be set up by outside agents, but are sometimes established by peoples themselves. These have to be understood in relationship to each other as working, even competing, models for coping. Outside agents, as already noted, have a rhetorical advantage. Alternatively, just as their definitions of phenomena can, if they wish, have an open-ended semantic quality, being subject to adjustments of meaning in the light of practical experience, so this same quality may apply to the categories of understanding held by peoples themselves.

However, there is one distinction which can broadly be applied to all cases, namely that between human and non-human agents. Our main point is that this distinction subsumes that between people and their environment.

Thus, so-called natural hazards, or 'acts of God', are ascribed a self-determinate capacity which may conflict with that of humans themselves. Even when natural hazards are given different identities and blamed, say, as the evil work of spirits, or when human ineffectiveness is explained as being the punishment for sins, the notion of conflicting human and non-human agencies still holds. The conflicts commonly arise from misunderstandings.

Shaw (Chapter 12) shows how the very idea of what constitutes a flood in Bangladesh, and what part it plays as an agent in human affairs, varies not only according to its severity but also according to the social status of whoever assesses it. For the rich living on high land in elevated houses, floods can be a resource which enriches large areas of low-lying cultivable land. For poor and land-hungry people living at lower levels, the same floods are disastrous, for they may eventually be required to abandon their dwellings and forsake their property.

In such cases gender differences may become critical. Bengali Muslim women are either supposed to remain indoors or remain in purdah. Purdah, a notion of closed-in personal privacy and propriety, may be lost if, as Shaw's cases suggest, families are obliged to flee from the floods to camps with minimal washing and sleeping facilities and almost no privacy. The belief is that a woman's loss of purdah makes families vulnerable to evil and noxious spirits which emanate from the floods. Women and children may become sick in the conditions of the camp. For such families the flood is not just an ecological hazard, but a moral hazard, for, through no fault of their own, their womenfolk have lost the moral and spiritual protection afforded by purdah. For women, too, their vulnerability becomes evident earlier than for men, though both are equally affected in the end.

One of the most amazing cases of admitted environmental misunderstanding by the government is documented for the former Soviet Union in Chapter 13 (Krupnik) and Chapter 14 (Vitebsky). The policy of *perestroika* (reconstruction) affects even the reindeer herders of the Soviet North. For decades their nomadic livelihood has been officially discouraged and threatened by the priority given to industrial development and oil and gas pipelines in their pasture lands. This policy is now being reversed as the government recognizes the ecological devastation of the Soviet North and reassesses the right of its citizens to determine much more their relationship to the state.

For the reindeer herders, cultural self-determination is an open issue and it is too early to say how full any return to nomadic pastoralism might be. But such issues are inseparably tied up with the area's ecological future: efforts to restore the ecological balance can only be successful if the northern peoples choose their own mix of traditional and modern modes of livelihood. This does not by itself ensure ecological harmony but is a *sine qua non* in any attempt to secure it. We are in effect witnessing the emergence of a judgement by the Soviet Union that peoples, their cultures, systems of subsistence and their habitats are part and parcel of each other and not to be distinguished separately as independently manipulable.

Previously the central government had imposed a kind of 'production nomadism' on the Even people, in place of their traditionally more holisitic, self-managed nomadism. It envisaged nomads as factory workers, with the men out at work with the herds, and their wives and children back 'home' in concentrated villages, with the women urged to produce goods for export unrelated to reindeer ecology (such as fur from raising arctic foxes). Apart from the fact that reindeer herding necessitated men's long absence from their families in the villages, the analogy with the factory completely misunderstood the family-based nature of traditional herding, in which all members had important and complementary productive roles to play. Further, the specially established villages became the new centres of Even activity, where schools, clinics, government offices and stores took on self-professed significance, while the herders became marginalized, literally living on the ecological periphery.

This contrast between centre and periphery inevitably degrades the outer landscape, which now became for government a material resource for exploitation rather than the Even traditional social map of movements, migrations, kinship and clanship.

What are the implications now for the Eveny in a future post-socialist society? Is there a parallel, Vitebsky asks, between this condition and the fact that the Eveny, like other native Siberian peoples, are also a post-shamanistic society? When they had a fully shamanic system, they could at least aspire to self-determination within its terms, adapting interpretations to acceptable versions of reality as is characteristic of shamanism. Thus, while the current push for decentralization seems to offer the Even once again the possibilities of self-determination, what form can this realistically take in the modern technological world which they have come to inhabit? Will they, in fact, return to shamanism as a self-managed and balanced means of reading the landscape? Or will they and others move in the direction they have been going: continuing to act as factory producers and at the same time reifying their culture and presenting it as if in a museum.

The imposition of such sharp distinctions as that between home and factory, itself reflecting that between domestic culture and exploitable environment, thus dislocates holistic social and productive systems. Yet, the offer to reverse this may also provide problems which have yet to be identified, let alone solved.

WORKING DEVELOPMENT

Within the field of development we commonly deploy hard distinctions between culture and the environment, and between these and human agents wishing to define and work the environment. Just as the meanings and messages attributed to the concept of development have become so polysemic, so there is no single set of understandings of, distinctions in or relations between culture and the environment which are characteristic of or unique to development. The concept of development particularly defined and applied to time and place is relevant here as a major statement about the environment and as a transformatory practice in the environment in most African, Asian and Latin American societies. Moreover, the development plan and project are also powerful in creating new performance contexts in which distinctions, say, between bush and farm, cleared and uncleared and cultivated or uncultivated, or the wild and tame, are managed and their interrelationships subsequently played out.

In relating cultural understandings of the environment to development, it might be useful to apply the notions of space, spatial metaphors and mapping or maps of meaning already mentioned. Thus we may think of development itself as a form of self-conscious or planned construction, mapping or charting both landscapes and mindscapes, and so incorporate both perceptions and representations of culture and environment. In this respect, much as Foucault (1972a; 1972b) conceived of architecture as constructed space, so development strategies, plans and projects might be thought of as spaces constructed through associated power and knowledge. Here, development establishes a very particular relationship between person and environment and between human agents for a specific purpose and with a distinctive practice. The specific objectives are thus applied within spaces bounded by this intentionality, will or agency, all notions which are inherent in the concept of development and the messages of development specialists. By this means the strategy, plan or project is marked out as a bounded space imbued with new meaning, language and intervention, so that human perceptions, beliefs and expectations of the environment may be endowed with acquired significance.

Within such spaces, the environment has often been isolated and observed by development specialists who bring their own distinctions, categorizations and knowledge to bear on it much as in another context the body has been subject to the clinical gaze. Indeed, the development gaze might be said to have its own history of negotiations between person and environment and between human agents, their distinctions and categorizations and in thus constructing its own environment, might be usefully divided into three general phases. Its history records a struggle between human and non-human agents over the extent to which each is thought of as separate and opposed, over how much status is given to other people's knowledge, and how much the environment is made exterior to the person.

In the first phase, possibly entitled colonial domination, the environment is separated out from human agents and perceived as an exterior non-human habitat subject to appropriation, domination, attack, conquest and domestication. Although the environment also may be perceived as having agency of its own or limiting and providing constraints on human agency, it is still to be dominated and tamed in the interests of human agents differentiated and selectively defined. The material non-human other is subjugated by specialist, imposed outside distinctions and categories disregarding local distinctions and categories and in the interests of order, rationality, standardization and certainty. Their inventory of land use, for instance, marks the appropriation of spaces primarily in the interests of resource availability and extraction in a language of predation and exploitation in the service of selected others, usually of outsider and specialist.

In a second phase, a higher status has been accorded to the conceptual otherness of local populations and to the interactive relationship between person and environment in the interests of improving and replenishing the latter. The wisdom of indigenous cosmologies might be recognized, but in the guise of outside advice backed by funding, technology, mechanization and the market, the distinctions and categories of the outside development specialist remain privileged *vis-à-vis* local distinctions and categories. These continue to be subordinated despite being privileged in rhetoric, just as local populations may remain subjugated – supposedly in their own interests as perceived and defined by development specialists.

In yet a third phase, that of complementary and constructed integration, the practical management of the environment rests not just on the integration of distinctions and categories of specialist and local population, but on the recognition of the idea of the environment as ontologically part of a people who give and draw sustenance from it. In such a holistic view neither person nor environment is privileged in the mutual envelopment. Human and non-human agents are inscribed in each other in that people identify with their surroundings in particular ways, are constituted by them and explain disorders or successes in terms of their proper mutual ordering. As Ingold (Chapter 3) says: if enfolded within the persons are the histories of their environmental relations, so enfolded within their environment are the histories of activities of persons. Thus people's own dichotomies and their respect for the attributes and capacities of their own environment at least have parity in status with those of the outside development specialist and may even become the starting point for any plan, project and analyses.

If the development gaze, then, sets up statements about the construction of and competition between human and non-human agents, and the environment and human perceptions of the environment, then the plan, project and strategy can be thought of as a performance in which those statements in all their distinctions, relationships and understandings are played out. Indeed it might be said that it is the event and action of the performance which specifically constitute the transformatory practices both of the environment and of the participants themselves. The performances or transformatory practices vary according to the degree to which the development specialists impose the design without the participation of the local population and write the script for or with their co-operation and according to the general status of the local population.

The naming or identification of actors or agents who undertake the transformations is important for they are the architects of construction. In turn, the conferment of authority on both the development specialist and the local agent requires the acquisition of certain attributes and capacities. The international or national development specialist requires a training in performance design and direction. For the local populations the performance involves the learning of new lines and cues often based on scripts or codes incorporating outside knowledge, naming and categorizations which equip, enable and enhance the performance. The performance itself may vary and can be categorized according to the degree to which lines and cues are based on outside knowledge and the degree of respect for and incorporation of indigenous knowledge in the script. The responsibility of the directors and producers for writing the script and allocating roles, attributes and capacities to the local actors and the degree of their participation has become an increasingly important criterion in evaluating the performance. Performances, then, come to vary according to the degree of privilege, intervention and empowerment directed from outside or placed at the disposal of the actors to write their own script. Within the constructed space, then, a particular performance has a script, structure and a design which is subject to evaluation, surveillance and reflexivity by the directors, the participants and the audience.

Just as development practice may be conceived of as a series of performances placed on a continuum according to participation of local actors in the transformatory design and practice, so the environment might be said continually to incorporate or be inscribed in the history or memory of past performances. Within development, then, it may be useful to think of the constructed space as both a discourse and transformatory practice bringing together cultural understandings of the environment with the recognition that, above all, the process of negotiation involves a hierarchy of power of things over people, of people over people and some people over things. Thus, control and therefore power is central to discussions of the environment and its relations to culture and human endeavour including development.

The development performance is primarily designed and has the capacity for transforming the environment in the interests of the utilization of resources, increasing productivity and for producing order out of disorder, chaos and wilderness through cultivation, harnessing, extraction or improvement. In the course of this transformation, cultivation practices on existing lands are improved, facilities and services expanded and new environmental spaces tapped through clearing, irrigation and forestation. To continue the theatrical metaphor, the performance is also enabled and enhanced by the provision of certain props including technologies and tools, credit, seeds, fertilizer and pasture improvement for technical intervention and empowerment as means to order, harmony and productivity. The question is: who maps out the spaces and decides the order, intervention and productive pursuits, and in whose interests is the environment separated out and dominated, tapped, exploited or otherwise acted upon?

IMPLICATE ORDER

Such holistic environmentalism, carried to its logical conclusion, privileges neither the humans nor the environment in which they live. Indeed, all are the environment, a redefinition which contradicts the term's basic sense of things surrounding other things. Elsewhere Ingold (1990) has suggested the use of Bohm's (1980) notion of implicate order to convey this mutual envelopment.

Whatever we call it, this holistic view of people and their environment carries the idea of at most only provisional centres. At one moment it is the herders or farmers who strategically fit their cattle or crops into temporarily favourable niches, at another time so-called natural hazards such as floods, perhaps characterized as the work of spirits as in Bangladesh, or benign and well-timed rains (the fruits of the rainmaker's efforts) occupy central place in the course of events. But even more than provisional centres is the notion that human and non-human agents are constantly changing places in the drama, now dominant and vociferous and now silent and defensive, and as likely to engage in misunderstandings as remain in harmony.

This ecological drama is both a metaphor of and for competing environmental theories. The invariably vociferous proponents of western-style environmental projects are sometimes, though still rarely, silenced by those expounding the lay views of subject peoples. Sometimes the dramatis personae are representatives of agencies and peoples, but sometimes they speak for themselves.

The question of representation and representativeness reminds us of the inevitable play of power and control that underlies the competition to define how a people and their habitat, how human and non-human agents, should be inscribed in each other.

Holism has, in social anthropology, been associated with structural-functionalism and with a conservative disregard for the movement of interests and power. Yet, it is clear from this discussion and from the chapters in this volume, that in its ecological sense used here, holism comprises a constant struggle between human and non-human agents, and between humans themselves when they wish to define and manage the 'whole'. For it is precisely over trying to define what are the boundaries of an environment, and what is acceptable environmental behaviour and what is not, that specialists and lay people alike argue, among themselves and with each other. We are then dealing with a holism whose boundaries are, to emphasize a dominant theme in the book, always being contested and negotiated.

REFERENCES

Bohm, D. (1980) *Wholeness and the Implicate Order*, London: Routledge & Kegan Paul.

Croll, E. (1983) *Chinese Women Since Mao*, London: Zed Press.

de Garine, I. and G. A. Harrison (eds) (1988) *Coping with Uncertainty in Food Supply*, Oxford: Clarendon Press.

Ellen, R. F. (1982) *Environment, Subsistence and System: the Ecology of Small-scale Social Formations*, Cambridge: Cambridge University Press.

Foucault, M. (1972a) *The Order of Things*, London: Tavistock.

—— (1972b) *The Archaeology of Knowledge*, London: Tavistock.

Freedman, M. (1969) 'Chinese geomancy', in *Proceedings of the Royal Anthropological Institute*.

Ingold, T. (1990) 'An anthropologist looks at biology', *Man*, 25 (2): 208–29.

Lan, D. (1985) *Guns and Rain: Guerillas and Spirit Mediums in Zimbabwe*, London: James Currey; Berkeley and Los Angeles: University of California Press.

Parkin, D. J. (1979) 'The categorization of work: cases from coastal Kenya'. In: S. Wallman (ed.) *The Anthropology of Work*, ASA Monograph No. 19, London and New York: Academic Press.

Richards, P. (1985) *Indigenous Agricultural Revolution: Ecology and Food*

Production in West Africa, London: Hutchinson.
—— (1986) *Coping with Hunger: Hazard and Experiment in an African Rice Farming System*, London: Allen & Unwin.
Sahlins, M. (1974) *Stone Age Economics*, London: Tavistock.
Schoffeleers, J. M. (ed.) (1979) *Guardians of the Land: Essays on Central African Territorial Cults*, Gwelo: Mambo Press.

Part II

Ecocosmologies

3 Culture and the perception of the environment

Tim Ingold

INTRODUCTION

Ecology is the study of the interrelations between organisms and their environments. Human beings, like other organisms, are enmeshed within webs of environmental relations. A central tenet of ecological anthropology, however, is that relations between humans and their environments are mediated by culture. It is almost an anthropological cliché to remark that culture is *the* human mode of adaptation. Yet as Steward wrote, in a classic introduction to the field that he christened 'cultural ecology', 'what to do about this cultural factor in ecological studies has raised many methodological difficulties' (1955:31). In retrospect, this reads like something of an understatement. Steward himself was markedly ambivalent, treating culture sometimes as a means by which humans adapt to their environments, and sometimes as a kind of superorganism that is itself undergoing adaptation, of which human beings are merely the flesh-and-blood carriers.

The essence of the difficulty is this. Cultures, it is supposed, are systems of symbols. As meaning-making animals, humans impose their symbolically constituted designs upon the external world (see Geertz 1964:39; Holloway 1969:395). If all meaning is thus culturally constructed, then the environment on which it is imposed must originally be *empty* of significance. But if we hold that culture is man's means of adaptation to the environment, and if the environment – prior to its ordering through cultural categories – is mere flux, devoid of form and meaning, it follows that culture is an adaptation to nothing at all, and to say that it is adapted is no more than to affirm that culture exists. We cannot, apparently, have it both ways. Either we must abandon the view, central to ecological anthropology, that culture is an adaptive system attuned to given environmental constraints, or we have to abandon the idea that human beings inhabit worlds that are themselves culturally constructed. Otherwise we would end up turning the kind of somersault that Steward did when he argued in one context, that culture prescribes how an environment is to be exploited, and in another, that for its successful exploitation an environment prescribes certain ways of doing things, that together form the core of a given culture (1955:37,41). Like Steward, we would be caught between the imperatives of culture and practical reason (Sahlins 1976).

I suggest here an alternative ecological anthropology that would overcome this dilemma. I start from the proposition that persons endure through a continuous intercourse with their environments. This intercourse is the life process. An adequate ecological anthropology must be centrally concerned with the mutual constitution of persons and environment in this process. Yet in rendering the process in terms either of an accommodation of culture to the imperatives of nature, or of an appropriation of nature within the categories of culture, orthodox theory erects an impermeable barrier between the 'interior world' of human subjects and their exterior conditions of existence, or between ideal form and physical substance. For it is supposed that persons can neither know nor act upon their environments directly, but only indirectly through the medium of their cultural representations. This supposition rests upon a cognitivist account of perception whose roots lie deep in the western dualistic worldview.

My aim is to substitute for this nature–culture dualism an understanding that proceeds from a notion of the mutualism of person and environment. To achieve this, an alternative theory of perception is required that shows how it is possible for persons to acquire *direct* knowledge of their environments in the course of their practical activities. Such a theory is available in the 'ecological psychology' of J. J. Gibson (1979; 1982). Gibson's ecological approach to perception, set up in explicit opposition to the prevalent cognitivism of mainstream psychology, offers a way out of the conceptual prison of the nature–culture dichotomy which is of immense significance for ecological anthropology. However, I need first to say more about the notion of the environment, which has received scant attention in all the arguments for and against various versions of environmental and cultural determinism.

ORGANISM AND ENVIRONMENT

Literally, an environment is that which surrounds, and therefore – at the very least – it presupposes something to be surrounded. As Lewontin writes, 'there is no organism without an environment, but there is no environment without an organism' (1982:160). We tend, however, to envisage the environment as a vast container filled with objects, living and non-living, mobile and stationary, like a room or stage-set cluttered with furniture and decorations. From this analogy comes the classic ecological concept of the *niche*, a little corner of the world an organism occupies, and to which it has fitted itself through a process of adaptation. If a vase be removed from an alcove, a niche remains for a small object that might appropriately fill the vacant space; by analogy it is implied that the ecological niche of an organism is independently specified by the essential properties of the environment, which impose the conditions of functioning to which any occupant must conform. Thus, the very notion of adaptation entails that niches exist in the environment *prior* to the organisms that fill them. The environment sets the problem, in the form of a challenge; the organism embodies the solution, in the form of its adaptive response.

However, this analogy ignores the most fundamental property of all animals: unlike vases, they both perceive and act in their environments. Indeed, perception and action are not really separable at all. One cannot, of course, describe an environment from the point of view of a vase, because the vase – being an inanimate object – does not interact with its surroundings, and does not have a point of view. Thus when I speak of the environment of the vase as the alcove in which it is placed, I am in fact relating both as components of my own environment, i.e. the relationship has its origin in my own observation. Similarly, the environment of the squirrel might be described as including the tree in which it lives. But so long as the tree is regarded in 'squirrel-neutral' terms as a ready-made object, built to independent specifications, it can only exist in the environment for an external observer. So also, it is only in the observer's environment that the squirrel exists as an object which, by virtue of its essential attributes, is 'fitted' to the tree. In short, the tree is not part of the environment *for* the squirrel, it is part of the environment *of* the squirrel *for* the detached observer.

How, then, should we set about characterizing the environment *for* an animal? One of the earliest and most original attempts in this direction was made in the *Bedeutungslehre* or 'Theory of Meaning' of Jakob von Uexküll (1982[1940]), a founding figure in the fields of both ethology and semiotics. Von Uexküll used the German term *Umwelt* – conventionally translated as 'subjective universe' – to describe the environment as constituted within the life project of an animal. Consider, for example, the meaning of a stone. In itself, i.e. as part of the environment for an indifferent observer, the stone is no more than an object with certain essential properties of shape, size, hardness and crystalline composition. Thus described, it would be an example of what von Uexküll called 'neutral objects'. But at some time or another, the stone may have been co-opted into the projects of various animals. A crab may have concealed itself beneath it; a thrush may have used it to break open snail shells; an angry human may have picked it up to hurl at an adversary. Within the *Umwelt* of the crab, the stone is a shelter, within that of the thrush it is an anvil and within that of the human it is a missile.

Von Uexküll insisted that these qualities are not attributes of the object itself, but are *acquired* by the object's having entered into diverse relationships with subject organisms. When the man picked up a stone to throw it, 'the stone became a missile – a new meaning became imprinted on it. It had acquired a "throw-quality" ' (von Uexküll 1982:27). Thus, far from fitting into a given corner of the world (a niche), it is the organism that fits the world to itself, by ascribing functions to the objects it encounters and thereby integrating them into a coherent system of its own. Hence its environment (its *Umwelt*) is the projection or 'mapping out' of its internal organization onto the outside world, or 'nature organized by an organism' (Lewontin 1982:160). Take away the organism, and the environment, in this sense, disappears with it, leaving only an array of neutral objects.

OBJECTS, QUALITIES AND AFFORDANCES

Independently of von Uexküll, Gibson argued along apparently similar lines, that animals perceive environmental objects in terms of what they *afford*, positively or negatively, for the consummation of behaviour. 'The *affordances* of an environment', Gibson writes, 'are what it *offers* the animal, what it *provides* or *furnishes*, either for good or ill' (1979:127). At first, the concept of affordance, central to Gibson's ecological psychology, seems to correspond closely to von Uexküll's concept of quality: both refer to the properties of an object that render it apt for the project of a subject. Thus we would include throwing, smashing and concealment among the many affordances of the stone. But there is a crucial contrast. Qualities, for von Uexküll, are subjectively 'added on' or affixed to the neutral object (the stone); they are contributed by perception to the world as encountered by each animal, respectively. Gibsonian affordances, however, are said to exist as inherent potentials of the objects themselves, quite independently of their being put to use or realized by a subject. Each object, Gibson argues, 'offers what it does because of what it is' (1979:139). It follows that whereas for von Uexküll, every animal is enclosed within its own subjective world, in a kind of 'reality bubble' accessible to no other than itself, for Gibson different animals can live in a *shared* environment, and moreover can share their perceptions of what it affords.

What happens if we apply these alternative perspectives of the animal environment, as an *Umwelt* and as a set of affordances, to the environment of human beings? If, as von Uexküll maintained, animals generally construct their environments by attaching meaning qualities to things, how can we continue to regard the cultural construction of the environment by human groups as in any way different? There is, as Willis notes, 'an interesting formal resemblance between the *naturally* constructed Umwelten of all animate species and the *culturally* constructed cosmologies of all human groups' (1990:11, cf. von Bertalanffy 1955). So wherein lies the contrast? One possible answer is that, unlike other animals, humans not only construct their environments but are also the authors of their own projects of construction. A beaver builds a dam, but the design for the dam comes into existence with the beaver itself – it has evolved, in the absence of a design agent, through a process of variation under natural selection. Not so with the human engineer, who not only builds dams, but designs them himself (Ingold 1989:505–6).

If humans perceive the environment as designers, they must do so in a way no other animal does, confronting it initially in a disorganized form as raw material, awaiting the imposition of form and function. Thus an animal may perceive a missile, an anvil or a shelter, but only a human will perceive a stone, which can be any of these things and much else besides (Ingold 1986a:3). Hence the human environment consists of 'neutral objects' waiting to be ordered in terms of a cultural project. Of course *we* may describe the environment of the thrush or the crab as including stones, or that of the squirrel as including trees, but this is *our* perception, not the animals'. And it is this same perceptual orientation that leads us to see the animal itself as a purely physical object, a thing of nature. If we identify the environment with 'nature', defined as an array of neutral objects, we would have to conclude – with von Glasersfeld (1976:216) – that for animals which lack the linguistically grounded, symbolic intelligence of human beings, the environment simply cannot exist. Non-human animals can no more apprehend the essential nature of the objects around them than they can apprehend their own natures, since they lack the reflexive capacity to treat their own being-in-the-world as an object of attention. 'The animal', as Marx wrote in the 1844 *Manuscripts*, 'is immediately one with its life activity. It does not distinguish itself from it . . . Man makes his life activity the object of his will and of his consciousness' (1964:113, cf. Ingold 1986b:219–20).

Although humans undoubtedly have the capacity to adopt such a 'designer orientation' towards the environment, I do not think this is the way it is normally perceived in everyday life. No more than other animals can human beings *live* in a permanently suspended condition of contemplative detachment. If the animal is always and immediately 'one with its life activity', so is the human for much (if not all) of the time. Thus with Gibson, I believe that our immediate perception of the environment is in terms of what it affords for the pursuit of the action in which we are currently engaged. The man throwing the stone did not, we suppose, first 'construct' the stone as a missile by attaching a meaning or 'throw-quality' to impressions of it received through the senses. Nor was the act of throwing merely the bodily execution of a command subsequently issued by the mind on the basis of this construct. Rather, it was the very involvement of the man in his environment, in the practical context of throwing, that led him to attend to the 'throwability' of the object, by virtue of which it was perceived as a missile. Such direct perception of the environment is a mode of engagement with the world, not a mode of construction of it.

It is clearly necessary to distinguish between the concepts of 'nature' and 'environment'. I shall call the former reality *of* the physical world of neutral objects apparent only to the detached, indifferent observer, and the latter reality *for* the world constituted in *relation* to the organism or person whose environment it is. Only for a subject that can totally disengage itself from its life in the world can reality *for* coincide with reality *of*. Thus an animal cannot engage with nature, or enter into an active relation with neutral objects, since the neutrality of nature is given only in *dis*engagement, in the absence of such relation. It may be a feature of the human condition that we can switch back and forth between engagement and disengagement, between outward-directed action and inward-directed thought.

My basic thesis, however, is that life is given in engagement, not in disengagement; or as Whitehead remarked, 'from the moment of birth we are immersed in action, and can only fitfully guide it by taking thought' (1938:217). Ecological anthropology, dealing as it does with human relations with the environment in the life process, must take the condition of active engagement as its starting point. We have therefore to overturn the Cartesian prioritization of cognition over action, or thought over life. Only by so doing can the dualism of culture and nature be replaced by the synergy of person and environment. To show how reality *for* emerges within this synergy, I must elaborate further on the Gibsonian theory of direct perception.

ON DIRECT PERCEPTION

Gibson's view represents a radical departure from the received cognitivism of most anthropological and psychological accounts of environmental perception. According to the latter, we must first know the world before we can act in it, and knowing consists in the organization of sensations impinging upon the passively receptive human subject into progressively higher-order structures or 'representations'. It is generally assumed that the information encoded in sense data is highly impoverished and, in itself, quite insufficient to specify the objects and events that subjects claim to perceive in their environments (see Michaels and Carello 1981:2–8, for a critical review). All knowledge of the environment has therefore to be reconstructed from these inadequate and fragmentary data, and this is achieved through processing the 'raw' sensory input according to cognitive schemata located in the head of the perceiver, not 'out there' in the world. Thus whatever patterning, structure or meaning we find in what we perceive is contributed by our own minds. Seeing is qualitatively distinct from knowing, for whereas the former consists in the receipt, by the private human subject, of transitory and meaningless sense data, the latter consists in the ordering of these data into commonly held and enduring conceptual categories. Only then do we know what we see. The only *activity* in perception, then, is mental activity, or as Gibson succinctly expressed the position he aimed to overthrow, perceptual activity consists in 'the operations of the mind upon the deliverances of the senses' (1982[1976]:397).

Central to the theory of direct perception is the rejection of this Cartesian dichotomy between sensation and intellection. As Reed comments, 'there is no distinction between seeing and "seeing as" in Gibson's epistemology' (1987a:105; cf. Gibson 1979:258). Perception is not a matter of the mental processing of sensory inputs into products (percepts) but involves the functioning of a total system comprising both the brain and receptor organs, together with their neural and muscular linkages, within an environmental context. In short, the whole animal (whether human or otherwise) perceives, not its mind alone, and the outcome is not a percept but a new state of the perceiver. Hence perception is a process that *goes on* continuously through time, rather than a fitting together, in memory, of a succession of discrete and instantaneous snapshots.

This process of perception is also a process of action: we perceive the world as, and because, we act in it. As we move around in and explore the environment, we actively seek and pick up information that specifies invariant properties and qualities of the objects we encounter. Visual perception, for example, involves the extraction of parametric constants underlying the continuous modulations of an *optic array* (i.e. the pattern of reflected light at a point of observation) for a moving observer. Crucially, the structures and meanings that we find in the world are *already there* in the information that we extract in the act of perception; their source lies in the objects we perceive, they are not added on by the perceiver. Therefore perceiving is, *ipso facto*, knowing – to have seen something is to have sought out the information that enables one to know it. But the knowledge gained through such perception is essentially *practical*; it is knowledge about what the object affords. Depending on the kind of activity in which we are engaged, we will be attuned to picking up a particular kind of information, leading to the perception of a particular affordance.

Affordances are properties of the real environment as directly perceived by an agent in a context of practical action. The reciprocal term *effectivity* denotes the action capabilities of the agent – what he or she is practically equipped to do (Cutting 1982). Thus the range of affordances of an object will be constrained by the effectivities of the subject, and conversely, the effectivities of the subject will be constrained by the affordances of the objects encountered. One corollary is that tools, since they enlarge the effectivities of their users, can radically transform the perception of the environment.

AGAINST CULTURAL CONSTRUCTION

I now return to my anthropological starting point, which was to contest the role of culture in the perception of the environment. General assertions that the human environment is culturally constructed are almost too numerous to cite, but Douglas' statement may be taken as fairly representative:

> As perceivers we select from all the stimuli falling on our senses only those which interest us, and our interests are governed by a pattern-making tendency. . . . *In a chaos of shifting impressions*, each of us constructs a stable world in which objects have recognizable shapes, are located in depth, and have permanence.
>
> (Douglas 1966:36, my emphasis)

Notice how the stress placed here on the meaning-making operations of perceivers effectively dissolves the reality of the environment in which they live, reducing it to a mass of stimulus prods which give rise to a chaotic flux of ephemeral sensations. According to this view, if perceptions are shared it must be because, thanks to language, people organize their sensory input in terms of conventionally agreed categories. 'Our internal perception of the world around us', writes Leach, 'is greatly influenced by the verbal categories which we use to describe it. . . . We use language to cut up the visual continuum into meaningful objects and into persons filling distinguishable roles' (1976:33).

The theory of direct perception asserts the precise opposite: that we *discover* meaningful objects in the environment by moving about in it and extracting invariants from the continually changing optic array. Language is not used for generating internal perceptions of our surroundings, nor is it necessary for perception to be shared. The awareness of living in a common world – the communion of experience that lies at the heart of sociality – does not depend on the translation of percepts, initially constructed by subjects from sensory data private to themselves, into the terms of an objective system of collective representations encoded in language and validated by verbal agreement (Gibson 1982[1976]:412). Sociality is rather given from the start, *prior* to the objectification of experience in cultural categories, in the direct perceptual involvement of fellow subjects immersed in joint action in the same environment.

Along with the constructivism of orthodox culture theory, we find an almost obsessive concern with classification systems: 'Our sense data', writes Ellen, 'are ordered through classifications' (1982:234), and not until we have classified things in the world are we said to be in a position to act on them. Again, Gibsonian theory asserts the contrary. Action depends on the perception of affordances, but 'to perceive an affordance is not to classify an object' (Gibson 1979:134). For example, I often use what I classify as a screwdriver in the context of painting – as a lever to remove the lid from the can, and as a whisk to stir the paint. Neither of these affordances – levering and whisking – has anything to do with the fact that I call the object a screwdriver. I could call it anything I pleased. In this practical context any similarly long, thin, rigid, graspable object will do, regardless of how or whether it is classified. Man has been defined, with some justification, as 'the classifying animal' (Berlin *et al.* 1973:214). But other animals, which presumably lack the human penchant for classification, get by very well without it. So, for most practical purposes, do we.

A further implication of orthodox theory is that a radical distinction has to be imposed between the world as objectively given to the indifferent anthropological observer, and the construction of that world by indigenous people (Ellen 1982:206). Many different terms have been employed to signal this distinction. Brookfield, for one, contrasts the *real* environment and the *perceived* environment. Environmental perception, he argues, is a mental activity, and the perceived environment is what the mind constructs through a selective response to particular stimuli (1969:53). Moreover:

> However closely the perceived environment may resemble the real environment, it is quite separate and distinct from it. Even though the real environment may . . . be the creation of human activity upon the natural landscape, it is only the perceived environment that is always and wholly a cultural artifact.
>
> (Brookfield 1969:64)

An alternative distinction is Rappaport's, between what he calls 'operational' and 'cognized' models. The former is the scientist's description, derived from 'observation and measurement of empirical entities, events and material relationships'. It corresponds to the 'physical world' of the people being studied. The cognized model is a description of 'the environment conceived by the people who act in it', and 'guides their action' (1968:237–8). Evidently, Rappaport's 'operational model' is a description of what I called earlier reality *of*, a reality accessible only to the totally disengaged observer. I reject the view, however, that the perceived environment, reality *for*, belongs to a separate domain of cultural artifice, that it is the outcome of an intellectual process of cognition and that such cognition is a necessary preliminary and guide to action. As I have shown, the environment, as distinct from nature or the 'physical world', is the same reality constituted in its relation to a subject, or group of subjects, in their active engagement with it. It is not separately cognized, prior to action, for it is by their action in the world that people know it, and come to perceive what it affords.

PRODUCTION AND CONSUMPTION

Another word for affordance is 'use-value'. Discussion of this concept has been plagued by the question of whether use-values are given as the physical properties of objects, or whether they are qualities assigned to things by cultural subjects. Marx defined use-values as 'articles capable of satisfying wants of one kind or another' (1930:169). To focus on their utility was to consider them with regard to their intrinsic physical features. Yet surely, Sahlins objects, the utility of a thing, at least for human consumers, will depend upon its incorporation within a system of symbolic values: 'all utilities are symbolic' (1976:150). Objects do not, in themselves, prescribe the nature or the context of their uses; they become use-values only through a system of signification which links each object to an idea or representation in the mind of a cultural subject. This representation, furnished by an expectation of how the object will be used or consumed, both precedes and motivates the act of its production. On these grounds, Sahlins dismisses Marx's somewhat tortuous attempts to establish the ultimate priority of production over consumption, to transform 'the preexistent image of production into its objective consequence' (Sahlins 1976:153, cf. Ingold 1986b:323–4).

By regarding use-values as affordances, the theoretical issue of whether they are naturally given or culturally constructed disappears. They are neither. Like affordances, they do not belong within an 'operational' description of the physical world, nor are they part of a 'cognized' system of cultural representations. Though they belong to the real world, they are the constituents of that world as engaged in the activities of people, that is as an environment or reality *for*. This point might best be demonstrated by comparing the dichotomy between action and perception with that between production and consumption. Sahlins' view of production is essentially equivalent to the cognitivist view of action: it begins with a representation in the mind of the producer, and ends with its realization in the form of a concrete object. It is thus a transferral of cultural design onto the 'physical world', establishing a division, within that world, between the natural and the artificial. Conversely in consumption, as in the cognitivist view of perception, raw materials detached from the physical world – analogous to sensory stimuli – are transferred to the consumer and assimilated in terms of a mental representational schema. If perception proceeds through the attachment of meaning by the perceiver to raw sense data, so consumption proceeds through the attachment of concepts of use by the consumer to raw material. In one case the process ends with the percept, in the other it ends with the utility; both represent the accommodation of the physical world to cultural design.

I take a different view of production and consumption, but one that accords closely with Marx's earlier thinking on the matter and the pragmatic realism of Gibson's ecological psychology. Rather than regarding production as the imposition of a cultural design upon the 'external' reality *of* nature, and consumption as the accommodation of nature within pre-existing cultural categories, I regard both production and consumption as twin facets of a mutually constitutive and continually evolving field of relationships between persons and their environments. The contrast between these views is indicated schemati-

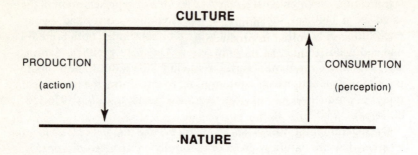

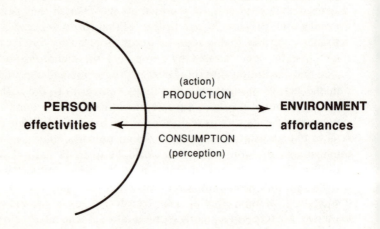

Figure 3.1 Two views of the relationship between production and consumption.

cally in Figure 3.1. In the process of production, people create their environments, not in the sense of inscribing meanings into things (to yield 'artifacts'), but in the sense that the environment is the embodiment of past activity. Objects in the environment, as Mead would say, are 'collapsed acts' (see Noble 1981:79), they are as they are because of activities undertaken by persons in relation to them. The history of an environment is a history of the activities of all those organisms, human and non-human, contemporary and ancestral, that have contributed to its formation. We should liken the environment not to a container or backcloth within or against which life goes on but rather to a piece of sculpture, or a monument, except in two respects: first, it is shaped not by one hand but by many; and second, the work is never complete. No environment is ever fully created, it is always undergoing creation. It is, as it were, 'work in progress'.

Just as perception is intimately involved in action, so consumption is intimately involved in production. Through both, the environment enters actively into the constitution of persons; i.e. in the mutually constitutive interrelation between persons and environment, production is a becoming of the environment, consumption is a becoming of persons. Like perception, consumption is an ongoing process and its outcome is not the utility but a new state of the consumer him- or herself. It would be wrong to think of the person–environment interface as one of external contact between separate domains; each, to use Bohm's (1980:177) term, is *implicate* in the other. A person's development is also the development of that person's environment, and these complementary processes result from a continuous interchange across the emergent boundary between them (Ingold 1990). Enfolded within persons are the histories of their environmental relations; enfolded within the environment are the histories of the activities of persons. Thus, to sever the links that bind any people to their environment is to cut them off from the historical past that has made them who they are. Yet this is precisely what orthodox culture theory has done, in giving recognition to the historical quality of human works only by attributing them to projects of cultural construction opposed to, and merely superimposed upon, an ahistorical nature.

To sum up, the cognitivist view in both anthropology and psychology encloses humanity in a world of its own – or rather many separate worlds corresponding to discrete 'cultures', each a system of shared and enduring symbolic representations. Beyond lies an external reality, known interchangeably as 'nature' or 'the physical world'. This reality is the source of raw sense data which are, in themselves, without order or meaning. In perception, these data, detached (as 'stimuli') from the environment and attached (as 'sensations') to human subjects, are ordered in terms of cultural schemata. Likewise in consumption, raw material is detached from nature and incorporated into culture. I am arguing, to the contrary, that persons and environment are mutually constitutive components of the *same* world, and that in both perception and consumption, meanings embodied in environmental objects are 'drawn into' the experience of subjects. These meanings are affordances or use-values. Hence the dialectics of the interface between persons and environment should be understood in terms of a dichotomy not between culture and nature but between effectivities and affordances – between the action capabilities of subjects and the possibilities for action offered by objects.

THE REDISCOVERY OF CULTURE

How, then, are humans different? In developing his ecological psychology, Gibson constantly stressed the continuities rather than the contrasts between human and non-human perceptions of the environment. If perception is a matter of discovering meanings in the environment through exploratory action, rather than adding them on through some kind of cognitive processing, then the apparently unique cognitive capacities of humans – including language and symbolic thought – will not lead them to perceive their environments in a radically distinct way from other animals. Where humans differ is in their ability to describe and render accounts of their actions discursively, to themselves and others. Language and symbolic thought are not necessary for us to *know* the world, but are needed to make such knowledge explicit. Their role, as Reed argues, 'is not to *create* knowledge out of merely potential meaningful input [but] to *make others aware*, . . . to share knowledge' (1987b:154). I do not deny the importance of knowledge-sharing practices in human society; my point is that the discursive representation of the environment in terms of cultural categories is not a precondition for our contact with it in production and consumption, or for our contact with one another in social life. The cultural construction of the environment is not so much a *prelude* to practical action as an (optional) *epilogue*.

Orthodox cognitivism makes little of the distinction between perceiving and imagining, but erects an absolute barrier between the perceived world and reality. By contrast, the ecological approach I have been advocating does not separate the perceived world from reality, but makes much of the distinction between perceiving and imagining. The capacity of human beings to construct imagined worlds is unmatched by any other species, and in this, both language and culture are directly implicated. But the imaginative reconstruction entailed in the discursive rendering of accounts implies a contemplative disengagement from the world. As objectively self-aware and self-interpreting animals, humans can describe their environment, and report on their actions within it, as though they had themselves stepped outside it, posing as mere spectators. But in so doing, the environment reverts to nature, reality *for* to reality *of*. Yet nature, in itself, is a world without meaning. It is the categories of culture, then, that lend significance to a reality rendered otherwise meaningless in consequence of its dissociation from action.

I conclude that it is fundamentally mistaken to model the ecological relations of human beings in terms of a confrontation between nature and culture. For the nature–culture dichotomy, far from describing a primordial division between mutually impenetrable worlds of matter and mind which people in their activities must perforce seek to bridge, is rather a consequence of the retrospective, analytic *decomposition* of our immediate and active perception of the environments in which we live and work. Perhaps the answer to Steward's question, 'what to do about culture?', is in fact to leave it out of the ecological equation. Anthropologists, no doubt, would be horrified at the thought. However, my case rests on the following observations:

1 Humans do not, in the ordinary course of life, experience the environment as a 'blank slate', i.e. as *space*, awaiting the imposition of cultural order; but rather as a structured set of affordances in the context of current action.

2 Acting in the world is the practitioner's way of knowing it, thus the acquisition of environmental knowledge is inseparable from productive practice. Perceptual skills and technical skills are therefore two sides of the same coin.

3 Culture is a framework not for *perceiving* the world, but for *interpreting* it, to oneself and others. We do not have to interpret things in order to perceive them; and much of what we perceive, we fail to interpret, i.e. our knowledge of them remains tacit.

4 'Nature', as an environment of neutral objects, is not a pre-existent given, but a product of the interpretative stance, which requires subjects to disengage themselves from the task at hand.

5 This may be something that only humans, with their capacity for objective self-awareness, can do. Because we are meaning-making animals, we are also unique in confronting the spectre of a *meaningless* environment.

6 Systems of cultural classification are not therefore a precondition for practical action in the world, but are invoked to recover the meaning that is lost when that action turns reflexively inwards on the self.

Finally, the same observations may be applied to that component of the environment comprising other human beings. I have spoken of ecological relations as if they were limited to an animal's interactions with inanimate objects, and with plants and animals of other species.

But the environment of any animal normally includes individuals of the *same* species, so that its relations with its environment must include interactions with conspecifics of the kind usually called 'social'. Again, anthropological orthodoxy has it that the relations that human beings have with one another are mediated by a symbolically constituted system known as 'society'. Hence it is supposed that only through society do we come into contact with other humans, just as it is only through culture (in this view) that we come into contact with non-human components of the environment. My argument is that we relate to others *directly* in terms of our perception of the possibilities they afford for interaction, rather than indirectly through the filter of social rules and categories. The latter are nevertheless fundamental to the way in which we call our own and others' social action to account, i.e. to what Hallowell (1960:346) called the *normative orientation* of conduct. The idea that human organisms come into being as unstructured raw material awaiting 'socialization' is a product of this normative orientation. Social life without rules is not chaotic, as ethologists have shown for non-human animals. But the vision of chaos is an inevitable by-product of the human activity of rule-making. Just as the perception of the environment as 'nature' is the product of a designer perspective, so it is as self-conscious regulators of their social activity that humans come to regard their own 'nature' as inherently disorganized, or mere potential.

REFERENCES

Berlin, B., Breedlove, D. and Raven, P. (1973) 'General principles of classification and nomenclature in folk biology', *American Anthropologist* 75:214–42.

Bohm, D. (1980) *Wholeness and the Implicate Order*, London: Routledge & Kegan Paul.

Brookfield, H. C. (1969) 'On the environment as perceived', *Progress in Geography* 1:53–80.

Cutting, J. E. (1982) 'Two ecological perspectives: Gibson vs. Shaw and Turvey', *American Journal of Psychology* 95:199–222.

Douglas, M. (1966) *Purity and Danger*, London: Routledge & Kegan Paul.

Ellen, R. F. (1982) *Environment, Subsistence and System: the Ecology of Small-scale Social Formations*, Cambridge: Cambridge University Press.

Geertz, C. (1964) 'The transition to humanity', in S. Tax (ed.) *Horizons of Anthropology*, Chicago: Aldine.

Gibson, J. J. (1979) *The Ecological Approach to Visual Perception*, Boston: Houghton Mifflin.

—— (1982) *Reasons for Realism: Selected Essays of James J. Gibson*, E.

Reed and R. Jones (eds), Hillsdale, NJ: Lawrence Erlbaum.

Hallowell, A. I. (1960) 'Self, society and culture in phylogenetic perspectives', in S. Tax (ed.) *Evolution after Darwin, Vol. II: The Evolution of Man*, Chicago: University of Chicago Press.

Holloway, R. L. (1969) 'Culture, a *human* domain', *Current Anthropology* 10:395–412.

Ingold, T. (1986a) *The Appropriation of Nature: Essays on Human Ecology and Social Relations*, Manchester: Manchester University Press.

—— (1986b) *Evolution and Social Life*, Cambridge: Cambridge University Press.

—— (1989) 'The social and environmental relations of human beings and other animals', in V. Standen and R. A. Foley (eds) *Comparative Socioecology: the Behavioural Ecology of Humans and Other Mammals* (British Ecological Society Special Publications, 8), Oxford: Blackwell Scientific.

—— (1990) 'An anthropologist looks at biology', *Man* (NS) 25(2):208–29.

Leach, E. R. (1976) *Culture and Communication*, Cambridge: Cambridge University Press.

Lewontin, R. C. (1982) 'Organism and environment', in H. C. Plotkin (ed.) *Learning, Development and Culture*, Chichester: Wiley.

Marx, K. (1930) *Capital*, vol. I, E. and C. Paul (trans.), from 4th German edn of *Das Kapital* (1890), London: Dent.

—— (1964) *The Economic and Political Manuscripts of 1844*, M. Milligan (trans.), D. J. Struik (ed.), New York: International Publishers.

Michaels, C. F. and Carello, C. (1981) *Direct Perception*, Englewood Cliffs, NJ: Prentice-Hall.

Noble, W. G. (1981) 'Gibsonian theory and the pragmatist perspective', *Journal of the Theory of Social Behaviour* 11:65–85.

Rappaport, R. A. (1968) *Pigs for the Ancestors: Ritual in the Ecology of a New Guinea People*, New Haven: Yale University Press.

Reed, E. S. (1987a) 'Why do things look as they do? The implications of J. J. Gibson's "The ecological approach to visual perception" ', in A. Costall and A. Still (eds) *Cognitive Psychology in Question*, Brighton: Harvester Press.

—— (1987b) 'James Gibson's ecological approach to cognition', in A. Costall and A. Still (eds) *Cognitive Psychology in Question*, Brighton: Harvester Press.

Sahlins, M. D. (1976) *Culture and Practical Reason*, Chicago: University of Chicago Press.

Steward, J. H. (1955) *Theory of Culture Change*, Urbana: University of Illinois Press.

von Bertalanffy, L. (1955) 'An essay on the relativity of categories', *Philosophy of Science* 22:243–63.

von Glasersfeld, E. (1976) 'The development of language as purposive behaviour', in H. Steklis, S. Harnad and J. Lancaster (eds) *Origins and Evolution of Language and Speech*, New York: Annals of the New York Academy of Sciences, vol. 280.

von Uexküll, J. (1982 [1940]) 'The theory of meaning', B. Stone and H. Weiner (trans.) from *Bedeutungslehre*, T. von Uexküll (ed.), *Semiotica* 42:25–82.

Whitehead, A. N. (1938) *Science and the Modern World*, Harmondsworth: Penguin.

Willis, R. G. (1990) 'Introduction', in R. G. Willis (ed.) *Signifying Animals: Human Meaning in the Natural World* (One World Archaeology, 16), London: Unwin Hyman.

4 The Dogon and their trees

Walter E. A. van Beek and
Pieteke M. Banga[1]

THE MASKS

Just before dawn, shrill cries echo through the sleeping village of Tireli, the quiet peace rudely interrupted as twenty young men dash through the steep narrow alleys winding along the hillside compounds. They shout at the top of their voices the high-pitched mask cries: 'He hee hee, be warned women, be alert men, the masks are here.' A few youngsters beat small wooden drums or tap sticks to arouse the villagers. Still dazed, the women slowly heave themselves from their sleeping mats in the compound and reluctantly enter their huts, where yesterday's heat still lingers. From their mats men greet the masks with a mighty call in the *sigi so*, the ritual mask language: 'Welcome, welcome, how did you spend your day, thank you for coming. Be strong and powerful.' Being men, they are allowed to look upon the shouting youngsters who behave as mask dancers but are not fully adorned as such. In fact, they seem sloppily dressed, not wearing the normal mask outfit which needs good and careful grooming. Some wear dilapidated masks half covering their faces, one wears a red grass skirt; the central piece of his costume, while a third has a strip of fibres tied around his head. The *puro*, the march of the masks, has come!

The so-called masks descend the rocky slopes to find the huge stacks of firewood on the first dune-ridge, where most of the women keep their fresh supplies of wood. The masks are looking for *ponu*-wood (*Detarium microcarpum*), a small fruit tree. Shouting, drumming and dancing, they overturn the neat piles of firewood and drag out all the *ponu* branches they can find. Other youngsters join them, some half-masked, others just for the fun of it.

The mask cries rise to an even higher pitch, the entire party returns to the village to display the offensive firewood, to general male indignation. In the village the compounds are also searched. Meanwhile, the older – and cooler – men are gathered in and around the main men's house, to discuss the gravity of the female offence and to decide on appropriate fines to offset the wrongdoing. A few fully clad masks from the other half of Tireli join in and add to the atmosphere of male dominance. However, this feeling is diminished by the presence of a woman, called Yasigi, one of the ceremonial mask sisters. Undaunted by any mask (clothed or not), this older woman freely mingles with the spectators and dancers, contrasting sharply with the rest of the Tireli women, who sit in their huts, quietly, though quite amused by the whole proceeding. At noon, the crowds disperse; the men slowly return to their homes and daily chores, feeling pleased about the day's work. The women have learned a lesson they will not easily forget. True, it has cost some money, as each husband pays his wife's fine and it will not be refunded by her. The women emerge from their huts, fetch water, cook millet mush and normal life returns again to Tireli.

Apart from being great fun for the men and mildly amusing for the women, the *puro* is a conflict between males and females in Dogon society about an environmental issue. The women need firewood for cooking and making pottery; a few battered trees grow alongside the creek on the nearby sandy dunes, protected by a mild taboo, but the women have to walk about 7 km to find suitable ones. The *ponu* provides good firewood, but the men enjoy its fruit too much to have the trees cut down. The fruit is not very nourishing, consisting mainly of a large inedible kernel, but the men like to suck its scanty covering.

The expression of this conflict is strictly Dogon: men oppose the women in a closed group, using the traditional means of control, the masks. The fundamental taboo in the whole complex of masks and mask dances is the fact that the women are not supposed to know that the masked dancers are costumed men. Of course they know very well, and can distinguish precisely who is dancing and can judge how good they are. But they pretend not to know in front of the men and joke mockingly about it in their absence. In the *puro*, however, the masks incompletely disguise the men, so the women are not allowed to see them and are confined to their huts. These rites can be held for any grudge the men of the village may have against the women, e.g. for quarrelling, or running away from their husbands. Recently, trees figure prominently in the rites, as in the event described.

We shall explore the reasons for this ecological issue in the relation between men and women and consider the functions of trees and shrubs in the Dogon ecosystem in some detail. Desertification, the ever-looming threat for this ecosystem and the cultural response to it are related to the way the Dogon view their own environment.

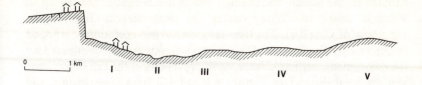

Figure 4.1 Cross-section of the escarpment situation near Tireli.

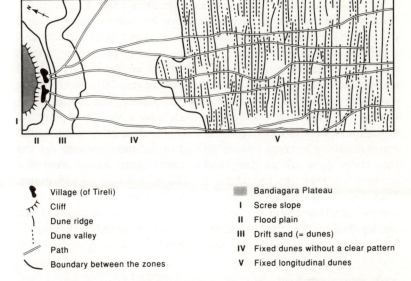

Village (of Tireli)	Bandiagara Plateau
Cliff	I Scree slope
Dune ridge	II Flood plain
Dune valley	III Drift sand (= dunes)
Path	IV Fixed dunes without a clear pattern
Boundary between the zones	V Fixed longitudinal dunes

Figure 4.2 Map of the geomorphological zones near Tireli (scale 1:50,000).

QUALITIES OF THE NATURAL ENVIRONMENT

Tireli lies near the Malian border with Burkina Faso, at the foot of the Bandiagara cliff, a NE–SW-oriented escarpment that forms the SE boundary of the Bandiagara Plateau. The 260 km-long escarpment is elevated from 100 m in the SW to 700 m in the NE (Barth 1970) above the Gondo Plain, that extends from the cliff towards the southeast. The base of the cliff, a relatively steep scree slope of 25–30°, has been the habitat of the Dogon since their arrival in the region. Together with the villages on top of the cliff, the string of escarpment villages, including Tireli, form the old core of Dogon settlements. The area is situated in the Sudan–Sahel zone, with a mean annual rainfall up to 500 mm, nearly all falling during the rainy season (June to the beginning of October). The tree–savannah-type vegetation is cropped intensively by the Dogon. Their ecological situation is dominated by the escarpment, with its scree, a small depression at the rim of the scree and the sand dunes (see Figures 4.1 and 4.2 for a cross section and aerial view, respectively).

In both figures, the following zones situated in the Gondo Plain[2] can be discerned in the neighbourhood of Tireli: (I) scree slope, (II) flood plain, (III) drift sand (= dunes), (IV) fixed sand dunes without a clear pattern and (V) fixed, longitudinal dunes.

Some characteristics of the zones are listed in Table 4.1. Table 4.2 shows the distribution of tree and shrub species over the various types. It seems that in most areas in the Sahel zone, the diversity of tree and shrub species and the number of trees and shrubs per species is least near the villages, increasing further away. From Table 4.2 for Tireli and probably most villages along the Bandiagara Cliff, the reverse is true: trees are concentrated close to the settlement. One reason might be that the conditions on the scree slope and in the flood plain are more humid than in the area of the fixed dunes; another might be the cultural rules governing ownership and use of trees growing around the village. Zone III, the drift sand (= dunes), can be considered as a gradient between the humid flood plain and the dry fixed dunes. However, as indicated with the tree density, the specifics of all these zones depend for a large part on the culturally co-determined land use. So, we shall explore the Dogon use of trees in view of their ecological history and emic view of their environment.

THE USE OF TREES

The Dogon value trees for several reasons. Fruit is only a minor consideration as most trees do not bear edible fruits. Some trees, e.g. the *oro* tree (baobab), are important for making the sauce for the daily millet mush, i.e. for seasoning and shortening. Baobab leaves flavour the sauce; when cooked with sesame they give a dark-green, rather slimy sauce greatly relished by the Dogon: 'It gives you strength.' The women stockpile dried leaves in the dry season as no daily diet is complete without them. The sweet–sour pulp of the baobab fruit is used in millet cream as well as being sucked raw between meals by children. The bark is stripped at regular intervals for rope fibres. The baobab is exceptional: on the one hand, it is used more intensively

Table 4.1 Characteristics of the Gondo Plain zones

Characteristics	Zones				
	I Scree slope	II Flood plain	III Drift sand (= dunes)	IV Fixed sand dunes without a clear pattern	V Fixed longi-tudinal dunes
Geology/ Geomor-phology	Slope (25–30°), con-sisting of large blocks of Cam-brian/ Ordovician sandstone. The present form of the slope has been developed during the Tertiary period and has hardly changed since the end of this period (Barth 1977)	Recent al-luvial sand and gravel	Recent deflation and deposi-tion of sand during the dry seasons	Sand dunes, which have been formed during the Ogolien (Late Pleistocene) (Barth 1977)	NE–SW or-iented longitudinal dunes, which have been formed during the Ogolien (Late Pleistocene) (Barth 1977)
Soils	Lithic Ustorthents	Ustoxic Quartzip-samment	Ustoxic Quartzi-psamment	Ustoxic Quartzi-psamment	Ustoxic Quartzi-psamment
Land use	Huts and granaries are built here. Fields, which are cultivated each rainy season with the use of manure (of cattle)	Fields, which are cultivated perma-nently with the use of manure (of cattle) com-post, and chemical fertilizers	Fields, which are cultivated each rainy season with the use of manure (of cattle) and chemical fertilizers	Jachère sys-tem. The fields are cultivated 6 years and are left fallow afterwards	Jachère sys-tem. The fields are cultivated 6 years and are left fallow afterwards

than other trees (leaves, fruit and fibres), while, on the other hand, its wood serves no practical purpose. It makes poor firewood, and

Table 4.2 The distribution of the most important tree and shrub species[3] in the Gondo Plain zones

Tree and shrub species Dogon names	scientific names	I	II	III	IV	V
Wenye	*Ficus lecardii* or					
	glumosa	x				
Baara	*Acacia arabia*[1]	x				
Kumu banu	*Ficus platyphylla*	x				
Kumu piru	*Ficus gnaphalocarpa*	x				
Si	*Celtis integrifolia*	x				
Kuygo	*Combretum micrantum*	x				
Siû	*Hyphaene thebaica*	x	x			
Omunu	*Tamarindus indica*	x	x			
Yuro (Bambara: néré)	*Parkia biglobosa*	x	x			
Mangoro	*Mangifera indica*		x			
Oro	*Adansonia digitata*	x	x	x		
Sèngè	*Acacia albida*	x	x	x		
Sa	*Lannea acida*	x	x	x		
Kamato	*Sclerocarya birrea*			x		
Mono	*Balanites aegyptiaca*	x	x	x	x	
Koybo	*Bauhinia reticalata*	x	x	x	x	x
Botskoko			x		x	x
Ponu	*Detarium microcarpum*	x	x	x	x	x
Kirè	*Prosopis africana*[2]			x	x	x
Aguno				x	x	x
Gurugu	*Guiera senegalensis*				x	x
Abana	*Combretum fragrans*[3]			x	x	x

Notes:
1 Identical with *Acacia nilotica* (von Maydell 1983).
2 The *kilèna*, mentioned by Dieterlen (1952:127), might be a Dogon homonym, though her determination is different: *Acalypha ciliata*. It might also be *alkilè* (*Diospyros mespiliformis*) (Dieterlen 1952: 136).
3 Given as *baban* in Dieterlen 1952.

consequently is never cut down. Other important fruit trees are *ponu*, *omunu*, *sa* and *yur* (in Bambara *néré*). Leaves are used as fodder for the goats and sheep – especially *sèngè* – and as manure for the fields.

In the western part of zone IV leaves of *gurugu*, *abana* and *aguno* are harvested during the rainy season and are used as manure for onion and tobacco crops in the flood plain.

In zone V the millet grown under the trees of *abana*, *koybo* and *kirè* flourishes more than millet growing further away. One reason is the slightly higher soil humidity in the shade of the trees, but more important, is the humus-rich soil produced by leaf fall.

One of the most important functions of trees and shrubs is the provision of firewood, especially in a poor country like Mali, where the income of the population is too small to import paraffin or kerosene. Suitable trees and shrubs for firewood are, according to the Dogon, *abana, gurugu, ponu, botskoko* and *aguno*. Less important are *sa, sèngè, omunu* and *yuro*.

During the rainy season, the Tireli women go each day into the bush to gather wood. Nowadays, they have to walk up to 1.5 hours (about 7 km) to reach the area with sufficient firewood. They carry 20 kg wood on their heads, sufficient for preparing meals for 10 or 11 days. So, for cooking, each woman needs 700 kg wood per year, i.e. the branches of 35 medium-sized trees, a total of 1.5 stere. In Tireli there are about 525 women. This means that a total of 18,375 branches will be burnt each year. The women also need firewood for brewing the millet beer. Given the scarcity of firewood, this is done very economically; the women place four to ten large pots in a double line along the fire close together to prevent the heat from escaping. Even so, beer is cooked for about 24 hours and no economizing can reduce that length of time. Thus, Dogon women generally acknowledge that villages with a good wood supply brew a far better beer than those with less. And Tireli beer is the best! The brewing of the millet beer requires about 875 medium-sized trees each year.

Firewood is also needed for firing pots. A Dogon woman produces her entire year's pottery at the end of the dry season, in a large open pit with dozens of large pots. The firewood is mixed with straw and dung and some economizing is possible, the process requiring about 50 trees each year. So the total amount of firewood needed for Tireli, a village of about 2,500 people, is 19,300 medium-sized trees each year, implying 386 tons or 550 m^3, i.e. 1,100 stere.

The Dogon also need timber for building houses and granaries. The house walls are built with sandstone blocks, plastered with mud. The granary walls consist entirely of adobe. But the construction of the roof and the floor requires about 13 trees (whole trunks), mostly Acacia, *ponu* and some *abana*. Five to eight trees are needed for the floor and the roof of each granary. The timber, however, is vulnerable to attack by vermin, e.g. termites. Estimates are that each house or granary needs new timber every 60 years and for the 600 or so houses and 1,200 granaries, 260 trees will be chopped each year.

Wood is also used (the larger branches) for fencing the onion and tobacco gardens. After the harvest, the fences are broken down and either reused or burned. The total length of the fencing is about 3,600 m. Ibrahim (1979) estimates that a small tree or bush is needed for every metre of fencing and 3,600 small trees or shrubs have to be chopped, but as this is reused as firewood, it does not require extra. Finally, several household objects are made from wood, e.g. hoe and adze handles, pestles and mortars and stools, but the consumption is small because these items last for many years. The annual wood consumption in a large village like Tireli would be: 386 tons for firewood, 21 tons for construction plus some 5 tons for additional objects, in total 412 tons (= 587 m^3 or 1,174 stere).

The Dogon covet leaves and fruits as well as wood but for the women, trees supply primarily firewood, though some fruits may be used. For the men, trees supply fodder and manure, wood for their huts and some fruit. The men use either leaves or the whole trunk, whereas the women use the branches. So, in times when trees become scarce, there is conflict between men and women embodied in, for example, the *puro*.

The scarcity of trees and shrubs also causes conflict between the conservation of the natural environment and the needs of the entire Dogon population. The trees and shrubs are at certain times harvested by the Dogon and taken to the village as part of a continuous flow of minerals and biomass from the periphery towards the centre of habitation. The leaves enrich the soil, and the nutrients are withdrawn by millet which will be harvested by men.

However, the savannah trees and shrubs also stabilize the soil against wind and water erosion. Shrubs are especially important because the foliage provides more soil cover than the trees. In places without natural vegetation, sand can drift away and be trapped elsewhere by shrubs. In this way embryonal dunes can form around *gurugu*, *aguno* and young *abana* trees. Where trees and shrubs are cut down, and leaves harvested, the stabilizing function diminishes.

Comparing the data of Tables 4.2 and 4.3, it appears that the trees of zones I and II are important because of their fruit, their leaves (for fodder) and their trunks and branches for timber (summarized in Table 4.4). In zone III the wood is used for firewood and timber. No leaves are harvested, but the soil beneath the trees is enriched with nutrients from leaf fall. Though the harvesting of fruit does not harm the trees, gathering firewood will destabilize the soil. Table 4.4 shows that as firewood and leaves are harvested in zone IV so erosion through lack of vegetation would be greatest, eventually leading to sand drifting.[4] The soil will also be nutritionally depleted.

So, the cultural habits of harvesting from trees are crucial in ecological analysis and estimation of erosion. The Dogon have their own interpretation of their natural resources, both capacity and

Table 4.3 The use of trees and shrubs by the Dogon

Species Dogon names	scientific names	Use fruit fruit	wood timber	wood fire-wood	sauces	leaves cattle fodder	manure
Baara	*Acacia arabica*		x				
Omunu	*Tamarindus indica*	x					
Néré	*Parkia biglobosa*	x			x		
Mangoro	*Mangifera indica*	x					
Oro	*Andansonia digitata*	x			x		
Sèngè	*Acacia albida*		x			x	
Sa	*Lannea acida*	x					
Botskuko				x			
Ponu	*Detarium microcarpum*	x	x	x			
Kirè	*Prosopis africana*		x				
Agouno				x			x
Gurugu	*Guiera senegalensis*						x
Abana	*Combretum fragrans*		x	x		x	

Table 4.4 Distribution of functions of trees over the Gondo Plain zones

Functions of trees	Zones I	II	III	IV	V
Fruit	x	x			
Sauce	x	x			
Cattle fodder	x	x			
Timber	x	x	x	x	x
Firewood			x	x	x
Manure				x	

limitation. Their attitude towards trees has its roots in history and fits into their overall view of their relationship with their environment.

THE HISTORY OF DOGON ENVIRONMENT

For the Dogon, as for the Tellem who previously occupied the area, the Bandiagara cliff offers a number of important advantages as a habitat. First, the water supply is slightly better than in the gently undulating sand dunes to the southeast. But as the Dogon have recently showed that they could cope with a receding water table, this could never have been the decisive factor in settling on the scree slope in historic times. The choice of habitat can only be explained by the constant threat of slavery and slave raiding. The cliff offers virtually the only natural defence for hundreds of miles around. Slave raiding was rampant in the area at least from the eighth- and ninth-century Islamic invasion (Barth 1857).

The cliffs were probably inhabited at that time (Bedaux 1980) by a similar people – horticulturalists, millet growers with a few livestock. They were not the ancestors of the Dogon. They are called Tellem (lit.: we found them) by the Dogon, who came into the area in about 1500. Though their place of origin is unclear, the Dogon probably migrated from the west in the wake of the Mali empire. They would have driven out the small Tellem population and established themselves as 'a spirited native people', defending tenaciously their independence against any Mossi, Fulani, Sao and, most recently, French claims of overlordship. They were fairly successful in this, and were never really subjugated before the twentieth century, despite hit-and-run slave raids by Mossi and Fulani, who carried off unsuspecting workers or women and sold them in the markets of Djene, San or Wahigouyia. So the population along the cliff probably remained fairly constant in precolonial times. After French colonization this balance was changed. The Dogon population, estimated at one hundred thousand at the turn of the century (Desplagnes 1907:130), was no longer checked by slave raiding or internal warfare, and quickly started to grow. It has now passed the 300,000 mark and still growing. Simultaneously the pax gallica opened up new land resources for these indomitable farmers. With increasing speed, the Dogon swarmed out into the open plains to start farming on a larger scale than hitherto possible. In the Gondo and Seno Plains, new villages sprang up, their very names bearing testimony to their recent origin: Anakana (new village), Anakila (last village), Pomonodonyu (low Pomonu, a Tireli clan). Between 1920 and 1940 most of these villages were established and continue to grow, while new wards of isolated compounds are being created between them (van Beek, forthcoming).

At present, the plains, where cultivable, are beginning to be densely settled. Starting from Tireli the first village is situated about 14 km from the cliff, implying that the zones for firewood collection of both villages are rapidly approaching one another. Still, the Dogon believe the plains are empty: 'There is plenty enough land', they stated repeatedly. For them, it still is simply a question of moving out and working hard, a little bit farther away. Of course the strict limitations of zones I and II, the scree slope and the flood plain, are glaringly obvious. Fields in these zones rotate between the oldest men of the various lineages: the scarcity of land is controlled by the scarcity of old people. Zone III is considered practically uncultivable, unless one has unusually large amounts of manure. Zone IV (the irregular dunes) is an interesting one. According to the Dogon, it is nowadays just bad, a no-good soil. The hard fact of diminishing resources has as yet not been culturally accepted, and probably will not be accepted quickly, as an exploration of the Dogon view of their natural habitat will show.

BUSH AND TREES, A DOGON VIEW

The Dogon realize that trees are essential for survival and value them, not so much as a production factor, as already outlined, but as a part of *oru*, the bush, a category sharply contrasted with *ana*, the village. The notion of *oru* is complex. On the one hand the bush is dangerous: no-one will ever sleep there without the protection of huts or people. The Fulani, who do sleep out in the bush are not considered fully human! (The pastoral Fulani in the area consider themselves protected by their cows from the dangers of the bush, but no Dogon takes this seriously.) Several types of spirit roam the bush and may attack people or exchange body parts with them. An often voiced fear is that spirits will exchange eyes with humans, rendering them blind. Vivid descriptions abound of spirits that change for a limited time into human beings, visit the market and disappear again. Besides these *jinu* and *yènèû* spirits, the elements of the visible bush are to be feared: animals, rocks and – finally – trees. The Dogon attitude to these reflects the second and more concealed notion of the bush: from the *oru* stem all wisdom, knowledge, power and life. The bush is the *fons et origo* of everything that makes life possible, e.g. the animals all know the future; they have a perfect awareness of man's activities: his intentions, mistakes, transgressions and frailties, and know what the future holds for humans. So divination can be performed with any animal. The fox divination (Paulme 1941) which is best known from the literature, is but one instance; divination can be performed with the song of the birds (especially doves), with the traces of the *key* (black ant) (though they are too small to be handled), with the sudden movements of an antelope, with the howling of the hyena, in fact with any non-domesticated animal with which interaction is possible.

Another consequence is that hunting is a magical skill not a technical one: only those people with potent magic, strong *sèwi*, can hope to deceive the animals. When a 'simple person' sets off into the bush with his bow and arrows or gun, all bush animals will be perfectly aware of his presence and intentions. Hunting, in Dogon culture, is a bridge between bush and village, and the hunter is not fully human at that. The hunter's mask vividly expresses this attitude: a fierce countenance, with large protruding teeth and a bulging forehead, reshape the figure into a non-domesticated human (Pern *et al.* 1982:120; Griaule 1938:318). A perfect hunter would have so many magical means, that he would not need a weapon: the animals will come to his door by sheer magical force. This kind of hunting lore is a cherished topic of public discussion among men.

Beyond wisdom and knowledge, life and death also stem from the bush. The main rituals aiming at procreating life (the *sigu*) and regulating death (the mask rituals) originated, according to the founding myths, with the bush spirits and animals. The main preservers of the cultural treasures, the *orubaru* are initiated in a 3-month period in a cave outside the village, living as animals as much as possible (no clothing, no speech, sleeping on the ground, no sexual interaction, etc.). In fact, the word *orubaru* means 'added to the bush' (Calame-Griaule 1968). 'If they are not like animals, they can never learn wisdom', an informant explained. In the *sigu* festival, held every 60 years, the Dogon notion of a normal lifetime – the surge of new life – results from men returning from the bush into the village. In a reversed fashion, the more dangerous power of the masks stems from the bush itself entering the village. Even the – seemingly – most human of all arts, speech, stems from the bush in the form of the secret language (*sigu so*; van Beek 1991).

Trees share this aspect of the power and life of the bush. 'All trees are medicinal', a healer insisted, 'you only have to know what for and how.' The same holds, less potently, for all herbs. Healing power comes from the bush; even the words used in spells, *anga tî*, has to be learned from either the spirits or the trees. A true *jojongunu* (healer), another intermediary between bush and village, speaks with trees at night in order to learn his craft. Some trees are 'initiated' (*yèm*) and walk at night, conferring among each other. Three species are known to be inveterate walkers, the *ji* (*Ceiba pentandra*)-*fromager*, the *omunu* and the *siwèlu*.

A typical story recounts how someone slept under a *fromager* near a neighbouring village. Waking up at night he found the tree gone, and stuck his knife in the ground. Before sunrise the *ji* returned and summoned him to take away the knife, or else the tree would kill him. The person took his knife back, but died within a month nevertheless. Folk stories abound with such tales.

Rocks also walk: those near the cemeteries are known to roam the scree beyond the village borders. In fact, anything in the bush moves and changes, in any season – sand dunes, gullies, trees and rocks. Only the village stays put as the only fixed point in the Dogon ethno-geography, inhabited by a series of succeeding populations (Toloy, Tellem, Dogon). They are the areas of stability. However, they also represent stagnation, the places where the forces of the bush whither away: life and death, wisdom and knowledge coming from the bush are applied in the village, but used up and worn down in the process. Knowledge dissipates – the people of the past inherently knowing more than those of the present – and power evaporates unless reinvigorated from the bush. (This view, in some way, closely resembles the ecological picture in which a constant flow of minerals and energy has to keep the population alive.)

So trees, in the Dogon view, are a part of a wise and powerful force 'beyond the village'. From the bush people are fed, the sick are healed, knowledge is acquired and discipline meted out. The proper attitude people should have towards the bush is twofold: respect (*bawa*) and work.

Respect is a key term in Dogon social life, operating in a fundamentally hierarchic system where age, sex and, to a lesser extent, knowledge and riches are the main parameters (van Beek 1992). Older people, in-laws and ritual officiators should be respected and similarly, other living things beyond the human sphere, i.e. the bush. The main non-human object of respect is millet (*yu*). Eating millet mush, drinking millet beer and millet cultivation are subject to certain taboos centring around respect. If respect is lacking, millet will vanish from the granary. Even speaking about millet one should be quiet and respectful: millet has ears. Other staples are less tabooed, yet are respected (cf. Dieterlen 1982).

The same holds with bush plants, particularly trees, which are associated with wealth. Folk tales abound about trees (especially the baobab) showering men with riches, when and if they show proper respect, which is expressed in several ways. Using trees for medicinal purposes implies a ritual conversation with the tree; cutting wood for construction or utensils should be done with care and restraint, using the proper axe in the proper fashion. Felling a whole tree is a difficult decision, never taken by a single individual, sometimes requiring a small offering. In return, the wooden utensils, like mortars, pestles, bowls, etc., are never burned, but left to decay slowly. Firewood is another matter, but even cutting it can cause problems. The *puro* showed one reason, but there are others. Women have to be careful when, where and how to cut firewood. They may not cut major branches, have to avoid trees near the village (unless owned by their husband) and should select trees in the *aû* (non-cultivated bush).

Trees are owned in principle by the owner of the fields in zones I and II, which together may be called the 'infields'. Ownership of these fields rotates in a complex way among the oldest men of the various lineages (Paulme 1941:267), and the trees go with the fields. Individuals who have planted and watered trees own them. The Dogon plant only the baobab and the *yuro*. Other trees are either not interesting enough, or die when uprooted (e.g. the tamarind). In the village the *wènye* is sometimes planted for shade in the compound and the *kumu* (*Ficus umbellata*), in public squares. In all cases trees are planted for reasons other than for firewood, i.e. for shade or fruits. Young trees, whether planted or growing spontaneously, may be protected from grazing sheep or goats.

Respect for trees also implies respect for the social organization of the village. Village and infield trees can only be cut with the explicit permission of their owners, and then only branches; these trees will never be felled. Trees in zones III and IV, the region between the permanent cultivation of zones I and II, and the Jachère system of zone V, belong in principle to the person who last used the field; these fields, laying fallow for decennia, were used in the past, before the pax colonialis opened up the distant plains for cultivation and permanent settlement (van Beek, forthcoming). Ownership is now vague, and women tend to ignore specific rights to trees when cutting firewood, another source of irritation with the men. Zone V trees, like the fields where they grow, belong to the lineages and sublineages of descendants of those who first cultivated them early this century. Usufruct of land implies usufruct of its trees, for all 'normal' purposes: cutting branches for firewood.

Cutting leaves for fodder is another 'normal' use not requiring permission from any owner. Harvesting fruits should be left to the owner; sometimes the baobab and very often the tamarind are protected against marauders by tying thorns around the trunk (van Beek 1992), or a ritual is carried out: a stone is hung on the lower branches or some *sa* bark tied to it. Thieves will suffer from constipation (the stone) or diarrhoea (the *sa*).

The general attitude towards the bush and trees is important in the Dogon dealings with the government organization responsible for conservation and reforestation, the 'Eaux et Forêts' – a government bureau working in the Sahel. Officers visit each village at least once a year to see whether trees have been felled. If so, they collect fines. This is a poor conservation strategy and the Dogon, with good reason, see it as another way the government sponges off them. The Eaux et Forêts officers arrive with armed gendarmes and wear uniforms. The Dogon treat them as they do any other government agency, with patient suffering and silent evasion. How can they avoid cutting trees? How can they replenish the bush? So they just pay up and shut up.

The second attitude towards the bush is one of work. Elsewhere (van Beek, forthcoming), we have stressed the Dogon notion of manageability: one should work hard in order to extract a living from the bush, and a depleting environment simply means working harder and longer. This strong work ethic is perceived as a corollary of respect, as work is a positive social value on its own. The workload diminishes with increasing distance from the village. The farther into the bush, the less work will be needed to change the life of the bush into a living for men. The onion gardens, hardly *oru*, call for hard labour, as do building houses and roads. Infield millet cultivation needs constant, but less intensive, manuring, while the fallowing system in zone V is the most work-efficient cultivation. Trees are real bush, and do not demand work; planting and watering (the only work possible for the Dogon) are done only within the village.

Nevertheless, work is crucial to make the transition of bush to man, especially as the bush is viewed as not only the ultimate source of living, but as an inexhaustible source. The village depends on the bush, and not vice versa. The Dogon may shape parts of it, enhancing their chances for survival and wealth, but in changing things of the bush to things of men, the truly fertile, life-giving aspects are lost. Whereas the bush is life, culture means entropy. So the Dogon are not interested in contributing to their environment, but transforming it by cultivation. The resources are not theirs to replenish. Fields are inherently plentiful, if only somewhat more distant nowadays; water has to be dug deeper. Wood, of course, can be conserved (a notion in perfect harmony with respect). It should not be burned indiscriminately, nor felled without good reason and ample discussion. Cooking should be –

and is – done with a minimal loss of heat (as with beer-brewing) and wood from old, discarded buildings can be reused. Consequently, working harder is a perfectly feasible solution to all environmental pressures. More of the same is demanded from men.

Still, within this general emic view of the bush–village divide, the Dogon perceive differences between villages. Tireli, on which the quantitative information has been based, is markedly different with regard to trees from some other villages such as its northeastern neighbour Amani. Looking from the scree, some 50 m above the sandy plains, a clear dividing line marks the border between Tireli and Amani. On the Amani side, a fairly dense cluster of trees contrasts with the sparsely covered sandy dunes of Tireli. This can be explained by several factors. In Amani, zone II is considerably larger and water more easily accessible. Crocodiles have been allowed to live in a permanent pond and have become the village totem. Two wood-burning activities have not developed in Amani: beer brewing and pottery. Amani women cultivate onions (unlike in Tireli and most other villages where it is men's work) and have taken over the income and specialized in the production of onion seeds and seedlings for other cultivators (Rompen 1984). This has resulted in a lower demand for wood.

According to the Dogon the difference is due also to an historical event of a very different kind. In the nineteenth century a blind bard (a prophet called Abirè) toured the plains and *falaise* area. From his miraculous birth in the north to his death in the south, he toured the settlements singing ballads, and prophesying the future. These ballads, called *baja ni* nowadays, form an integral part of the Dogon funeral proceedings. One of the prophecies concerned Tireli. The elders of Tireli, according to the ballad, were annoyed with him for unstated reasons; they had the reputation of being 'hard people'. They did not believe that Abirè was really blind, and had announced that they would 'operate' on him to see whether he could see. Abirè, like a good prophet, immediately knew what they were up to, and did not enter Tireli. He cursed Tireli: the village would never have a 'forest', i.e. a thicket of trees between the scree and the dunes. So the evil ways of the ancestors, i.e. their lack of respect, has robbed Tireli of a part of its resource flow.

Let us return to the *puro*, in which the women were disciplined by the masks (men) for cutting a fruit tree for firewood. One might read this ritual as a cultural device to preserve a scarce resource. Indeed, some other checks on cutting trees are to be found in Dogon religion apart from the general attitude towards the bush, as stated above.

Places with much water, associated with the water spirits, are feared and the wood forbidden. Felling an 'initiated' tree will call for the same kind of *puro*. Still, the emic system does not envisage a replenishing of the system by human agents through the exertion of men in the ritual sphere. The bush–village opposition is at the same time a hierarchy, an irreversible entropic system running downwards. Thus, the *puro* may be viewed more as an expression of the importance of *bawa*, respect, than as 'cultural wisdom' or 'the big ecologist in the sky'. Lack of respect by the women for the male preferences of taste is what is punished. Lack of respect for the bush generates a response in which the bush (masks) comes into the village to discipline. The appropriation by men of this function is fully consonant with the Dogon view of their environment. Through these rituals, men have appropriated for themselves both the life-giving and life-threatening aspects of the bush. The fact that they eventually have to pay their wives' fines is a nice irony of culture. Notwithstanding the male ritual definition of the situation, it is woman, not man, who shares fertility with the bush, guaranteeing the continuity and expansion of life.

NOTES

1 An earlier version of this article has been presented to Prof. J. Zonneveld, on his retirement from the chair of Physical Geography, University of Utrecht. Field research among the Dogon has been carried out in several expeditions from 1979 through 1989 financed by the Netherlands Foundation for the Advancement of Tropical Research (NWO/WOTRO; grant W52-246), the University of Utrecht and the Dapper Foundation. For some expert criticism on the forestry aspect we thank Dr Hans van Dijk of the Agricultural University of Wageningen.

2 The Bandiagara Plateau falls outside the scope of this chapter. For a thorough description of a village on the plateau, see Bouju 1984.

3 For Table 4.2 we have collected most tree species in their fertile form, to have them identified later. Comparison with Dieterlen (1952) showed a correlation of about 85 per cent, which is sufficiently high for present knowledge of this vegetation. A number of trees mentioned in Dieterlen (1952), however, were not found on the plains. Two reasons, beyond the limited sizes of both samples, can account for that. Vegetation on the plateau differs from that of the plains; second, some tree species may have died out since the early fifties; anyway, nowadays, they are found only towards the wetter south.

4 However, it is not zone IV, but III, where erosion processes already occur. Desertification not only results from felling trees and cutting shrubs to fulfil the demand for wood, but is also a consequence of other land use. The cultivated fields are cleared of shrubs and other plants. Only trees are left. So the fields, which are only cultivated in the rainy season, are not

overgrown during the dry season. The fertile topsoil can be blown away and desertification processes can continue, as in zone III. In zone II the soil is permanently cultivated, so the fields are covered with crops throughout the year, with no erosion. In zones I, IV and V the fields are only used during the rainy season. But in zone I the fields are too small and the soil contains too much clay to be blown away. In zones IV and V relatively few fields are cultivated; most fields are overgrown by fallow vegetation, by which the soil is protected against wind action.

REFERENCES

Barth, H. (1857) *Reisen und Entdeckungen in Nord- und Central-Afrika in den Jahren 1849 bis 1855*, Gotha: Justus Perthes.
Barth, H. K. (1970) Probleme der Schichtstufenlandschaften West-Afrikas am Beispiel der Bandiagara, Cambaga- und Mampong-Stufenländer, *Tüb. Geogr.* Studien 38.
—— (1977) Der Geokomplex Sahel, *Tübinger Geogr.* Studien 71 (Sonderband 12), Tübingen.
Bedaux, R. M. A. (1980) 'Tellem, Reconnaissance Archéologique d'une culture de l'ouest Africain au moyen âge', Dissertation, State University of Utrecht.
Bouju, J. (1984) *Graine de l'Homme; enfant du Mil*, Paris: Société d'Ethnographie.
Calame-Griaule, G. (1968) *Dictionnaire Dogon (dialecte Toro): Langue et Civilisation*, Paris: Klincksieck.
Desplagnes (1907) *Le plateau central Nigrien*, Paris: Larose.
Dieterlen, G. (1952) 'Classification des vgtaux chez les Dogon', *Journal de la Société des Africanistes*, XXII: 115–58.
—— (1982) *Le Titre d'Honneur des Arou (Dogon, Mali)*, Paris: Socit des Africanistes.
Griaule, M. (1938) *Masques Dogons*, Paris: Institut d'Ethnologie.
Ibrahim, F. N. (1979) *Desertifikation, Wüstenbildung – ein Weltweites Problem*. Düsseldorf.
Paulme, D. (1941) *Organisation Sociale des Dogon*, Paris: Jean-Michel Place.
Pern, S., Alexander, B. and van Beek, W. E. A. (1982) 'Masked Dancers of West Africa: The Dogon', *Time Life*, Amsterdam.
Rompen, K. (1984) 'Vrouwen van Amani', Utrecht, unpublished manuscript.
van Beek, W. E. A. (1983a) 'Harmonie en schaamte bij de Dogon', *Prana*, 32: 44–53.
—— (1983b) 'Sacrifice in two African communities', *Nederlands Theologisch Tijdschrift*, 3: 121–32.
—— (1991) 'Enter the bush: a Dogon mask festival', in S. Vogel (ed.) *Africa Explores; 20th Century African Art*, Center for African Art, New York and Prestel Munich, pp 56–73.
—— (1992) 'The innocent sorcerer: coping with evil in two African societies, Kapsiki and Dogon', in T. Blakely, D. H. Thompson and W. E. A. van Beek (eds) *African Religions: Experience and Expression*, London: Currey.

—— (forthcoming) 'Processes, and limitations of Dogon agricultural knowledge', in M. Hobart (ed.) *The Growth of Ignorance*, London: Routledge.

von Maydell, H. J. (1983) *Arbres et arbustes du Sahel: leur caracteristiques et leur utilisations*, Eschborn: Switzerland.

5 Women's crops in women's spaces
Gender relations in Mende rice farming

Melissa Leach

This chapter explores the cultural understanding of the environment in relation to gender differences among the Mende of Sierra Leone. Given that static cosmologies and sets of symbolism associated with the environment and with gender[1] are analytically restrictive starting points, it looks instead at the *use* of the environment as a context through which cultural constructions of both environment and gender are created and recreated. It argues that such a dynamic approach is analytically more useful for their understanding, especially how they interplay through social and economic change. It draws on and brings together two sets of interpretive concepts: space and its mapping; and performance, event and action as contexts through which relationships are instantiated. While focusing on rice farming among Mende speakers in Sierra Leone as a case study, it hopes to illustrate this analytical approach.

Ardener (1981) has argued that 'structural relationships, such as in hierarchies or other ranking patterns, and systems of relationships like those of kinship, (can be) treated . . . as "social maps" which are frequently, but not always, realised "on the ground" by the placing of individuals in space'. In turn, where there is a map 'on the ground', it speaks; makes statements about social relationships. For Ardener *et al.* the justification for, and analytic usefulness of, 'social map' as a broad folk term referring to both physical and metaphorical space derives in part from the frequency with which spatial metaphors occur in our own language. The Mende language also conflates the spatial and the social, e.g. as in *hinda* (place; also affair or business), *wa* (big or important), *mumu* (small or unimportant), *kulɔ* (in front of; *nya gulɔ* = ahead of me physically; also 'doing better than' me). Space seems part of the way in which the Mende understand physical and social relations, resonant with language and with aspects of history and social organization.

This chapter attempts to 'dynamize' Ardener *et al.*'s static approach to 'social maps' by linking it with recent, agency-based approaches to the study of gender relations. Strathern has suggested that rather than starting with two categories and sets of symbolism labelled 'male' and 'female', it is more useful to regard a gender difference as 'instantiated each time a difference between the sexes signifies the relation of an active agent to the source of or reason for his or her actions' (1987:299). Social relationships come to be seen not as static, and able to be analysed by beginning with categories (e.g. male and female), but as fluid and negotiable, able to be created and recreated through performance, event and action. Spatial patterns are important loci for affecting the directions which such instantiation takes. They can reflect and in turn reaffirm, through the repeated actions they condition, social relationships. But performances associated with certain kinds of space also provide opportunities for actors to press their interests in moments or actions which speak slightly differently about the structure, thus altering or renegotiating relationships. Therefore, while in Ardener's terms space speaks about existing relationships, its utterances can also be a source of their renegotiation.

Processes of historical change, in affecting both the layout of spaces and conditions for their use, affect the directions negotiation may take, which may alter the social map or its meanings. In attempting to tackle this mutual instantiation of relationships and understandings through performance and action, 'space' here is also used in a second way, rather as Guyer has suggested recently that the notion of 'rhythmic structures' might be incorporated into studies of history. This is as an etic analytic and descriptive tool; a mediating interpretive concept through which we can more clearly see, and thus convey, the 'shifting nature of social and cultural reality' (Guyer 1988:247).

The present discussion focuses on the Mende rice farm as an environment, arguing that the set of actions involved in the use of spaces in upland rice farming has always been an important locus for the instantiation of relationships, creating and recreating differences between men and women, men and men and women and women along particular lines. It first looks at its general cultural construction as a type of space, in relation to cosmology but also to the farming process. This reveals the importance of various types of space in how farming is understood culturally. Moving to the division of tasks involved in converting, and working within, spaces, the chapter then attempts to show how they provide a general 'map' of social relationships. Central to this argument is the notion of men clearing 'bush spaces' within which women subsequently work, planting rice and vegetable intercrops. The title refers to 'women's crops in women's spaces' because in this area there appears always to have been a notion that 'we make farms for the women'.[2] It relates in one sense to their food-providing role but in another to the relative position of men and women in, or as converters of, spaces; which, as I shall show, is associated with the construction of gender relations more generally.

In a shifting cultivation system in high forest, moreover, spaces are created and recreated annually. This constant fluctuation is itself central to Mende understandings of their environment. But it also turns agriculture into an annual performance with opportunities to play around and elaborate upon its major themes: to construct the spaces slightly differently according to changing interests. These interests may be 'about' social relationships as much as agricultural issues, and the statements made in creating and defining bush spaces is one way in which those relationships (including those between the sexes) are negotiated and renegotiated.[3]

The last part of the chapter addresses ongoing, longer-term shifts in farming patterns associated with the increasing popularity of tree cash crops and swamp (rather than upland) rice farming. It links changes in the types and uses of space by different categories of person with shifts in gender relations in social and economic life. Changes in farming pattern, by altering the range of possible actions and spaces and the meanings they carry, are altering the contexts through which gender relations are constructed. In this the meanings attached to the term 'we make farms for the women' are altering. How the map of bush spaces is changing, and what this tells us about the map of relationships, will be discussed.

The fieldwork was carried out from October 1987 to December 1988 in a village of approximately 500 people on the edge of the Gola Forest in the Eastern Province of Sierra Leone. *Ngola* means 'forest' in Mende. The dominant environment in this high-rainfall area is closed canopy tropical rainforest over a landscape of rolling hills. A mixture of ethnic groups evolved into a now Mendephone population and settled in a village pattern after warfare in the late-eighteenth and nineteenth centuries. The gazettement of 748 km^2 of rainforest as the Gola Reserves by the British colonial administration in 1926 (Gola East and West) and 1930 (Gola North, the present study area) mean that large areas of primary forest have persisted despite the pattern of agriculture, based on forest clearance and the shifting cultivation of upland rice of indigenous varieties, which emerged with the growing food needs of nineteenth-century settlements. Low population densities along the edge of Gola North have allowed fallows for 10–20 years

– sufficient time for tree species which coppice to recover. Farm work used to be organized in large domestic groupings or *mawɛisia* (sing. *mawɛɛ*) based on a group of agnatic kin, affines and clients. Today rice-farming households are smaller, usually based on the (generally polygynous) conjugal unit with additional kin, and sometimes paid labour groups, who assist during peak periods. This shift seems to have begun around the late 1950s–60s, coinciding with the widespread adoption by men of smallholder coffee and cocoa production as cash crops. The last part of the chapter addresses this set of changes.

THE CULTURAL UNDERSTANDING OF FARM SPACE

The cosmology which has evolved in the forest (*ngola* or *ndɔgbɔ*, the general term for 'bush') revolves around its opposition to the safe humanness of the town (*ta*) (Jedrej 1974). The village and its welfare are associated with *ngafanga*, 'the spirits of people who are, or were once, alive' (ancestral spirits being divided into *kɛkɛni/mamadani*, 'the remembered', and *ndebla*, 'the spirits of those who existed before living memory'). The wild areas beyond are associated with non-ancestral spirits (*jinanga*), relatively local, often associated with imposing natural phenomena; thus *ndɔgbɔjusu* inhabit the 'deep bush' (*susu/jusu* = deep/recess), *tingɔi* and *njalɔi*, deep pools and water falls and *tɛmuisia*, hilly areas and imposing rock formations. 'Compared to the relation of the Mende to their ancestral spirits, the relationship between *jinanga* and the Mende are more anti-social, surreptitious and apparently random' (Gittins 1987:60). Whereas ancestral spirits are venerated in a group social sense, *jinanga* can become associated with individuals who venture into the bush, bringing either welcome changes (increasing wealth) or unwelcome changes (leading astray, and then abandoning the victim). Because of this, and linked with changes associated with secret society initiation in the bush, Jedrej (1980) has identified it generally as a source of change; associated with potency, danger and uncertainty.

Neither the elements of this cosmological map nor the contrast between town and bush can be related *a priori* to gender differences. Men and women can have contact with the ancestral world (often through dreams) and if they have 'eyes' with *jinanga* (most are of unspecific gender or occur in alternate male and female forms). The town–bush opposition affects everyone, being related both to these spiritual dangers and to the physical hazards of the forest. The first settlements were hunting encampments with the forest as a source of wild, dangerous animals. Warfare brought about the possibility of enemies emerging out of its dark cover, and war towns, led by warrior leaders, were fortified against raids by rivals during periods of political instability (Abraham 1978). Settlement history was 'about' carving safe spaces out of the forest.

The upland rice farm (*kpaa*) is seen as intermediate in the town–bush opposition (Jedrej 1980). Like the town, it is a human space, but temporarily carved out of the bush. Like *ta* it is light, hot and dry, but it remains close to and surrounded by the cold, dark bush which is always threatening to reinvade, and is then allowed to fall fallow after one or two years' cultivation. Only human presence and activity maintains, or 'holds' (*hɔu*), it as a human space, as with the precarious nature of warring early settlements which could and did often revert to bush, the inhabitants 'scattering' if the leader died or departed. The remains of earlier fortifications in the forest (Innes 1969) and previously cultivated land can be associated with *tumbuisia* – spiritual entities sometimes referred to as 'previous inhabitants' and regarded as legitimate overlords of the land, who became associated with groups which subsequently worked there (Gittins 1987:60). Land also became loosely associated with the ancestors of the group which first cleared it. But essentially, any *mawɛɛ* (regardless of family origin) working an upland farm has the status of 'stranger' with regard to any of the spirits of the area and must continue to 'show them goodness' throughout the year by sharing and offering food if their work is to be successful, acknowledging that they are only temporary occupants.[4]

Given that settlement and farming history have, over time, converted a high-forest environment into a mosaic of village, farm, forest and bush in various stages of regrowth, this idea of the relative humanness and non-humanness of spaces is central to local understandings of the environment. More important still is the awareness (by men and women) of the constantly shifting, temporary and precarious nature of any space at any time.

CREATING SPACES: UPLAND FARMING AND GENDER RELATIONS

It is when we turn from 'views of the environment' to what people actually do in relation to it that gender differences emerge. If we look at upland rice farming, we become involved in analysing a 'division of labour'; but rather than seeing it as some kind of determinant organizing principle it can be shown to be itself related to the cultural construction of gender and of the farming environment. That is, divisions are mutually instantiated (and reaffirmed or renegotiated) through the annual performance of upland farming.

In upland farming, men clear the space in which women work, selecting the farm site, brushing undergrowth, felling large trees and, at the end of the dry season and carefully timed, burning the vegetation. Thus they enter, delineate and carve out a (temporary) 'human' farm space in the bush. Women rarely visit the site (January–April) except to carry food to the men. As they say 'this farm business/place is for the men'. But with the start of the rains (May–June), the farm becomes a more female space, acknowledged by the clearers in statements such as 'we just do the brushing – after that the farm is for the women'. The women broadcast and plough in rice mixed with the seeds of intercrops, planting 'hungry' foods, weeding and scaring monkeys and birds. They protect and sustain the farm space and make it productive.

Men are involved by building a fence and a hut. Young male kin of the household head or wives are often used (or employed as labour groups) to assist with ploughing, and work within the women's space. They tend to be low-status and work as dependants, thus the social map of the upland farm 'speaks' about differences between men. But each farm may 'speak' differently each year. A young man regarded in a senior kinsman's or patron's farm as dependent in another context may, as a married farm-household head, have cleared space for his own wife. Equally, the division between clearers and sustainers is not run strictly according to biological sex. Husbandless women, as female heads of household, clear their own bush spaces, and create and recreate annually their farm-household head status usually through paying male labour or calling on their own kin. However, they face economic difficulties in doing so and tend to be among the poorest households.

A few male farm-household heads show great interest in planting rice and essential foods, experimenting with new varieties and organizing, and assisting with, their planting. But their numbers are small, in contrast to Richards' (1986) stress on rice production and the performance of the whole agricultural cycle, as being intimately associated with male status. It appears that the different historical, social, economic and ecological conditions in the Mende area of the Southern Province in which Richards worked would make the statement 'we make farms for the women' inconceivable.

In the Gola forest area, however, the notion that male status comes from carving out spaces which women and lower-status dependants subsequently consolidate and sustain is resonant with other aspects of historical experience and social organization. Within the nineteenth-century warrior culture, status and leadership roles depended primarily on skill in warfare (Abraham 1978). Warleaders would carve new territories out of the forest, creating safe human spaces in fortified towns but also, by banishing rivals and allocating land to followers, defining larger areas of territory. Women and non-fighting followers would 'hold the town' literally and metaphorically while the warriors were out conquering new territory, while the group of followers, including late-coming families who had sought the warrior's protection, through their allegiance and farming activity consolidated it as his. Mende link warriorhood explicitly with men's bush clearance for farming. In these circumstances, men are hyped up like prize fighters, attacking the forest, appearing to assert male identity and strength.

Within a kinship system with strong patrilineal tendencies, men define the 'genealogical space' (cf. Ardener 1981) which women subsequently fill and consolidate by coming in as wives 'for' the husband's group (and, through the institution of the levirate marriage, inherited by it), and producing children which – although the physical offspring of both parents, mother contributing spirit and father substance, are regarded as belonging to his kin group. Women can also consolidate the agnatic kin group as daughters or sisters, through being given as wives to incorporate incoming strangers. Those strangers not important enough to found their own groups also fill genealogical space for their *hota kɛi* (stranger-father), often becoming indistinguishable from family members over time through the genealogical fictions allowed by the non-specificity of Mende kin terms. The dangers that beset a kin group as a solid 'space' are not from a threatening environment but from other rival groups. Statements like 'we want to hold our house/group', however, given as explanations of politically strategic marriages, seem to be echoed in farm-household members' determination to spend time on their farms even after planting, 'watching our rice grow' as they put it; they are, in effect, 'holding' the space.

In terms of residential arrangements, the male kin group defines the space of the *kuwui* (compound), but it is 'filled' by the women's sleeping house or *pɛlɛ wa* (lit. 'big house') which, in the past, included all the women under a family head (including his dependants' wives), consolidating his status. Men physically build the houses and kitchens. Women work within, sustaining the group physically (preparing food) and genealogically (producing children).

The clearing of bush space provides an annual re-affirmation of this status and set of relationships to wives, their kin and the few dependants on which the heads of most small farm-households can now legitimately call. It also annually instantiates the notion of complementarity in gender relations. Within the upland farm, male and female tasks are different but complementary and mutually dependent, making food production necessarily a joint venture, central to the cultural construction of gender (MacCormack 1980). It runs through procreation and ritual spheres (through the existence of the two main societies, *Sande* and *Poro*) as well as other aspects of economic production (e.g. female spinning and male weaving of cotton), making marriage ritually safe by their respective initiation procedures – the ideal union. The upland rice farm is thus an illustrative social map which speaks about gender relations more generally.

However, its utterances can also be altered to make particular statements, in order to reinforce or renegotiate relationships. This often exploits the finer divisions of meaning attached to particular kinds of space, or the action of working in, or converting, them. A striking example occurred in 1988 when one man defined and set out to clear an area of primary forest equivalent to four large upland farms to be divided between himself, his brother, his sister and a stranger-client. Known as a *ngolagbaa* (forest farm) such areas are rarely cleared today because of the extreme effort involved in felling mature trees and relatively poor rice yields, especially in the first year. In any case this farmer showed very little interest in the farm after clearing. Moreover, while assisted during the brushing stage he deliberately (and apparently perversely) took on the tree felling almost entirely single-handedly, claiming to use medicine/power in doing so. He was politically ambitious, and clearing this most difficult, dangerous kind of space seemed to be a statement of male status and identity to the kin farming within it (whose respect and allegiance he sought) and to others aware of his achievement. It also appeared to be a renegotiation of control over his three wives whose jealous squabblings over the last year (largely precipitated by his own interference) had split them apart such that all wanted to farm independently and visit relatives during the farming season. Their husband's effort appeared to back up his efficacy in making them work within the household farm, however, while the necessity to plough and protect the crop from the forest monkeys in such a large area (or have no rice) eventually brought them together and reaffirmed, temporarily, the 'ideal' of a co-operative group of co-wives working to complement their husband.

DIVIDING SPACES: PRIVATE PLOTS, INTERCROPS AND FEMALE—FEMALE RELATIONSHIPS

So far, women working within cleared space have been treated as a homogeneous group. Moreover, the cleared space has been assumed to be an undivided one fulfilling the interests of the farm-household as a unit. However, sub-divisions of the 'women's space' – spaces within spaces – present a 'social map' of differences between women, and an opportunity for their annual reaffirmation or renegotiation.

The first division is into *kpaa wa* (lit. 'big' farm) and *kpɔkpɔ*. *Kpɔkpɔisia* are small additional individual portions of the upland farm cleared by a household head and set aside; a separate enterprise from the production of household rice. Within the original large *mawɛɛ* system they were intended for male dependants to feed their own nuclear families; now they tend to be made either for wives or by unmarried sons 'for my mother'; i.e. a wife–son unit. A wife can negotiate with her husband for this extra independent space but will usually not expect to try until she reaches a certain age and status (especially *vis-à-vis* co-wives) and, once she does, her entitlement will be assumed. Having a *kpɔkpɔ* is usually associated with, and reflects, the status of a senior wife who participates in household decision-making, organizing farm labour and perhaps selecting subsequent wives. In turn, it annually instantiates her superior, more independent status *vis-à-vis* junior co-wives who, partly as a practical consequence of senior wives' involvement with their *kpɔkpɔisia*, perform more work within the household space, affirming their dependent status in relation to husband and seniors. The division of female space thus reflects and reaffirms the 'order of arrivals' of wives into a household, a central determinant of wife–wife status. It can, however, be overridden by favouritism – the 'beloved wife' – who is often young and junior. This is usually not revealed directly in the farm as a social map because favourites are often excused farm work; several men had glamorous favourite wives whom they visited in larger towns, for example. However, it can show up through co-wives' attitudes of exclusion, as in the case of two older women who deeply resented their husband's lavishing of attention on a younger wife. Their periodic emphasis on their husband having 'made this farm for us, not for her' seemed to represent both a carving-out of the farm as their own social space, and a reassertion of their centrality to the household (which could not subsist without a farm).

The second involves the planting of intercrops. Unlike *kpɔkpɔisia*, the social allocations of space involved here do not involve men; they divide already cleared space, and men – except for a few – are mostly uninterested, writing them off as 'small things'. Men's interest is largely confined to rice, and despite assertions that 'we make farms for the women', most do try to buy rice to make up the 'hungry season' shortfall in July–September using their cocoa and coffee revenue. Women, as food providers in the wider sense of meal providers, have multiple interests. Many plant cotton to spin during the dry season. They need vegetables for sauces, of which there are many varieties: cassava leaf, potato leaf, greens, *krin krin*; peppers, tomatoes and garden eggs used in soups and beans (a sauce or a meat/fish substitute). Benni is grown as a palm oil substitute. Maize and various root crops (cassava, yams, cocoyams, sweet potato) are planted as snacks for children and farm workers, and as 'hungry season' staples. In theory the latter are a joint interest, but in practice women are responsible for daily meal provision throughout the hungry season and must ensure that there *is* a staple. While men buy rice in the hungry season when supplies run low, it is women who must eke them out with rice substitutes or fill the secondary gap when they are finished. Many men class 'hungry' staples as 'small things'.

Intercrop planting patterns constitute a social map of wife–wife relationships constructed among themselves, but statements made often concern their relations with their husbands, and are an instance of non-gendered differences being 'about' gender (cf. Strathern 1987:15). Although their cooking is a group responsibility, in practice there are various reasons why individual wives might want to maintain separate crops: for marketing, separate cooking for herself and children, feeding her own farm workers, visiting kin or strangers and as inputs into her own exchange networks. In addition to those owned by all, and scattered or planted throughout the *kpaa wa*, individual interests in intercrops can be defined spatially in various ways. Seeds scattered with rice can be broadcast in separate sections of the farm (in which the rice is jointly owned but intercrops are not), delimited by lines of fallen branches; crops such as maize, beans and root crops can be planted in easily identifiable places, such as along the line of a half-burnt tree trunk, and pepper and garden eggs can be grouped to make a 'garden'. If planting in the absence of a co-wife, women sometimes use children as 'witnesses' of their crop locations.

As a map the social division of intercrop space thus reflects the social and economic organization of women's activities within the household and their outside interests. Individual rice plots can also be reconsidered in these terms (i.e. in relation to the use of rice rather than the status of having a plot). Despite variation, they can be seen to reflect several 'principles' in wife–wife relations. First, is the 'order of arrivals'. Junior wives do more housework and cooking and have less opportunity to pursue individual interests; senior wives are expected to be more independent and sometimes to contribute to household expenditure with palm oil and rice by selling vegetables. Second is the difference between wives who have married uxorilocally or from a village in the same chiefdom, who are embedded in local kin networks and need intercrops frequently for exchange with female kin or to feed visiting relatives, and those who have been 'brought in' from outside. The latter have less opportunity to maintain space within the kinship system outside marriage and are more confined to their husband's genealogical space; their lesser need for their own rice and intercrops reflects this.

Third, that spaces are divided at all reflects the acknowledgement among co-wives of the need to maintain personal space and distance more generally. Women within polygamous hierarchies are conscious of the possible tensions arising from close relationships and feel that it is good to have your 'own things' to avoid conflict if other wives feel that you are being extravagant. Reasons for separate planting reflect this, for example: 'I have many friends and relatives and if I want to give rice away I will be able to do it of my own accord. If I have to ask to use the family rice there might be problems'; or 'It is good to have your own things so that you are not always asking your mate'. Thus interests in private farm space (*hinda* = place) reflect interests in private social and economic space (*hinda* = 'business'; metaphorical space) and the desire to avoid open negotiation within wife groups: wanting private 'crop space' is like wanting private kitchen space. Patterns of joint versus separate intercrop ownership thus often reflect (and make statements about) social relationships between wives rather than (sometimes as well as) individual economic interests. For example, two middle-aged, similar-status wives shared the planting of intercrops, reflecting their 'joint' approach to social and economic life more generally, 'in opposition' to the relationship between their husband and his young favourite wife. The determined planting in separate spaces of three similar-aged wives fraught with jealousies turned out, from looking at the subsequent disposal of the crops (all picked indiscriminately on each other's sections), to be little more than a gesture.

The fact that the tensions involved in the last example had heightened considerably since the last farming season shows that the construction of women's crops in women's spaces is, like the creation of farm spaces itself, an annual performance. The map can change from year to year in response to shifts in interests and wife–wife relations; its utterances often seem to reaffirm or renegotiate them.

ABANDONING SPACES: THE END OF THE FARMING CYCLE AND GENDER RELATIONS

Women's multiple interest in intercrops also creates a gender difference at the end of the rice-farming cycle; in the experience of fluctuating spaces and their conversion. The rice harvest, co-ordinated by women using kin and friends for assistance remunerated with rice, is usually completed over a period of 2–3 weeks in late November–December. Male concern with the farm, perhaps rejuvenated with storing the harvest and assessment of how much may need to be bought, ends at this point. The key to the store is handed to the senior wife. Male attention turns to the cocoa and coffee harvest, the dry season 'town business' and negotiations over land for, and the start of brushing, next year's farm. Thus, the old farm is abandoned to return to *ndɔgbɔ*, not *kpaa*. The former term can refer to secondary bush up to the length of fallow which might be cleared for farming, and thus in the category of bush, rather than semi-human, space.

Men's experience of the fluctuation of spaces of thus one of abrupt, one-off conversion; it is also strongly governed by the annual cycle:

Ndɔgbɔ – *Kpaa* – *Ndɔgbɔ*
Bush (clearing) – Farm – Bush (no rice)

Women continue to be interested in this reverting-to-bush farm (*njɔpɔ*) space because their intercrops are harvested gradually. Leaves and vegetables are gathered throughout the dry season and into the following year. Digging root crops tends to follow the same pattern although a 'clearing out' of cassava from the old farm may be undertaken around April ready for planting on the new farm. Women talk of going to 'look for' rather than picking vegetables in the *jɔpɔi*. They do so as and when required, reflecting a hand-to-mouth, 'small–small' approach in contrast with men's more dramatic, one-off actions and the women's talk and demeanour implies a sense of uncertainty about what they will find: 'I shall pick garden eggs if I see them'.

The composition of the sauce in the diet is variable; if okra leaf is unavailable, potato leaves are used, reflecting the practical uncertainties created by reinvading bush; it becomes more difficult to locate crops, fences break down and certain crops may have been eaten by forest animals. As the dry season progresses, women return empty handed from such expeditions. However, several recolonizing species are useful as food or medicine, and the gathering of wild plants 'planted by God' becomes more significant than the harvest. Both types of plant are seen as useful if found but finding them is uncertain. This use of space is perhaps echoed in the experience of the conversion of space; in both, the boundary between human and non-human is blurred. Women's experience of the fluctuation can be summed up as:

Kpaa – Ndɔgbɔ

farm – abandon to bush

(enter cleared space) – gradual process

Whereas men define and divide up spaces abruptly, envisaging them as more or less 'human', women move in areas within and between the spaces, a fluid movement, 'managing' in the face of the uncertainties, but seizing opportunities (e.g. collecting useful wild plants) so created. An analogy can be seen in their experience of economic life more generally. Men's cocoa and coffee incomes and one-off purchases of rice delimit 'budget space' marital financial arrangements. But in meeting their own financial obligations, women experience its benefits unreliably, pushing them into the uncertain, but productive (if pursued cleverly), terrain of crop stealing and exchanges with kin as sources of income, blurring many boundaries such as those between locally legitimate and illegitimate activities.

In the *jɔpɔi*, however, women do control the cut-off point at which they will no longer tolerate the difficulties of 'managing'. The point at which the *jɔpɔi* is finally abandoned to bush depends more on the subjective assessment that 'this place is too bushy now' – paths become overgrown and awareness increases of the encroaching spiritual dangers of the forest – rather than on the crops having finished or the next year's space having become available. In household management, the analogy holds when women occasionally draw a cut-off point by creating 'palaver' with a husband who is perceived to be behaving 'beyond the pale', financially. Equally, the (rare) last resort in a tension-filled, too-uncertain marriage (as to a too-bushy farm space) is to 'seek space' in a new one. The language used is the same: *ngi gbua nya hini woma* (I have come out from behind my husband); *ngi gbua njɔpɔi na* (I have come out of that bush). Women's usual coping strategies tend to involve not turning to new spaces (a new marriage may be no better) but negotiating for a variety of intermediate 'spaces in between' and for private individual spaces.

CHANGING SPACES: TREE CROPS, SWAMPS AND GENDER RELATIONS

The foregoing allusion to women's perception of an inability to rely on men leads into discussion of the shifts referred to at the start of this chapter. In farming terms, these involve the increasing significance of rice swamps (*kpete*) and cocoa and coffee plantations (*tuhani*) as spaces. The trends are related. Small rice swamps have often been cultivated in the past as individual endeavours or small additions to the farm. As an alternative to upland farming for main food production, swamp rice cultivation has received much attention in the literature on Sierra Leonean rice farming primarily putting forward the Asian wet-rice model as a form of agricultural 'improvement' (cf. Richards 1986). Drawbacks include the labour supply problems associated with swamp preparation and water control. However, the hilly landscape of the Gola Forest area has abundant inland valley swampland, which can be cultivated without water control, and although preparation is difficult (weeds which recolonize fallow swampland tend to be deep-rooted, and tree roots must be dug out if the rice is to take root evenly), my data suggest that the clearing period requires less labour than an upland farm of equivalent size.

Men in the study area see a year spent swamp farming as a 'rest' as much, it seems, because it releases their labour during the optimistic, leisure-and-politics filled dry season as in its reduction on the total demand. This need to rest is perceived as greater now that tree cash crops place a double demand on the farming cycle: 'Once we just did rice farming. Now all our work is scattered.' The availability of cocoa and coffee revenue to buy rice for the hungry season justifies making farms smaller; upland or – more often – small swamps producing a bushel of rice or less. What was once an occasional addition to the upland-farm enterprise now more often constitutes a farm-household's rice-farming activity for the year and, therefore, some households in Madina have given up upland farming altogether. Both this trend, and its unsteadiness and annual variability, are illustrated in Table 5.1. Individual plots, which in the past were sometimes upland (*kpɔokpɔisia*) and sometimes swamps, are now almost always swamps.

These shifts in farming pattern have many economic implications which bear on, and work through, gender differences, including labour and budget responsibilities. Here we are concerned with the kinds of spaces, swamps and plantations that are made salient through cultural understandings of the environment; and how such spaces, and their

Table 5.1 Household farm types in the study village, 1987 and 1988

Number of households making:	1987	1988
Upland only	48	24
Upland and swamp	4	8
Swamp only	8	28
Total	60	60

conversion, are associated with gender differences in the division of labour. The remainder of the chapter explores how the relations differ from those in upland farming, and how far we can see this as a social map of shifts in gender relations more generally.

Both tree-crop plantations and rice swamps lack the intermediate, temporary character of the upland rice farm. Coffee and cocoa trees have long life cycles (>20 years) and once planted represent, in effect, permanent human occupation of bush space. Annual brushing of undergrowth to facilitate harvest and pest control prevents the bush from reinvading. Elements of the forest remain in the form of large trees left during first clearing to provide shade, but constant brushing around these is regarded as 'releasing them from the bush', humanizing them, while those which are a particular source of uncertainty in cosmological terms (e.g. cotton trees are thought to harbour *jinanga*) are often deliberately removed. Inland valley swamps can be planted with rice for 4–5 years in succession before the invasion of grassy weeds such as *gbali* indicate that they should be left fallow, and can usually be recultivated after a further 3–4 years. Thus, they represent more nearly permanent cultivation than do upland farms. Indeed, language associates swamps with the idea of permanence generally in the phrase *kpete hɛini* (lit. 'swamp sitting'; 'permanent site, base, headquarters' (Innes 1969)). In both swamp and tree-crop cultivation, long-term acquaintance with the spirits of the area in a general and personal sense (even rice swamps tend to be cultivated by the same household every year) converts the status of the farmer from insecure newly arrived stranger (as in upland farm space) to 'incorporated' stranger who still 'shows goodness' by offering food – but courteously rather than deferentially. Plantation and swamp spaces seem, generally, to be regarded as safer spaces, lacking the sense of uncertainty which *kpaa*, with its ceaseless fluctuation, presents. A strip of coffee and cocoa gardens now encircle almost all the villages in the Eastern Province, providing a permanent buffer between the town and the ever-changing mosaic of bush and upland farm space beyond.

Swamps and tree-crop gardens also have different associations with gender. Cocoa and coffee plantations, although able in practice to be owned by women, are, largely as a result of the cultural constructs through which they were introduced and through which their revenue is disposed of, regarded as 'for the men'. Men, who generally plant and inherit them, use their revenue to support wives and dependants. Married women very rarely plant tree crops and when – as at cocoa and coffee harvest – they work in their husband's plantations, they do so for him and in his space. Perhaps as a balanced consequence, rice swamps, which are in practice made most regularly by those households which take tree crops most seriously, seem to be regarded as more fundamentally 'female spaces' than upland rice farms. Men rarely assist with planting. Male household heads with large plantations take minimal interest even in rice yields. They can buy to make up shortfalls. In such households, the phrase 'we make farms for the women' comes to mean less a clearing of space for, than a disowning of responsibility.

Space conversion also has different meanings in swamp farming. The distinction between space clearers and space 'holders' is often blurred by the overlapping demands on male labour of swamp and plantation brushing during June and July. In households with insufficient resources to meet this bottleneck by paying labour, women do it themselves – especially removing and piling-up vegetation. Even when men carry out the entire operation, it lacks the drama of forest clearance in upland farming, being tedious, muddy work involving cutting of small, persistent weeds and bushes in a space already made safe by previous years of cultivation. Mende consider that it lacks the male status associated with fighting, warriorhood and the carving out of territory which women subsequently sustain.

That women can and do clear swamps themselves means that they do not represent and reaffirm the mutual dependence of different male and female actions as does upland farming. Nor does it represent the meeting of joint production needs within a single space. Instead, it implies turning to separate spaces to pursue interests which women increasingly seem to perceive as separate also. This is revealed most clearly by exploring the divisions which, in upland farming, are of the space cleared by the men: individual rice plots and intercrops. In a swamp household farm, individual plots which dependants want to make must also be swamps, but valleys are often too small for more than the farm itself. Wives' individual swamps become (often widely) separate spaces, if instead, as is often the case for women who have married within their own village, she requests land from her own family. This in turn implies separate space conversion: whereas husbands cleared *kpɔkpɔisia*, wives must use paid labour, or their own male kin, to clear individual swamps. Thus women define and create their own bush spaces, independently of husbands and co-wives. This constitutes a map of gender relations in social and economic life more generally. Unfavourable trading terms between declining cocoa and coffee prices, and escalating, volatile rice prices, combine with the social and political dangers of tree-crop ownership at village level, necessitating heavy investment in protective medicine or *halɛi* and less money for subsistence. Husbands often cannot fulfil financial obligations to provide clothing, food and medicines; wives increasingly feel that husbands are unreliable. 'Perhaps he will help, perhaps he won't', reflects most wives' present attitude. Some younger women express this more strongly: 'The men here do nothing to help us.' Security lies in independently pursued coping strategies, drawing on own-account enterprises in agriculture, trade, kin networks, friends and lovers in seeking separate social and economic space. Thus wives have much in common with widows and divorced or separated women – the latter trend growing in the context of declining rigidity over brideprice and levirate marriages. Such female-headed households (there were 13 in 1988) tend to pursue swamp cultivation as a food-producing option. This use of bush space, in which women organize the clearing and carry through the entire food-producing cycle using independent resources, thus reflects a more general situation: either they have no husband or husbands are seen as unreliable.

CHANGING SPACES AND WOMEN'S INTERCROPS

Finally, this separation of male and female activities is reflected in the intercrop planting patterns caused by changes in the spaces in which rice is grown. Most of the intercrops grown on upland farms are unsuitable to plant in swamps because the soil is too wet. Thus, rice swamp farming does not meet the multiple interests of women which the upland farm space provides. Alternative spaces for intercrops must be found. Men choose the type of farm space in their own interests without serious consideration of wives' wider range of apparently small, but summarily important, concerns – again a metaphor for gender relations more generally. As with individual rice plots, their coping responses imply having separate spaces independently from husbands, another link with female household heads. The range of women's spaces imply different experiences of the environment and different social divisions and sharing of space between women.

One option is to plant vegetables (*hakpa*) in a 'second-year' plot, rebrushing the reinvading undergrowth, and often intercropping sauce leaves and vegetables with cassava, maize or groundnuts.[5] Sometimes cultivation is in the household's own *jɔpɔi* if an upland farm had been made the previous year, but women often seek land from own kin or friends or join with women from other households (two married sisters made adjacent groundnut/vegetable plots in 1988; another woman joined a friend from a nearby kitchen on her household's *jɔpɔi*), thus defining their own space. In this situation, they usually clear it themselves or with (often) paid labour. Deciding to create *hakpa* space in a group means making a small, insecure space easier to 'hold' and the presence of nearby farms more 'human'. A group provides more personal security from the threat of the bush which, as in upland rice farming, begins to reinvade throughout the harvest.

A second option is to create a permanent garden (*gadi, hakpa yadi*) – either every dry season in a swamp which is being planted with rice during the rainy season, or on a river terrace. The vegetable garden involves both permanent cultivation (sometimes alternating rice with vegetables) and the concept of one-off harvesting (necessary to make way for rice or next year's vegetables), rather than experiencing reinvading bush. As a use of space it has more in common with men's cocoa and coffee plantations than with upland intercropping, and this conceptual link is implied by the use of the English word garden (*gadi*) for both. Permanent vegetable gardens mean production for the market rather than for subsistence. While visiting relatives, women have learned of the vegetable gardening projects in villages throughout the Eastern Province (promoted by the Eastern Integrated Agricultural Development Project and then by CARE since the early 1980s). The latter have promoted and assisted with inputs for tree-crop gardens for men and vegetable gardens for women and have helped to fix the idea of two separate (male and female), *gadi* spaces/cycles producing for the market.

A final option, which is becoming increasingly important with changes in farming patterns, is for women to gather vegetables on each other's upland farms. Informal arrangements over 'gathering rights' are made constantly between women with upland farms and those without, reflecting and, in turn, instantiating links between networks of female kin and friends, and connecting with other exchanges of goods and services within such networks. More formal arrangements are sometimes made: one young woman whose husband made no farm for her at all in 1988 arranged to scatter all her intercrop seeds on her mother-in-law's farm; several older, female heads of household from swamp farms who wanted to plant cotton did so on their daughters' upland farms. This kind of inter-household sharing of space also takes place if a woman has planted in her own space unsuccessfully, e.g. one such woman in the 1988 study subsequently collected all that she needed from her sisters' farms. These networks are not static. Looking back to the section on wife–wife relationships in intercrop planting, it now becomes clear that the *kpaa wa* is also a social space in which *inter*-household relationships between women are played out through intercrops. As there, the performance may serve to affirm or renegotiate such relationships. Presently, the distribution of farm types between households across the village is different each year according to which kinds of space household heads decide to clear, and this represents an annually shifting context for making statements about female–female kin links more generally.

CONCLUDING COMMENTS: SPACE, GENDER AND DEVELOPMENT

The shifts in the use of farm space indicated in this chapter might be summed up as follows. Upland rice farming involved men clearing space and women securing it, and represented a coming together of different but complementary activities in, and in relation to, an uncertain environment. Swamp farming, tree-crop cultivation and vegetable gardens, on the other hand, imply a shift towards independently cleared and secured, 'male' and 'female' spaces – each associated with a more permanent, less uncertain use of the environment. While this could be seen as a 'map' of a situation in which marital and intra-marital obligations are becoming more difficult to sustain and in which the relevant locus of uncertainty has shifted from the environment to gender relations, this would oversimplify both the changes themselves and their links with social relationships. Perhaps the most characteristic feature of both farming patterns and gender relations in the study village at present is their interhousehold and annual variability. Yet this absence of regularity is itself significant, reflecting that the major change is the removal of a locus for directioning, not the setting up of a new one. The expectation that all would be involved with an upland rice farm every year meant that its social map provided annual reaffirmation of social structures for all.

Its disappearance has opened up a range of new contexts through which the cultural construction of gender and the environment can interact.

This chapter has tried to indicate the usefulness of an approach based on the mapping of spaces (both physical and metaphorical) in interpreting the changes in Mende farming implied by this case study, both because of its resonance with Mende views of the environment and gender relations, and because as an etically applied analytical concept it has enabled their interplay to be seen more clearly. In conclusion, mapping, integrated dynamically with the use of spaces through concepts like instantiation, action and performance, may be a useful approach to thinking about the cultural understanding of the environment and gender relations more generally, and both in the context of development. It is recent and rare for project planners addressing agricultural or other environmental issues (e.g. social forestry or water supply) to attempt to take full account of gender roles in relation to the environment. Even those who have tried to incorporate the local understandings on which these are based have tended to do so in a static sense and by taking them at face value. Dynamic social maps may be a more useful basis for planning development interventions, in that they take into account how gender and environmental understandings interact, and allow agriculture (or local management of trees or water supplies) to be seen as a performance in which the set of actions and the meanings which actors attach to them may also address other concerns.

Development projects themselves are also powerful in creating new performance contexts in which relationships and understandings are subsequently played out, becoming loci for the directioning of social relationships (including gender) which may reach far beyond the project's intended scope. The vegetable gardening projects mentioned earlier, which have set a locus for women's separate pursuit of cash-oriented interests, and thus for the renegotiation of gender relations along new lines, are one such example. In providing a 'way in' to understanding these wider issues, considering such dynamic 'social maps' may be a useful approach towards appraising development interventions and assessing their implications for social, and people-environment, relationships.

NOTES

1 Starting from these would follow a precedent set by much earlier anthropological work, which has treated the environment in terms of

formal cosmology, exploring the sets of symbolism and spiritual entities associated with land, plants and water, and examined how they link up with the symbolism and possibilities culturally attached to gender. (See MacCormack and Strathern (1980).)

2 At least as far back as the 1930s when a missionary's account (Crosby 1937) stated that 'the growing and preparation of food is not a man's prerogative . . . she (the head wife) talks about "my farm", "my rice" etc.'.

3 This wider interest (and the focus on gender) differentiates my work from Richards' (1987) from whom the notion of agriculture as a performance has been borrowed. He has focused primarily on agriculture as a performance through which agriculture gets done; I am interested in agriculture as a performance through which social relationships more generally are played out.

4 This analogy was made to me by an informant in 1988.

5 Women from upland farms sometimes make second-year plots as an extra source of independence or cash, as do young men.

REFERENCES

Abraham, A. (1978) *Mende Government and Politics under Colonial Rule*, Freetown: Sierra Leone University Press.

Ardener, S. (ed.) (1981) *Women and Space: Ground Rules and Social Maps*, London: Croom Helm.

Crosby, K. H. (1937) 'Polygamy in Mende country', *Africa* X (3):249–64.

Gittins, A. J. (1987) *Mende Religion*, Nelletal: Steyler Verlag – Wort und Werk.

Guyer, J. I. (1988) 'The Multiplication of Labour: historical methods in the study of gender and agricultural change in modern Africa', *Current Anthropology* 29 (2):247–72.

Innes, G. (1969) *A Mende–English Dictionary*, Cambridge: Cambridge University Press.

Jedrej, M. C. (1974) 'An analytic note on the land and spirits of the Sewa Mende', *Africa* 44:38–45.

—— (1980) 'Structural aspects of a West African secret society', *Ethnologische Zeitschrift Zurich* 1:133–42.

MacCormack, C. (1980) 'Proto-social to adult: a Sherbro transformation', in C. MacCormack and M. Strathern (eds) *Nature, Culture and Gender*, Cambridge: Cambridge University Press.

MacCormack, C. and Strathern, M. (eds) (1980) *Nature, Culture and Gender*, Cambridge: Cambridge University Press.

Richards, P. (1986) *Coping with Hunger*, London: Allen & Unwin.

—— (1987) 'Agriculture as a performance', paper presented to workshop on 'Farmers and Agricultural Research: complementary methods', Institute of Development Studies, Sussex.

Strathern, M. (ed.) (1987) *Dealing with Inequality: Analysing Gender Relations in Melanesia and Beyond*, Cambridge: Cambridge University Press.

6 Ideas and usage

Environment in Aouan society, Ivory Coast

Jan P. M. van den Breemer

Since the work of Brokensha *et al.* (1980), interest has grown among anthropologists in the study of local knowledge systems for development purposes, especially the ecological ideas of indigenous peoples. This interest was stimulated by environmental and energy crises and by efforts to find solutions to them in, for example, social forestry, nature conservation and sustainable land use. Social scientists and ecologists commonly suggest that forest-dwelling groups show respect for nature and act as genuine conservationists of their natural environment (Persoon 1991). Hunters and gatherers are thought to possess ecological wisdom and so act as model park guards. Sometimes social scientists discover ecological codes in myth or ritual, e.g. Jungerius (1986) and Richards, who states:

> African cosmologies often embody notions which far from being 'illogical and anti-scientific', and therefore 'barriers to progress', serve to protect the community and its lands from the depredations of the individual and so act in the long-term interest of environmental conservation.
>
> (Richards 1975)

When observing religious beliefs and rules, these viewpoints may be justifiable. However, increasingly, cases have been discovered in indigenous people's behaviour which actually destroy their environment (see Lemaire 1984; Zwier 1985; Persoon 1987). A reasonable inference therefore is that, despite religious ideas and norms oriented towards maintenance of an ecological equilibrium, certain processes have influenced these people to ignore them.

This is an in-depth study of the Aouan of the Ivory Coast in which religious (and conservationist) ideas about nature are combined with a devastating use of the forest within the same group. How is such a combination possible? How did it come about? In the case of the

Aouan at least, the relation between cosmological notions and environmental conservation is less direct than Richards might suggest.

The Aouan live in the southern part of the sub-prefecture of Prikro, (still) a forest region, about 300 km north of Abidjan and 150 km east of Bouaké, in the Comoë river basin. In 1972-4 they numbered about 1,500,[1] and there were about 2,000 established foreigners. Autochtones and allochtones were spread over four villages and many small satellite settlements. The Aouan belong to the wider group of the Ando-Djé, who, in turn, are an old subdivision of the Ando-federation, a kingdom situated in the transition zone of forest and savannah. Their principal staple is the yam, cultivated with taro, maize, banana and manioc. Cocoa and coffee are their cash crops. In general, there is no land scarcity except for cocoa cultivation. The Aouan show great diversity with regard to religion: some have been converted to Christianity or Islam, but others also deliberately adhere as far as possible to traditional religious ideas and practices (see van den Breemer 1984a).

First, I shall broadly outline some fundamental religious ideas, especially the relation between village and the surrounding bush in the Aouan conception. It will become obvious that here is a system of ideas which, supported by rules and taboos, obliges people to maintain an ecological equilibrium. Then I shall briefly indicate how, according to the Aouan, their environment has greatly changed over time. They explain that many changes are due to increased human intervention in the forest, especially the acceptance of certain destructive innovations. The third section poses the following questions: why have the Aouan accepted such innovations, and why could their traditional religion no longer fulfil its conservational role? The answers lie in the Aouan's perception of their society and its internal processes of social change.

THE RELATION BETWEEN PEOPLE AND NATURE IN THE AOUAN CONCEPTION

At the core of the Aouan conception of nature and people are two important distinctions. The first is that between the god of heaven, Nyamien, and the earth goddess, Assie. Nyamien, who is simultaneously heaven and god of heaven, is the creator who is thought to have brought into existence Assie (earth and earth goddess). Nyamien is considered to be a god in retirement, whilst Assie is active, imposing rules and sanctions and seeing that they are applied.

The second distinction is that between forest and village – *bo* and

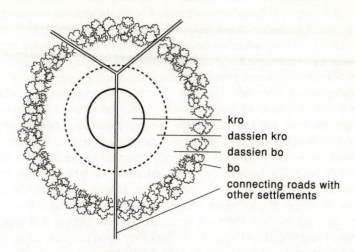

kro
dassien kro
dassien bo
bo
connecting roads with
other settlements

Figure 6.1 The spatial division in and around the Aouan village.
Source: van den Breemer 1984a: 282.

kro. *Bo* is the all-encompassing environment surrounding *kro*. *Kro* is
an open space within *bo* and in this space some things belong and
others do not. *Kro* is separated from *bo* by a region (*dassien*), which is
kept free of wild vegetation.[2] *Bo* contains the wild plants and animals,
rivers, pools, rocks, savannah and the non-human godlike beings
(*amoin*), and the forest spirits (*bessin*). The *amoin* govern *bo*, assisted
by the *bessin* who bestow life and rule over plants and animals.

The village and *dassien* must be kept free of wild vegetation.
Weeding is the women's task. The *dassien* around the village forms a
barrier, especially to snakes and scorpions, keeping them in the place
where they belong – the *bo*. People, especially women, belong in the
kro and must live separately from the *bo*. Sexual intercourse and
human reproduction must occur in the village and is strictly forbidden
in the *bo*, where plant and animal reproduction occurs.

The division of space (the *dassien* separating the houses from the
forest) means that villagers rely on the *bo* for physical subsistence, for
food and drink, medicinal plants, house-building materials, tools and
(formerly) clothing. To survive, villagers must cross the *dassien* and
communicate with the beings who reign in the *bo*. This is permitted
provided that Assie's rules are obeyed.

Different forms of boundary crossing exist, for example the establishment of a new settlement or farm. Men are not allowed to live just

anywhere and establish a settlement. They may stay in the *bo*, but they may not bring women. Permission to live and reproduce in a place is only given after it has been marked as *kro* by the ceremonial planting of a tree (a branch of the *fromager*, of *Ceiba pentandra* L, see Visser 1977:529). This ritual must be performed by a representative of the holder of the stool in that area, namely the chief of the longest-established matrilineal group. He requests Assie's consent and brings corresponding offerings.[3] Likewise, it is impossible to lay out a field in the forest at will. Only men are authorized to do this. If the forest is virgin, the man must belong to the village community, which implies that the right to land use had already been granted to an ancestor by agreement with Assie. Again, an offering must be made to Assie. Women are not allowed to do this, nor are established foreigners. If the field is in a previously cultivated forest (*afoufouin*), then the man must obtain permission from the person who first worked and offered there, or his heir. A foreigner may ask for and obtain this type of forest. Once social and religious orders have been acknowledged then the boundary can be crossed and the field or settlement established.

Various rules and taboos prevail for crossing the boundary, for instance no-one may work in the field during the week following the death of an adult person, sexual intercourse in the *bo* is strictly forbidden, human blood, especially menstrual blood, must not come into contact with the *bo* and its supernatural beings, and fields must not be established on steeply sloping land because Assie appears there and this is dangerous to man. Because of the *bo–kro* distinction, these negative rules imply that it is man's duty to maintain social order, to live in the *kro* separated from *amoin* and *bessin* in the *bo*, and protect the *bo* in places susceptible to erosion.

There are also special rest days (*fokien* or, translated into French by the Aouan, *mauvais jours*), on which work in the field is not permitted. All Aouan and Ando have one common day of rest (Friday). Other general days differ from village to village, and are sometimes described as 'the days of Assie or the forest', or 'the days of the village'. These different explanations did not seem to worry the informants, because the result is the same – *bo* and *kro* both need days of rest to recover from boundary-transgressing activities without disturbance. The regional rest days concern certain parts of the forest and always coincide with the general days. No-one is allowed to enter the part of the forest concerned and they can be regarded as an additional guarantee against overstepping the boundary too frequently – or can remind man to allow *bo* sufficient rest. The system of prescribed rest days maintains the relationship between *bo* and *kro* and the social order within the *kro*, and social life is allowed to develop on rest days, protected against excessive pursuit of individual gain.

Furthermore, there are bans on certain plants and animals: 'The Earth has as taboos the rice plant, the kola tree and the goat; these must not touch the Aouan Earth.' No informant could explain the ban on planting cola nuts. Nevertheless, there had been limited planting for many years on the young cocoa farms to provide shade later on. The ban on keeping goats could not be explained either. However, established Baoulé foreigners have been seen entering the village with a goat carefully wrapped in a burlap sack, 'so that its droppings would not fall on the earth', otherwise Assie would be furious. For the ban on rice cultivation no other explanation could be given other than the ancestors had wanted it that way. An interesting comment was: 'Our Earth does not like rice.' When the Aouan return from a family visit to the north of the Ando land and bring back rice, which can be cultivated there, it has to be husked or, if not, the chaff must be burnt immediately so that not a single grain can fall on the earth and germinate. Otherwise, the Earth Goddess will withdraw her gold and her fertility, will no longer allow rainfall, and will destroy forest/plantations by fire, resulting in poverty, disease and death: rice cultivation leads to environmental devastation and the downfall of human society.

Given the fundamental importance of the distinction between *bo* and *kro*, the conditions and rules regarding the crossing of the *dassien* and the task ensuing from these rules, the three plant and animal taboos also contain the socio-ecological message, an assumption supported by data.

Informants state that rice and cola cultivation is permitted in the north Ando country but not in the south in areas were gold digging used to take place. As there is a general need for these products, the interdiction of rice and cola cultivation can be explained as an expedient to reach regional interdependence within the Ando kingdom and to maintain unity and order. In view of the geographic situation of the Ando territory, these interdictions imply that cola and rice are reserved for savannah and may not be cultivated in a forest area.

In terms of maintaining ecological balance, the bans on rice and goats are interesting. Biologists (Furon 1968; de Vos 1975:155) argue that goats, in comparison to sheep (which the Aouan are permitted to keep), cause more damage with their hooves, can consume more vegetation, and being expert climbers, can destroy the vegetation at greater heights. Against this and the background of the Aouan classification system, the ban can be interpreted as necessary for maintaining the differences between forest and village.

Rice cultivation (in contrast to the yam, cocoa and coffee plants) needs a great deal of sunlight and requires the cutting down and burning of vast forest areas, certainly when grown as a monoculture for the market. In consequence, the intense heat of the sun dries the soil, and erosion takes place. Therefore rice cultivation does extensive damage to the differences between village and forest, and the ban can be explained as something that maintains such differences.

Here then is a classification system which, through rules and taboos, constrains people apparently to maintain order in the *kro* as well as in the relationship between *bo* and *kro*, and so maintain an ecological equilibrium (see van den Breemer 1984a; 1985).

THE AOUAN PERCEPTION OF ENVIRONMENTAL CHANGE

According to the Aouan their environment has changed considerably over time, for example when referring to the past they often used the expression 'at the time of the dense forest'. The dry season is much longer than it used to be, rainfall has decreased, is more irregular and heavier. It was said that in the olden days it would drizzle for days on end but more recently large parts of the forest became parched during the dry season with extensive forest fires. These fires first occurred at the end of the 1950s. Soils which formerly suited cocoa cultivation no longer do so because of the changed rainfall pattern, dehydration, and the increasing penetration into the forest of the harmattan with its great differences in temperature. The Aouan say that they used to harvest cocoa pods twice a year (May and November), whereas today trees produce only once a year (November). Now the Aouan have to travel to the south of the Ivory Coast just to buy fresh cocoa pods. There are no gorillas left and the number of chimpanzees and other apes has decreased considerably. Indeed it was not difficult for the Aouan to talk at length about the consequences of the changed rainfall pattern. However, their explanation was brief: 'We, humans do not know; it is God who knows; it is the fury of Assie.'

They also referred to changes in human intervention in the forest: first, due to population growth through natural increase and immigration; second, the acceptance and spread of cocoa and coffee cultivation (perennial cultures) since about 1920 transformed large tracts of forest into plantations; third, in the early fifties the hunting rifle became widespread; and, last, the cultivation of rainfed rice was introduced in the late 1960s, completely devastating huge areas of forest, notwithstanding Assie's ban on rice growing in Aouan soil. Another important factor in environmental change, that emerged from my detailed study of the spread of cocoa and rice cultivation is the conversion to Islam or Christianity, which, beginning in the 1920s, encouraged certain groups and individuals to defy Assie's rules and taboos on forest and land use and weakened the sanctions of chiefs and elders.

THE AOUAN CONCEPTION OF SOCIETY AND SOCIAL CHANGE

How could the Aouan accept innovations which are so destructive in ecological and in religious respects? The commonly given explanation that most of these innovations lead to a higher income in kind as well as in money is not satisfactory. When the specific characteristics are examined (that is: who, from which social category, accepted or transgressed first; who resisted and why; why at that time and place, and not at other times and places), it is evident that the processes are determined by the participants' view of society, its structural relations and processes.

Aouan society has always been characterized by social inequality based on matrilineal descent. The principal distinction is between leaders and followers: matrilineally hereditary leaders, who were the first to arrive in the area and therefore enjoy the right of demanding obedience, and hereditary followers (formerly slaves and at present established foreigners) who arrived later and pledge obedience. The hereditary leaders had the right and duty to prove their leadership over followers and to build up a flourishing settlement. Consequently, they always tried to concentrate as many people as possible in their settlements, especially slaves and foreigners, who on the basis of their matrilineal descent always kept their subordinate status. Social relations and dependants are extremely significant in this system of thought.

However, this social inequality deriving from matriliny eventually evoked an emancipatory reaction, the origins of which are obscure, but nevertheless stimulated by the (descendants of the) slaves. The latter enjoyed many rights, often had a free father, and were permitted to cultivate their own cocoa and coffee plantations and become wealthy, but had no right to leadership and could not claim the ultimate right to guard and distribute land because of their maternal origins. Aspirations grew through cocoa and coffee cultivation and conversion to Islam or Christianity. Such innovations offered opportunities unavailable under matriliny and also had consequences for the environment and the use of land.

As conversion proceeded and belief in the religious sanctions of the chiefs weakened, some people argued against the rules of Assie, resulting in parts of the forest becoming accessible for agricultural exploitation, while the prescribed rest days for community and forest were respected less and less. Perennial cultures were also involved, which meant that over time large areas of forest were transformed and withdrawn from the system of shifting cultivation. This process accelerated when foreign wage labourers were engaged to plant, tend and harvest crops. These labourers entered Aouan society and many asked for permission to stay and start their own plantations. Thus, successful cocoa and coffee cultivation was emancipatory for many Aouan in two respects: first, it provided financial independence and second, it enabled him to develop his own clientele of dependants, labourers and established strangers, something which previously had been reserved to only a few of the correct matrilineal descent. But this social process took place at the cost of the environment.

Agriculture was originally highly communal – a group of married men made a circular clearing in the forest, after the oldest had selected a site and made an offering. This man attributed a sector of the circle to each participant within which each man and his family planted their crops. A man could only enlarge his field by extending his sector from the circle centre. After a few years a new complex of fields was started in the same way in another clearing, and the first remained fallow for the forest vegetation to recover. According to the informants, no importance was attached to personal land rights in those days.

With the development of cocoa and coffee cultivation – and conversion to Christianity and Islam – such communal agricultural methods could no longer be sustained. Each man chose a large, square plot of land for himself and his companions and made offerings at a selected site. Gradually, more importance was attached to individual claims to land which had been personally cultivated, resulting in less co-operation and a process of 'individualization in agriculture'.

'Emancipation' and 'individualization' do not, however, imply that for the Aouan the acquisition of dependants and social relations have not remained the supreme good. Even today the Aouan achieve this by calculating their benefit in terms of relations and dependants rather than money.

During my observations of the establishment of rice growing, another kind of social process came to light. In the spring of 1966 the government started a campaign to persuade farmers to adopt rice cultivation. The Aouan refused to co-operate on the grounds that:

'Our earth does not like rice.' But in spite of this 'religious' resistance they finally conceded in 1969.

Around 1960 many plantations were at the end of their lifespan and cocoa production in several villages began to decrease. Consequently, it was no longer profitable for the Aouan to engage labourers for a share in the produce and so the recently established foreigners were increasingly deprived of employment opportunities. In 1966, some of the foreigners, who had experience of rice cultivation and were interested in earning money, began to grow rice secretly. When this was discovered by the Aouan, deep dissension arose between them and the foreign rice growers. The dispute was settled by the government in favour of the latter and the Aouan were compelled to set aside land for rice cultivation for the established foreigners if they so requested. In 1967, many established foreigners began to grow rice on a large scale and engaged large numbers of cheap labourers from their homeland. They began to grant money loans against a high interest in kind to impoverished Aouan.

Some Aouan (Muslims and members of a locally subordinate family who arrived later) started to sow rice secretly in a corner of their own foreigners' rice field. Upon discovery, the Aouan concerned were condemned as 'thieves' and violators of the existing order. They had to supply sacrificial animals 'to appease the fury of the earth'. However, early in 1969 one Aouan (a Protestant this time and a member of the same subordinate family) openly announced that he had no other choice but to plant a rice field. He had run into financial difficulties and felt obliged to borrow from foreigners (against high interest in kind with the risk of remaining in debt). This incident led to an official declaration by the highest politico-religious leader of the Aouan, that henceforth all Aouan (including those not in debt) were permitted to cultivate rice.

This decision, at the collective level, permitting all Aouan to cultivate rice is based on the awareness of the threatening reversal of the relationship of hereditary leader to follower, which is fundamental to Aouan society. The followers who had arrived last and were supposed to remain dependent and form a permanent labour pool for the Aouan were now permitted by the government to cultivate large rice fields and earn a great deal of money. Some Aouan had ended up in such a critical situation that they were compelled to borrow from these same foreigners. The interest in kind was so high that this could only lead to permanent dependence. Consequently, the Aouan territory was in danger of becoming a region that had been conquered peacefully by the peoples from the north, and the Aouan were in danger of being downgraded to followers in their own territory. The only way to prevent this reversal was to cultivate rice oneself, to cultivate a crop which rapidly provides money (within 5 months from sowing) in the specific period of the year in which it is urgently needed. Consequently, they accepted the cultivation of a crop which is more damaging to the environment than any of the existing crops. Rice growing necessitates large-scale deforestation when grown as a monoculture for the market. Assie, whose influence had weakened over the years, had no other choice, in the light of this threat to Aouan society, than to permit this violation. Rice cultivation became accepted by the Aouan responsible for the cult of the Earth, in an effort to escape from a threatening social change and to restore the old social order. The ideas of the Aouan about the society and its processes predominated over their ideas about the environment[4] (see van den Breemer 1984a, 1984b).

CONCLUSIONS

In the introduction I raised the question of how the Aouan could combine religious (and conservationist) ideas about nature with a devastating use of the forest. What has happened? There are two main historical reasons for this discrepancy between norm and practice. First, the acceptance of cocoa and coffee cultivation and conversion to Islam or Christianity during the 1920s. Their spread in Aouan society implied that ideological impediments to exploit the forest were removed or weakened, while the cocoa and coffee cultivation effectively transformed large parts of the forest into plantations for long periods. However, analysis of the social system has shown that both ecologically destructive processes have their roots in the aspiration towards emancipation, for instance in the reaction against the traditional social order.

Second, is the acceptance of rain-fed rice cultivation at the end of the 1960s. This ecologically destructive innovation came about to prevent an undesirable socio-economic development and to restore the correct social relation between the first-established or autochthones and the newly arrived subordinate allochthones. In other words, the relationship between ideas of nature and the human use of it, is less direct than might at first be assumed. A system of ideas exists about the social order, about the right socio-political relations and about what is socially or politically desirable or not. It is the relationship between these two systems of ideas – about nature and about society – that should be examined, and it is the interrelationship between both systems which determines individual or group behaviour in the use of the environment.

With regard to this relationship in the Aouan case, three statements can be made. First, here is a system of social ideas which customarily recognizes and legitimates hereditary leadership and social inequality. It is oriented towards attracting people from outside and binding them to compound and settlement. Historically, it has indeed led to the immigration of foreigners and to their integration at a subordinate level.

Second, we find a system of religious ideas oriented towards the protection of the social and ecological order. However, given the social need for immigrants and thus for demographic expansion, a logical contradiction exists between the ideas about society and the religious ideas about the relationship of human society to its environment.

Third, there are two social processes: first, one of emancipation and individualization through the acceptance of perennial crops, new religious ideas, individual land use and the building up of a personal clientele of labourers and established foreigners. This social process implied demographic growth as well as increased human intervention in large forest areas. Second, we find a process of social restoration, in which an ecologically very destructive annual crop was accepted as a means to prevent new socio-economic developments. Thus the contradiction between ideas of the social order and those of the ecological order has been developed, so far, at the expense of the latter.

Presently, the way in which the Aouan use their environment exacerbates the development of this contradiction. On the one hand, the still existing preference for the cultivation of the yam as a staple crop and the way in which it is cultivated, seem to be in accordance with the traditional Aouan ideas on nature (van den Breemer 1989). On the other hand, land use has greatly changed over time. The agricultural area has expanded enormously as a consequence of the social need for foreign immigrants and emancipation. Areas hitherto forbidden could be opened up for agricultural purposes by Muslims and Christians, also in the context of emancipation. New crops were accepted, first by slaves and other subordinates, then by the Aouan who feared they were losing their superior position. Land tenure changed: individual claims on the usufruct of personally cultivated land have become important in order to be able to distribute land to one's own immigrants and to build up a personal clientele. Thus, confronted with ecologically interesting cosmological ideas one has, for the purpose of environmental conservation, to evaluate their actual social relevance by examining the relationship between the ideas of the environment and those of human society in its historical and logical dimensions.

NOTES

1 A few undergraduate students took part in the research among the Aouan, which resulted in the following important sources for my study: van Loopik (1974) and Visser (1975; 1977). The research has been made possible by the Netherlands Foundation for the Advancement of Tropical Research (WOTRO) and by the State University of Leiden, Netherlands.
2 The drawing of the spatial division in and around the Aouan village was made by Paul Bijvoet in Leiden. The Baoulé also know the twin concepts *blo/bro-kro*, although less emphasis is laid on them in the literature than in my study of the Aouan, for example, Trouchaud (1965:93–4) and Etienne (1966:368). For the Asante see, McLeod (1981:39–40).
3 A comparable ritual also exists among the Baoulé. See ORSTOM 1965, vol. 1:39; vol. 2:49, 51. For the foundation rituals and the alliance with the earth among the Agni, see Amon d'Aby 1960:169–70.
4 The study of the Aouan perception of environmental change was not the main object of my fieldwork. It arose in the context of my research, the aim of which was to investigate the Aouan's original resistance to and final acceptance of rainfed rice cultivation.

REFERENCES

Amon d'Aby, F. J. (1960) *Croyances religieuses et coutumes iuridiques des Agni de la Côte d'Ivoire*, Paris: Editions Larose.

Brokensha, D., Warren, D. M. and Werner, O. (eds) (1980) *Indigenous Knowledge Systems and Development*, Washington: University of America Press.

de Vos, A. (1975) *Africa, the Devastated Continent?* Den Haag: Junk Publishers.

Etienne, P. (1966) 'Phénomènes religieux et facteurs socio-économiques dans un village de la région de Bouaké (Côte d'Ivoire)', *Cahiers d'Etudes Africaines* VI(3): 367–401.

Furon, G. (1968) 'The gentle little goat: arch despoiler of the earth', *Unesco Courier* 11:1.

Jungerius, P. D. (1986) *Perception and Use of the Physical Environment in Peasant Societies*, Reading Geographical Papers 93, University of Reading.

Lemaire, T. (1984) 'De Indiaanse houding tegenover de natuur', in W. Achterberg and W. Zweers (eds) *Milieucrisis en filosofie*, Amsterdam: Ecologische Uitgeverij.

McLeod, M. D. (1981) *The Asante*, London: British Museum.

ORSTOM (Office de la recherche scientifique et technique outre-mer) (1965) *L'étude régionale de Bouaké*. Abidjan: Ministry of Planning.

Persoon, G. (1991) 'Ecological balance and innovations: cases from the forest', in J. P. M. van den Breemer, H. T. H. van der Pas and H. J. Tieleman (eds), *The Social Dynamics of Economic Innovation Studies in Economic Anthropology*, Leiden: DSWO Press.

Richards, P. (1975) 'Alternative strategies for the African environment. Folk ecology as a basis for a community orientated agricultural development', in P. Richards (ed.) *African Environment, Problems and Perspectives*, London: Int. Afr. Inst.

Trouchaud, J. P. (1965) 'L'implantation actuelle de la population', in *L'étude Régionale de Bouaké*, Paris: ORSTOM.

van den Breemer, J. P. M. (1984a) 'Onze aarde houdt niet van rijst. Een cultureel-antropologische studie van innovatie in de landbouw bij de Aouan van Ivoorkust', PhD dissertation, University of Leiden.

—— (1984b) 'Classificatiesysteem, emancipatie en innovatie bij de Aouan van Ivoorkust', *Antropologische Verkenningen* 3(2): 44–67.

—— (1985) 'De betekenis van het taboe op de rijstbouw voor de Aouan van Ivoorkust', *Antropologische Verkenningen* 4(2): 200–22.

—— (1989) 'Yam cultivation and socio-ecological ideas in Aouan society, Ivory Coast. A contribution to crop sociology, *Sociologia Ruralis* 29, 3/4: 265–79.

van Loopik, A. (1974) 'Enkele notities betreffende de achtergronden van de sociale en territoriale organisatie van de Aouan, Ivoorkust', Doctoraal stageverslag, part 1. Leiden: ICA.

Visser, L. (1975) 'Plantes médicinales de la Côte d'Ivoire', *Mededelingen Landbouw Hogeschool Wageningen* 75(15).

—— (1977) 'L'igname, bonne à manger et bonne à penser; quelques aspects de l'agriculture Ahouan (Côte d'Ivoire)', *Cahiers d'Etudes Africaines* XVII(4):525–44.

Zwier, G. J. (1985) 'De Indiaan als wijze ecoloog. De "edele wilde" in een modern jasje', *Onze Wereld* 42–4, April.

7 Ritual topography and ecological use
The Gabbra of the Kenyan/Ethiopian borderlands

Günther Schlee

In this chapter the Gabbra in the Kenyan/Ethiopian borderland are the main example used to discuss holy sites, routes of pilgrimages, meanings attributed to the landscape such as the way it is linked to myths and the manner in which the ritual topography, the ensemble of these meaningful features, contributes to the symbolic constitution of social identities. As the ritual status of an area is sometimes linked to restrictions on land use, can such 'conservationist' aspects of belief systems be seen as ecological adaptations? However, less emphasis is placed on answering this question in the chapter and more on considering the role places and the beliefs about them have for the constitution of community. By helping to establish and maintain a community with a certain system of production and enabling it to articulate with nature (i.e. the non-human parts), these beliefs, and the whole culture of which they form a part, do also have, of course, an ecological aspect.

The chapter then considers examples from neighbouring societies and even continents and social configurations as different from the Gabbra as modern nation states. This provides a catalogue of similarities and contrasts with regard to concepts of space, forms of territoriality and land tenure, different shapes and structures which pattern the surface of the earth as it is appropriated by different forms of societies and converted to different forms of use. As pastoral nomads appropriate space like hunter-gatherers and very differently from agriculturalists and modern nation states (which divide it up in bounded surface areas) to meet their economic requirements and to adjust to the distribution of their specific natural resources, ecology becomes significant here also.

THE *JILA*-JOURNEYS OF THE GABBRA

The Gabbra are Boran-speaking camel herders forming two local clusters: the Gabbra Miigo and the Gabbra Malbe. The former are an eastern branch; they live in the northern part of Wajir District in Kenya and the adjacent parts of Ethiopia. Due to their high mobility and the erratic changes of pasture conditions they may also be found far outside their usual areas of residence. In 1986 I talked to some near Agere Maryam, 250 km north of the Kenyan/Ethiopian border at the northwestern fringe of the Boran territory, whose southeastern neighbours the Gabbra Miigo are normally regarded.

The area occupied by the Gabbra Malbe lies generally more to the west. In the Marsabit District they number some 23,000 (Rep. of Kenya, 1981). A smaller population lives on the Ethiopian side, especially in the Mega Woreda (District) of the Arero Awraja, Sidamo Administrative Region.

The Gabbra have lived for many centuries on the fringe of the Islamic world, in an area of interaction of African and Middle Eastern cultures. The Gabbra Miigo have nominally accepted Islam in the last decades, at least with regard to their contacts with outsiders. One elder once explained to me that in town they are Muslims and in the bush they are Gabbra. Their traditional culture, which for some centuries has been their ideological stronghold against Islam, is itself in many aspects reminiscent of Islam. Some such similarities may predate Islam (Jensen 1960: 101f.), while others may be due to either of the two periods in which Islam flourished in the southern Horn (Schlee 1985). Most Gabbra Malbe still resist conversion to Islam, although they are exposed to some social pressure of the type Baxter (1966) has described for the Isiolo Boran, and Christian missions, starting with the destitute as they do among the Rendille (Schlee 1982), to try to gain a foothold in their society.

The Gabbra Miigo perform periodic rituals on Hees mountain in the Borena Awraja. The holy sites of the Gabbra Malbe are certain mountains and craters located mainly in the Arero Awraja of Sidamo or in the Gemu Gofa Region. A few sites of minor importance are on the Kenyan side of the border. Of the five phratries ('drums') of the Gabbra Malbe, Gaar, Galbo, Alganna and Odoola have their own holy sites, while Sharbana shares those of Alganna. The Gabbra Malbe go on pilgrimages or en masse migrate to these sites at certain times determined by a combination of their solar and lunar cycles (cf. Schlee 1989a: 54–144; 1989b; briefer descriptions of the calendar in Schlee 1984: 29–32; 1985: 31). The date has to be in an appropriate month of a given year in the 7-year cycle: for Gaar phratry a Thursday-year, in the other phratries the subsequent Friday-year, normally after two or three such cycles, i.e. once in 14 or 21 years. These pilgrimages are closely connected with age-set promotions which take place on these journeys. In the Friday-year 1986 I joined the ritual journey of the Galbo phratry.

The information about Gaar is based on the written account of a key informant who is literate in Swahili. Informants from other phratries were also interviewed. Similar migrations to the sites were carried out by the Sakuye. Material has been collected since 1979 and for a more comprehensive account see Schlee (forthcoming).

All groups studied have age-set systems of the *gada* type, but even among the Gabbra there are four different systems with regard to the length of initiation intervals, number of sets per generation and the distribution of offices to different sets (cf. Schlee 1989a: 54–144; 1989b).

Figure 7.1 shows that the holy sites of these different Gabbra groups are closer to each other than the extreme regions of the territories they occupy in profane years (note the convergence of arrows on the map). It also shows that the main direction of the pilgrimages is from south to north. In the case of the Miigo this tendency is not as pronounced, since many Miigo live in Ethiopia to the east and even to the north of Mount Hees. Among the Gabbr Malbe, however (as district records in the Kenyan National Archives from colonial times show), there has been a remarkable trend of southward expansion in the first half of this century, so that now, generally, they are found well south of their original area. Thus, these *jila* journeys can be seen as periodic migrations back to their origins, as confirmed by the clan origin myths of the Gabbra and the significance they attribute to their holy sites in that context.

What has not been adequately illustrated in Figure 7.1 and needs clarification is that not all households have the same starting points for the journey. Hamlets in the north join the cluster around the *yaa* (the mobile capital comprising office holders) when it passes in their vicinity. Others regularly live in Ethiopia around the holy sites or even north of them and join the *yaa* only when it has reached the *laf jila*, the 'land of festivities' or the 'ceremonial country' and starts to perform rituals at the various prescribed stages. At that point the journey changes character: the first part of the journey is a practical one and problems of access are discussed on it: how can hundreds of households and thousands of camels cross vast stretches of rough territory in time for the ceremonies? Once this has been overcome and the 'country of ceremonies' is reached, the journey itself acquires a significance: the correct route to certain locations has to be followed and reached by certain dates, the right animals have to be sacrificed in the right place and the correct words must be said by the appropriate

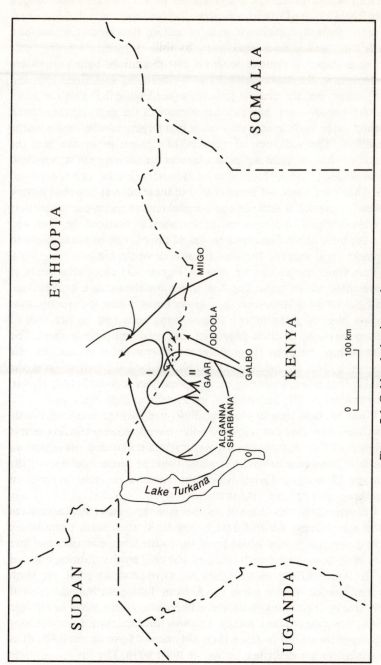

Figure 7.1 Gabbra holy sites and movements.

persons whose genealogical and age-set position entitles and obliges only them to perform these rites. Delegations must collect ritual paraphernalia like sticks or gum of certain tree species or bur-like seeds from well-known areas.

These stages in the *jila* journeys of different Gabbra groups are sometimes at the same locations with the routes sometimes crossing each other. But the general pattern is (see Figure 7.1) that the more westerly groups have their ritual sites more to the west and the eastern groups to the east, so that they move in a largely parallel south–north direction. The localities of the Gabbra phratries in the land of festivities thus roughly depict in a smaller area the way in which these phratries are normally located in relation to each other in a wider area. This, however, does not mean that Gabbra groups at any level have a defensive territorial attitude and claim exclusive rights over particular stretches of land. It simply means that most of the time the Gaar *yaa* and the bulk of the Gaar households and herds can be found more to the north and more to the west than those of the Galbo.

Two Gaar routes can be seen in Figure 7.1; the Galbo route is represented by an unbroken line which continues as a broken line. This has to do with alternating age-set lines visiting different places; age-set lines of grandfathers, fathers, egos, sons and age-set lines of fathers and sons of other people who succeed and precede them. The relationships between them differ from system to system. In this chapter I want to approach the topic of the *jila* journeys from the spatial dimension, including the temporal perspective (Schlee 1989a), only insofar as it is necessary to understand spatial relations.

If one of these journeys is singled out, represented on a larger-scale map and the dates of the sojourns in different locations marked (Figure 7.2) we can discern a long, gradual northward movement of the *yaa* Galbo over several years and then the ceremonial part of the journey (2 weeks), during which the *yaa* moves along a chain of inselbergs and around one of them.

Unfortunately, this chain of inselbergs in the plains (remnants of the Ethiopian plateau which formerly stretched much further south) are very conspicuous, impressive features, visible from afar and therefore they have been loaded with meaning not only by the Gabbra, but also by the Anglo-Ethiopian boundary commission which employed them as land-marks, so that today the Kenyan–Ethiopian boundary, a cut line, free of vegetation, undulates ribbon-like from hill top to hill top. Thus, the Gabbra are forced to cross an international boundary whenever they want to reach their holy sites. (Some of the difficulties this involves are described in Schlee 1987; 1989c.)

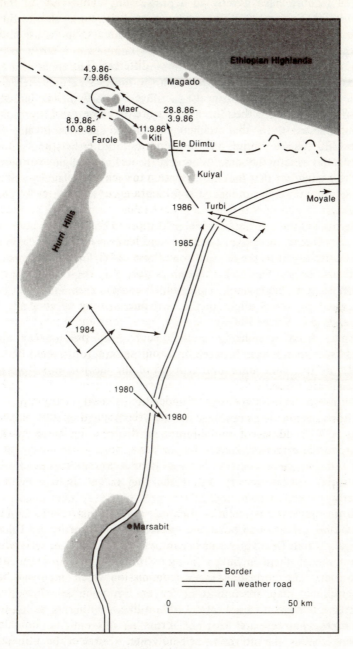

Figure 7.2 Galbo Gabbra ritual migration.

The Gabbra have a verse of a praise song about each of these mountains (Schlee 1987). Other aspects of their relationship to these mountains are no less pragmatic and instrumental than the use made of them as landmarks by the boundary commission. When asked about the significance of these mountains for them, the Galbo Gabbra usually give answers of a rather technico-magical nature: such and such a lineage has to perform the sacrifice of a particular animal at a given lunar date at a location associated with their clan history, this being important for the wellbeing of herds and people and for successful age-set promotions, above all because fathers and grand-fathers did exactly the same. Whatever the feelings, religious or other, one can safely say that the entire physical surface is overlaid by a ritual topography which prescribes rules for actions and avoidances for each locality.

Because of the association of sacrificial sites with the origin myths of the constituent lineages of Galbo, a ritual journey past this chain of mountains re-enacts the original constitution of Galbo out of elements of diverse origin. This idea of Galbo as having a composite structure, rather than as undergoing segmentation from a common origin, as suggested by these origin myths, is confirmed by other kinds of evidence (e.g. Schlee 1989a).

Apart from re-enacting mythological time, the journey also establishes spatial links between different mountains or even different peaks of the same mountain and given lineages; in other words: lineages are mapped.

Although there is no neat equivalence of lineage structure and territorial segments as reported for the Tiv (Bohannan 1954; Sahlins 1961: 329) we do have a spatial representation of some lineages which figure in the origin myths (see Figure 7.3).

The difference between the Tiv and Galbo is that the Tiv are a highly territorial peasant society, and (according to the Bohannans and possibly even more so in Sahlins' interpretation) very much concerned with pushing their boundaries forward. The internal subdivisions of the Galbo, on the other hand, are not localized. Houses of Ali Umur, Kuiyal, Mamo Deera and Saleda can be found in the same settlement and none of them is linked in any distinctive way to their holy mountain. The correspondences between the social map and the geographical map are important for the symbolic constitution of society but have no implication for residence or access to natural resources whatsoever, at least not at the lineage level.

Nevertheless, the utilization of holy areas is restricted by a number of rules reminiscent of modern ideas like wildlife protection and

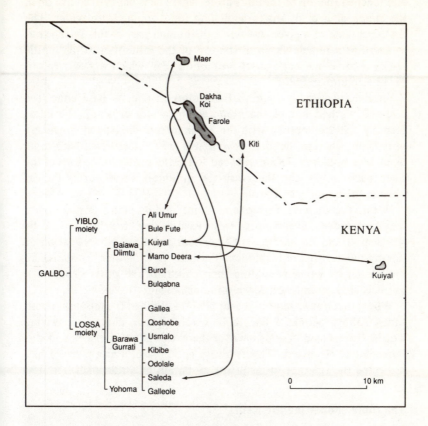

Figure 7.3 Galbo lineages and their sacrificial sites.

environmental conservation. The Farole mountain, an untypical, but most important example for the Galbo, has been studied in detail.

THE HOLY GROUND AS TRADITIONAL NATURE RESERVE

The pilgrimage of the Galbo is called *gaaff jila galani*, 'the time (*gaaff*) when they go home (*galani*) [to hold] the ceremonies, festivities (*jila*)', so-called because the localities are associated with origin myths. The most important is about the ancestor of the Worr Farole (people of Farole) segment of the Barawa lineage cluster who was seen by herdsmen in the bush with a brother. The future clan ancestor was caught and integrated into human society, while his brother fled and reached the top of Mount Farole, where he is believed to live on in the shape of a giant snake with long fur dripping with water. The firstborn male of a given age-set of the human part of this lineage has to sacrifice a female sheep at the top of the mountain to his reptile senior relative in every age-set promotion year, which was carried out on 13 September 1986.

Special rules apply to both the mountain and its base cone (the material washed out of the mountain by water erosion), the latter forming a sharp contrast with the wider surroundings; and consisting of red soil, whereas the plain beyond it is grey, interspersed with some black lava boulders. The area of red soil rising gently to the foot of the steep rock slopes, together with the mountain itself, forms the *laf Farole*, the country of Farole.

Within this area it is forbidden to hunt, and no plants or plant parts may be removed; even fibrous twigs used as toothbrushes have to be left behind and no herding sticks or tent poles are cut. Swearing or talking indecently are forbidden. This rule is, of course, honoured in the breach by women scolding their children (and other situations), but it is also often heard as an admonishment.

When, in a non-ceremonial year (1984) I climbed the mountain with some Gabbra people, I had to be careful not to choose the wrong words. Once I said: 'Let us try over there; this is a bad place', and was immediately corrected: 'This is a very good place, a nice place.' I had neglected the rule not to insult the mountain or a part of it.

The route connecting these sites

The Gabbra are used to walking long distances. The routes depicted in Figures 7.1 or 7.2 do not show the scale of the distances walked by individuals, as some people move backwards and forwards on the routes continuously, visiting people who have remained behind or leaving the routes to visit their satellite herds.

Even more astonishing are the roundabout routes the Galbo take on the *jila* journey. The shortest route from their position on 4–7 September just north of Maer to their position on 8–10 September would have been along the eastern flank of Maer to its southern side. Rather than moving this way the Galbo – with houses, families, loading camels and herds – moved in a wide circle around the mountain on the far side. One reason was that a ritual gate between Maer and Farole had to be passed on 11 September in a west–east direction. This gate, composed of stacks of thorny branches, seems to be a miniature version of a larger gate, the poles of which are the two mountains themselves. It is therefore plausible that the line connecting the two peaks had to be crossed from the west, but even that does not explain the actual route taken. Some Galbo who claimed that they were going the proper way and that others were taking a short cut, went around Maer in an unnecessarily wide circle.

After leaving the settlement position in a west–northwesterly direction and having walked 2½ hours (corresponding roughly to 8 km given the slow speed of such a migration with young and old, herds and households), it was decided that we should turn left, i.e. southwards. As the trek was long by then and everybody was waiting to turn left and go around the mountain, we all turned simultaneously, moving as a wide front through the plains rather than travelling in single file. Thus some had to walk longer distances than others in a circle around Maer. At that point a man came running back and forth and reminded those who had walked in a narrower circle to go further west and move in a wider one. The words he used were *aki aada godaana!* – 'migrate according to the custom!', i.e. along the customary route. Where compliance with custom leads to fatigue it is often neglected and so everybody just continued to walk ahead.

I had walked about an average distance, neither the shortest nor the longest way, and when we arrived at the new settlement some people were already resting while others had not yet arrived. No-one could unload the camels because the *qallu*, a ritual specialist and the senior man, had not arrived. He would choose the exact location for his house and everybody else would settle south of that in a given sequence. The *qallu* arrived 40 minutes later, took his time to choose a site, so that we could only start to unload our camels an hour and a half after our arrival. The reason for this delay was explained by the *qallu* thus. The proper way leads not only around Maer but also around a couple of smaller hills west of it collectively known as Doofi. We had only gone round the small Doofi hills (*Doofi didiqo*), while he and some followers had also circumvented the Big Doofi (*Doofi gudda*), which lies further to the west. The western route is the appropriate one, since the fathers and grandfathers of the age-set promotion candidates had also gone that way. If one does not take the proper route, then it waits to be taken. In addition to the claim the Gabbra have on their holy grounds – a claim which has had to be defended against the Boran – the holy sites and the routes connecting them have a claim on the Gabbra. The way cannot be kept waiting, you have to walk it.

Attempts at interpretation: The perspective of ecological determinism

Rappaport (1967) analysed a cycle of labour-intensive pig-raising over more than a decade in a small community in the Bismarck mountains of New Guinea, which is then followed by a wholesale slaughter of almost the entire pig population in a large-scale communal ritual to which potential allies are invited. This feast is a prelude for war, in which territorial rights in potential cultivated land are redefined. Then the peaceful phase of pig-raising begins again.

Marvin Harris (1978) has taken Rappaport's book as one of his examples for showing how ritual practices, beliefs and values are adaptive responses (not consciously so) to the ecological environment. Other examples used by Harris with a similar intention are the Jews' and Muslims' abstinence from pork and the 'fierceness' of the Yanomamö. I. M. Lewis (1976) has criticized this view of ritual as too utilitarian and suggests that Rappaport reduces the significance of sacrificial feasts to calorie and protein intake. This may be further simplification, even in relation to Harris' condensed presentation of Rappaport's (1967) book. But whether sacrifices are there for helping oneself directly to food – by eating the victim – or indirectly – by inviting allies who help you to fight your neighbours so that you can snatch their gardens, cultivate yams and start a new cycle of pig production, the basic line of interpretation remains the same: ritual is an adaptive response to the environment, especially to the parts of it which have a food-producing potential, and the ultimate values are those of the stomach.

It is tempting to apply the perspective of ecological determinism to Gabbra ritual; especially since the rules concerning the *laf Farole* (hunting and plant-use restrictions) seem quite clearly concerned with environmental preservation.[1] Can we describe the whole complex of rituals as a system to preserve environmental resources and to allocate them to certain groups? I suggest that we resist this tempting interpretation as too reductionist and as ignoring too many other factors.

The Gabbra, although they have holy mountains, are not a mountain people. Their economy is based on camel nomadism in the vast arid plains. The mountains are relatively unimportant for this pastoral form of land use. They do, however, facilitate a visualization of origin myths and social structure and thus contribute to social coherence, which may in turn enable the Gabbra to defend their more important ecological resources in the lowlands against outside intrusion. While highly functional, we cannot dismiss this more indirect ecologically adaptive value of Gabbra ritual – but at this level of generalization everything that constitutes society can be interpreted as environmental adaptation since society itself is a metaphor for the way in which people organize themselves and their needs and articulate them with environmental resources. The argument becomes trivial.

Attempts at interpretation: Territorial aspects of identity

Rather than contributing directly to the Gabbra economy the holy mountains seem important identity symbols at various levels of social organization. Lineage identities and interrelationships are visualized by the means of the holy mountains and associated ritual acts.

To ask whether lineages are territorial or non-territorial, localized or not, is a standard ethnographic distinction in the description of segmentary lineage systems and clan systems. Can the link between certain lineages and landscape features in this context be interpreted as evidence of a localized or partly localized character of these lineages? Certainly not. Neither in non-ceremonial years, nor in ceremonial years is there any clustering of residential units around their respective holy sites. In non-ceremonial years the movements of Gabbra with links to holy places, just like those without and with whom they live in mixed hamlets, are determined by practical considerations like availability of pasture and water and, in recent years, access to markets, shops and schools. In ceremonial years the individuals who have to perform rituals at certain stages of the journey move with the *yaa* or the settlements around it and go from that base, with a group of age mates for a few hours or a day to the religious sites. Thus, there is no residential dimension to this spatial association.

Was there ever localization of lineages around their holy sites in the past? Such a question might be inspired by the example of the immigrant Chinese in South-east Asia who keep the memory of the exact locality their ancestor left many generations ago and derive an important aspect of their identity from a village they have never seen. But in the Gabbra case evidence even for former residence around these sites is completely absent.

The origin myths of the Gabbra lineages typically state that the lineage ancestor (a boy or a man) with his household and camels, was found by members of some other lineage at some place, the very place where today his descendants hold their sacrifices. Whether or not this ancestor had lived there for any length of time is not stated. To summarize: Gabbra lineage and phratry identity have a local aspect which has nothing to do with residence for the nomadic Gabbra only visit their holy sites periodically. The *jila* journeys re-enact the original constitution of each phratry by visiting the places where the ancestors were 'found' in a given pattern by a prescribed route. The cognitive map guiding these movements does not mark contiguous surface areas and lay claim to such (with the exception of the *laf Farole*) but the points and lines (routes) connecting them.

EMIC REPRESENTATIONS OF TOPOGRAPHY – SOME COMPARISONS

I am grateful to Ingold for pointing out that he had used exactly the same phrase 'points and lines' in his description of how hunters and trappers appropriate space (Ingold 1980: 155); thus we are, of course, still within the metaphor of drawing a map. If we talk about the real surface of the earth, these 'points' and 'lines' translate as 'places' and 'paths', a terminology Ingold, following Gibson (1979: 33–6), prefers in a later publication (Ingold 1986: 147 ff.).

A number of correspondences with hunters and gatherers, especially the Australian material Ingold discusses, are indeed quite striking. The links between the Aborigines and their native land is thought of as a mutual claim; the land belongs to the people, but the people, in their perspective even more importantly, belong to the land: 'it is truer to say that the country owns them and they cannot remain away from it indefinitely and still live' (Elkin 1938: 40–1, quoted in Ingold 1986: 139). A man–land relationship of this kind is difficult to equate with a term like 'ownership' drawn from the jural English or other, dominant languages. Australian anthropologists therefore face the problem of how to phrase the defence of Aboriginal land rights when they are dealing with lawyers who evaluate whatever is said along the dimension of correspondence/lack of correspondence with established legal categories. A defence phrased in terms which try to come close to non-European categories may in such a situation easily become self-defeating.[2] Another problem is that this link between people and the land has been described by anthropologists as being primarily of a religious nature, not as economic, but ' "The apparently non-economic aspect of the man–land relationship is only so to us" (Hamilton 1982: 90). For the very provisioning of society is thought to depend upon the proper conduct of ritual activity, whose object is periodically to revitalize the environment, thereby securing the reproduction of all animal and plant life' (Ingold 1986: 140–1).

The claim the country has on the people, or more analytically, the fact that social relationships with regard to places are phrased as relationships between these places and people in which the former appear animated and even possessive, reminds us of the road which expects the Gabbra pilgrims and cannot be kept waiting (Schlee 1987). But does the ritual also 'revitalize the environment'? The negative instance makes the point clear: omission of rituals entails misfortune. In local oral tradition one can find numerous examples. These oral traditions stem from the same cultural environment and may illustrate the local shapes this nearly universal idea takes in lowland North-east Africa: there are Rendille traditions about negligent Gabbra (Schlee 1989a: 184, original text 1979: 263), and Boran traditions about other Oromo, for example that people from the Awash valley, east and northeast of Addis Ababa, once failed to perform their regular *muda* journeys to the Boran *qallu*. Consequently, blood came out of the udders of their cows, women did not give birth, or babies were born blind, etc. (cf. Schlee 1984: 148).

Apart from maintaining and reproducing cosmic order and reproductive capacity, the rituals also benefit everything in their proximity. For all important Rendille and Gabbra rituals, the camel herds have to be present. If the rituals take place outside the settlements, new thorn-bush enclosures have to be built to enclose the camels. In the busy 2-week period during which all the *jila* ceremonies are performed, the camels stay within the enclosures, deprived of pasture. Elsewhere I have enumerated all these occasions and conclude that during a 17-day period without water, the camels had been prevented from browsing for ritual reasons (presence at sacrificial sites, migrations to other such sites) for all or most of 7 days and some hours in the eighth day.

> When asked about the effects of this extended period of thirst and the little time left to browse, the Gabbra responded: *Aadan quufsa* – 'the ceremonies satiate', or 'the law satiates (the camels)', meaning that the divine order requires the rituals and therefore cannot allow them to have negative effects on the camels. Camel herds would get lost or decline if the rituals were not carried out properly and cannot possibly suffer from them being carried out.
>
> (Schlee 1988: 146–8)

But the positive working of the rituals can also be spoilt. In another paper on the *jila* journey, which focuses more on political aspects and interethnic relations, I have explained why some recent Boran occupants who had settled in the *laf Farole* since the last *jila* in 1972 had to be expelled from these holy grounds. Apart from the claim that they had used up the scarce water in the natural cavities in the rocks of the mountain, and also species of vegetation important for the rituals, it was also thought that their mere presence would spoil the rituals: they were a polluting influence. This is a case of defensive territoriality with regard to a small, ritually important area, particularly acute in a certain period. In everyday life, the Gabbra do not mind living in pluriethnic neighbourhoods (Schlee 1987).

In the case of some or most Australian Aborigines this relationship of mutual appropriation between country and people does not exist between a bounded surface area and those who live on it, but between certain focal places and certain people linked to them by their clan histories and individual biographies. These ceremonial places are inhabited by totemic ancestors, to whom particular songs, stories and ceremonies pertain.[3] These places are linked by the paths of ancestral travel (Strehlow 1965: 138 about Aranda, Ingold 1986: 149). In other words: these spatial representations are zero-dimensional (places without a specific extension) or one-dimensional (vectors, lines, paths) rather than two-dimensional (bounded surface areas). Ingold (1986: 148) perceives two-dimensional tenure as a consequence of agricultural production.

This zero- and one-dimensional appropriation of space by hunters and gatherers implies the absence of boundaries. As the two-dimensional perception of land rights is deeply ingrained in our own culture, it took the anthropologists in Australia a long time to acknowledge the absence of boundaries (Ingold 1986: 148-9). But even in agricultural societies, where the clearing and appropriation of a field clearly involves a two-dimensional, bounded area, at higher political levels we find power concentrated at the centre, radiating out, becoming weaker and weaker and not ending at a defined boundary. According to Schiel (1989), in precolonial Javan kingdoms 'the realm is not defined by a boundary but structured by a centre of power' (my translation).

This unbounded perception of space seems to be widespread among Malay societies, and can even be found in a modern urban context. Evers demonstrates the consistency of this cultural pattern:

> by drawing examples from conceptions of geographical, social, religious and political space and their combination in an image of the city. As Malaysian towns and housing developments are built according to a Chinese bounded conception of space, the absorption of Malay rural-urban migrants is impeded and Chinese control over urban commerical activities is maintained.
>
> (Evers 1977: 205)

If we regard the entire breadth of possible perceptions and appropriations of space (or the varieties of which we are aware), at one end of it we find the zero- and one-dimensional forms predominant among hunters and gatherers and possibly pastoralists also. In the middle are agricultural societies and ancient kingdoms, where zero-dimensional and two-dimensional forms of structuring space exist side by side. At the other extreme is the modern nation state, which derives an important aspect of its identity from its territory, visualized on maps as a compact two-dimensional shape and which is 'defined' (from Lat. *fines*) by a boundary.[4]

This is not a line of development in the evolutionist sense and can only partly be linked to any historical chronology. The perceptions of space by hunter-gatherers and pastoralists may be similar, but probably this is due to similar forms of access to their respective resources: both hunter-gatherers and pastoralists move on when the return from local resources falls below a certain level, i.e. they are mobile.[5] The similarities in their respective perceptions of space may ultimately be linked to their mobility and are to be regarded as parallel developments rather than the one cognitive system having been derived from the other. Thus, nomadic pastoralism has not evolved from hunter cultures but, in terms of culture history, fairly recently from mixed farming.[6] In many cases people may have turned to pastoralism thousands of years after their ancestors had ceased to be hunters.[7] That pastoralists in given cases have absorbed hunters and/or borrowed elements of hunter cultures, is, of course, not precluded by this caveat.

If we look at European history, which exported this model of territorial organization to the rest of the world, we find its development to be fairly recent. If we compare a sixteenth-century map of France with a nineteenth-century one, or Germany in 1800 with Germany in 1900, we perceive a contrast between scattered territories tied by a variety of links ('personal' property, loan, church estates) and a variety of centres and the compact shape of modern nation states. In France, a new sovereign had to be found after the old one was beheaded.[8] The new sovereign was the nation, which in addition to a common language and a common culture had to be defined by a common boundary.

Due to modern cartography, printing techniques and the electronic mass media, the shapes of the territories of nation states have become handy, transportable emblems of identity, just like flags or heraldic arms.

Such portable emblems with respect to places are neither limited to bounded surface areas nor to modern communication technology. The

Farole mountain can be seen from hundreds of kilometres away, and its visibility adds weight to the swearing formula *Farole ten!* (our Farole!) when making an oath or stressing a point. Converted into a figure of speech, the mountain can serve as an identity emblem even when it can no longer be seen. Having outlined the range of variation in social representations of space, we now return to the question of where the pastoral nomads of Northern Kenya and Southern Ethiopia fit in this scheme. A trapper need only appropriate a trap line, a one-dimensional entity, but a nomad has to ask himself also about the extent of a grazing area. We should therefore look for more examples of zero-, one- and two-dimensional representations of space among these nomads and try to determine their relative importance, and especially ask ourselves which role (their own or imposed) boundaries play for them.

While this proposal goes beyond the scope of this chapter, it should be said that an analysis of how the Rendille talk about space (Schlee 1990) also reveals the importance of routes and places. The concept of bounded surface areas appears alien to them: where we find it, it is identified by a loanword. Of course, Rendille do understand what a boundary means when one is imposed and enforced on them, but there is little in their own ways of ascribing meaning to spatial relationships which could give legitimacy in their eyes to such boundaries. The problem of the social meanings of spatial relationships requires detailed philological analysis of what people say in addition to on-the-ground observation of what the places talked about look like and what people do there.

NOTES

1 The preservationist character of these rules may even be too explicit to fit into the ecological-determinism theories of the sixties, since these attribute the effectiveness of ecological regulation to the *unconscious* working of religious and other cultural rules.

2 Williams (1983: 94–109), in a discussion of 'Yolngu concepts of land ownerships' analyses how these concepts were presented in court and failed to be recognized as 'property'. The judge, who does not appear to have found his task easy, found that '[I]t seems easier, on the evidence to say that the clan belongs to the land than that the land belongs to the clan' (p. 94). Property, as she defined it, 'in its many forms, generally implies the right to use or enjoy, the right to exclude others, and the right to alienate'. And, proceeding from this definition she concluded: 'I do not think that I can characterize the relationship of the clan to the land as proprietary' (p. 98). It was held against the Yolngu that they had 'no written records or anything corresponding to them' (p. 98) and that their sacred objects could

not be equated with title deeds. The clans holding the land were unstable because they changed their composition by births and deaths and did not exclude non-clan members from the use of the land, having a 'permissive' attitude towards it (p. 96). The court, of course, did not deal with the question of which legal concepts of the Euro-Australians were close enough to Yolngu categories to be acceptable to them.

3 The songs may have an African parallel in the *dikir* songs of the Gabbra about each of their holy mountains (cf. Schlee 1987).

4 Here, we set aside the three-dimensional appropriation of space: questions of the air space, mineral deposits in the soil, urban development, how high you may build, etc.

5 For different forms of mobility cf. Ingold 1986: 165–97.

6 A possible origin of pastoralism in hunting cultures has been longest maintained in the case of arctic reindeer herders. But even here Vajda (1968) shows that nomadism in the steppe south of the taiga was well developed much earlier and that arctic nomadism is not an independent development but the local adaptation of a complex of ideas and practices which were already well established elsewhere.

7 For quite recent examples of agriculturalists turning into pastoralists cf. Barth 1961 and Haaland 1969: 64ff.

8 I am aware that I simplify here. The prerevolutionary French monarchy had already some 'national' elements.

REFERENCES

Barth, F. (1961) *Nomads of South Persia: the Basseri Tribe of the Khamseh Confederacy*, London: Oslo University Press.

Baxter, P. T. W. (1966) 'Acceptance and rejection of Islam among the Boran of the Northern Frontier District of Kenya', in I. M. Lewis (ed.), *Islam in Tropical Africa*, Oxford: Oxford University Press, pp. 233–50.

Bohannan, P. (1954) 'The migration and expansion of the Tiv', *Africa* 24: 2–16.

Evers, H.-D. (1977) 'The culture of Malaysian urbanization: Malay and Chinese conceptions of space', *Urban Anthropology* 6(3): 205–16.

Gibson, J. J. (1979) *The Ecological Approach to Visual Perception*, Boston: Houghton Mifflin.

Haaland, G. (1969) 'Economic determinants in ethnic processes', in F. Barth, (ed.) *Ethnic Groups and Boundaries*, Bergen/Oslo: Universitets Forlaget; London: Allen & Unwin, pp. 58–73.

Hamilton, A. C. (1982) *Environmental History of East Africa*, London: Academic Press.

Harris, M. (1978) *Cannibals and Kings*, New York: Vintage Books.

Ingold, T. (1980) *Hunters, Pastoralists and Teachers*, Cambridge: Cambridge University Press.

Ingold, T. (1986) *The Appropriation of Nature: Essays on Human Ecology and Social Relations*, Manchester: Manchester University Press.

Jensen, A. E. (1960) 'Beziehungen zwischen dem Alten Testament und der nilotischen Kultur in Afrika', in S. Diamond (ed.) *Culture in History. Essays in Honor of Paul Radin*, New York: Columbia University Press, pp. 459–66.

Lewis, I. M. (1976) *Social Anthropology in Perspective*, Harmondsworth: Penguin.

Rappaport, R. A. (1967) *Pigs for the Ancestors: Ritual in the Ecology of a New Guinea People*, New Haven: Yale University Press.

Sahlins, M. D. (1961) 'The segmentary lineage: an organization of predatory expansion', *American Anthropologist* 63: 322–45.

Schiel, T. (1989) 'Modernisierung und Paganisierung. Staatliche Entwicklung und "traditionelle" Gesellschaft auf Java', unpublished habilitation thesis, Bielefeld.

Schlee, G. (1979) *Das Glaubens- und Sozialsystem der Rendille: Kamelnomaden Nordkenias*, Berlin: Reimer.

—— (1982) 'Annahme und Ablehnung von Christentum und Islam bei den Rendille in Nord-Kenia', *Ostafrikanische Völker zwischen Mission und Regierung* 101–30. D-8520 Erlangen: Lehrstuhl für Missionswissenschaften (Prof. Moritzen), Jordanweg 2.

—— (1984) 'Nomaden und Staat: das Beispiel Nordkenia', *Sociologus* 34(2): 140–61.

—— (1985) 'Inter-ethnic clan identities among Cushite-speaking pastoralists', *Africa* 55(1): 17–38.

—— (1987) *Holy Grounds*, paper for a workshop on 'Property rights and problems of pastoral development in the Sahel', Manchester, April (proceedings in preparation by P. T. W. Baxter).

—— (1988) 'Camel management strategies and attitudes towards camels in the horn', in J. C. Stone (ed.) *The Exploitation of Animals in Africa*, Aberdeen: Aberdeen University African Studies Group, pp. 143–54.

—— (1989a) *Identities on the Move: Clanship and Pastoralism in Northern Kenya*, Manchester: Manchester University Press; New York: St Martin's Press.

—— (1989b) 'Zum Ursprung des Gada-Systems', *Paideuma* 35: 231–46.

—— (1989c) 'Nomadische Territorialrechte: das Beispiel des kenianisch-äthiopischen Grenzlandes', *Die Erde* 120(2): 131–8.

—— (1990) 'Policies and boundaries: perceptions of space and control of markets in a mobile livestock economy', a contribution to the EIDOS Winterschool on 'Trade, State and Ethnicity', Bielefeld, 16–20 January.

—— (in preparation) *Heilige Berge und Pilgerfahrten im kenianisch-äthiopischen Grenzgebiet*.

Strehlow, T. G. H. (1965) 'Culture, social structure, and environment in Aboriginal central Australia', in R. M. Berndt and C. H. Berndt (eds) *Aboriginal Man in Australia*, Sydney: Angus & Robertson.

Vajda, L. (1968) *Untersuchungen zur Geschichte der Hirtenkulturen*, Wiesbaden: Otto Harassowitz.

Part III

Changing to order

8 People's participation in environmental projects

Carol A. Drijver

During the last 10 years, 'environmental projects' have become increasingly important in the development field (Anonymous 1985a; Harrison 1987). The term has been used loosely and has a number of meanings. It may refer to such activities as reforestation, erosion control, establishing nature reserves or environmental education. In this chapter I propose not to employ 'type of activity' as the criterion determining whether or not a project can be defined as an environmental project so much as its objectives, i.e. a project such as planting rubber trees or building dykes and dams are not necessarily environmental projects; indeed these types of interventions may either cause serious damage or conserve the natural environment. Only when the principal objective is the sustainable management of nature and/or natural resources should the term environmental project be employed. When this is a secondary objective then it may be more appropriate to conceive of the development project as having an environmental component. Thus, where afforestation activities are included in an irrigation project this may be an example of an environmental component rather than an environmental project. The latter may itself have several components each composed of a separate but linked set of interventions and activities.

Also, in the last 10 years, the agencies managing the projects have had little time for in-depth evaluation and reflection, thus, possible lessons to be learned from recent experiences have not been adequately reported and recorded. The Centre for Environmental Studies in Leiden recently allocated part of its research capacity to the systematic evaluation of the environmental projects in order to improve their design and implementation. This chapter deals with different types of environmental projects, and in particular emphasizes the importance of a 'participatory' approach. Following a short introduction on methodology, four case studies are examined for their

Table 8.1 Classification of environmental actions (on the basis of different environmental objectives and different forms of action)

Several forms of action		*for several environmental objectives*	
strategy plan programme for project measure	conservation rehabilitation of promotion	sustainability of economic functions of nature ethical and aesthetic values of nature	

implications for the future planning and implementation of environmental projects.

AGENCY AND THE ENVIRONMENT

Environmental actions can be categorized into two main parts according to whether they promote the sustainability of economic functions of nature or whether they promote natural ecosystems and species from an ethical or aesthetic viewpoint (immaterial values of nature). Thus an environmental project may aim, respectively, at conserving, rehabilitating or recreating the sustainability of economic functions or the immaterial values of nature. As shown in Table 8.1 this gives six (three times two) possible different objectives for a project.

Table 8.1 shows that an environmental project may be aimed at the conservation of a herd of elephants (ethical value) and also at the promotion of sustainable fisheries (sustainability of economic functions). Another important distinction between projects is that between those with a direct impact on the physical environment, e.g. erosion control, reforestation or energy-saving stores and those with an indirect impact, e.g. education, consciousness raising and the promotion of environmental legislation. This chapter focuses on projects with a direct impact on the physical environment.

Environmental projects like other development projects may be categorized according to the degree of participation encouraged of those undertaking and/or benefiting from the project. In centralistic environmental projects, the objective and the modes of implementation are largely determined by a small group, usually consisting of representatives of donor organizations, local government and the project staff, perhaps assisted by consultants. The local rural population may be used as informants and sometimes consulted for their opinions. However, this does not necessarily give them any real control or participation in the direction of the project. In contrast, in participatory projects, the objectives and modes of implementation are, to a large extent, the outcome of choices and decisions made by the local community itself, although this does not necessarily involve all its members. This chapter suggests that the main characteristic of participation projects is that the local community has a decisive say in the objectives, design and implementation. It will generally accord with its participants' priorities and consequently, they will be strongly motivated to contribute. The role of the project staff, officials and consultants is then not primarily to take decisions, but rather to act as catalysts and intermediaries.

One major means of differentiating participatory projects is to distinguish between participation as a means or as an end (Oakley 1984). At present, participation is often seen as a means to a more effective or efficient realization of the objectives of sustainable management of resources. In this case the focus is on the results of participation. When participation is seen as an end, major importance is given to the process of participation itself. It has been suggested that the importance of participation as an internal process within the local communities cannot be practised when projects have been predesigned, defined and controlled by development experts. In line with this view it has been argued that the usual project approach in development co-operation be replaced by a more flexible programmatic approach. The latter approach, however, is hardly applied in practice, and the distinction between programmes and flexible projects is difficult to sustain. To elaborate the process of participation it is necessary to identify which local people should participate in which phase of the project and to determine how they can participate and why it is necessary to investigate further the concept of 'participation'.

De Groot (1989) presents many different dimensions of participation, five of which are relevant for the analysis of people's participation in environmental projects. The first emphasizes the 'social reach' of participation, i.e. its width and its depth. A wide social reach means that numerous sections of the local community actually participate in the project. The depth of social reach is the extent to which the specific target groups of the project participate without intermediaries. For instance, often in projects which aim to improve the situation of the rural poor, a deep social reach may be said to be attained when farmers with few resources participate. In environmental projects it may be other groups besides the poor that are defined as the primary target groups. For instance, in the battle against overgrazing, the participation of the owners of large herds is essential and here the depth of the social reach may be said to depend on the extent to which these owners participate.

De Groot's (1989) second dimension, the 'functional reach', focuses on the content of participation. Again a distinction can be made between width and depth. A wide functional reach of the participation means that people participate in many of the project components and phases, although the number of issues in which people participate and the moment at which they do so is in itself no guarantee of effectiveness. Moreover, if people frequently take part in decisions involving only minor details, the participation in that particular project shows a wide but superficial reach. Third, the decision power of the participants may be nil if people only labour or provide information. If people give opinions and formulate questions but project staff take the decisions, then the people may be said to have some participation in decisions. If the people themselves take all the major decisions concerning the design and implementation of the project and the role of project staff is restricted to that of catalysts and intermediaries, then the relevant terms for their participation may include autonomy, self-reliance, self-help and self-design.

According to De Groot's (1989) fourth dimension the direction of participation is less important. The participants may support the planning and implementation of an activity or not. If, for instance, people refuse to plant a tree selected by the project staff because they prefer another species, they might still be said to be participating. Indeed, this form of opposition from participants, which may influence and change project policies, may prevent unsuitable interventions and therefore may eventually contribute to the general success of projects. The direction of participation in this case is towards adjustment, for people may resist projects feeling that they may damage pre-existing practices and values in which they have an interest. Last, it is important to know why people participate and why they support, adjust or resist the project. Only when motivation is identified, can a better understanding of how and under what conditions participation might be intensified. Motivation might be based on the expectation of material advantage, e.g. certainty of a good harvest, or informal benefits such as transport systems, medical services or project funding. Non-material motives such as status, social pressure or expressing interest and the wish to learn can also be important. Motivation can be less positive when it is to check

Table 8.2 The four case studies reviewed in this chapter

project	country	objectives
Waza National Park	Cameroon	conservation of nature from an ethical and aesthetic viewpoint
Amboseli National Park	Kenya	conservation of nature from an ethical and aesthetic viewpoint and the promotion of sustainable use
Guesselibodi	Niger	rehabilitation of nature for sustainable economic use
Sukhomajri	India	rehabilitation of nature for sustainable economic use

whether the project is likely to threaten certain existing interests.

To examine this in more detail four cases of environmental projects in developing countries are reviewed (see Table 8.2). The Waza National Park in Cameroon and the Amboseli National Park in Kenya are projects that aim to conserve species in natural ecosystems from an ethical and aesthetic viewpoint. In the Guesselibodi project in Niger and the Sukhomajri project in India, the principal objective is to promote the sustainability of the economic functions of nature. The cases illustrate some differences in approach and methodology: the Waza National Park is an example of a centralistic project while the Sukhomajri project has been developed to incorporate a participatory approach; the others combine both types of approach.

THE WAZA NATIONAL PARK IN CAMEROON

The Waza National Park is an area of about 1,700 sq km in North Cameroon. The scarcely populated eastern half is part of the Logone river floodplain. Two tribes, the Kotoko and the Mousgoum, have their settlements on the plain. The Kotoko have based their life on specialized forms of fisheries on the floodplain and they practise a floating rice culture (van der Zee 1988). The Mousgoum (relative newcomers) live in small compounds and combine cattle herding, agriculture and fisheries (van Dijk (in preparation)). Because of regular inundations this extensive plain is covered with perennial grasses (Drijver and Schrader 1988), which, during the dry season, have abundant fresh green leaves resulting in herds of several ethnic groups such as the nomadic and sem-nomadic Fulani and the Arab-

Choa entering the floodplain to feed. Although at present hunting without a licence is prohibited, it still occurs (van Dijk (forthcoming); Korthof 1988). Formerly a variety of wildlife could be found in the region, but with the gradual increase in land-use activities, wildlife has been replaced largely by cattle. In 1936 the colonial government established a Waza forest/hunting reserve which allowed existing settlement and herding activities but restricted tree logging and hunting. In 1968 the reserve was transformed into a National Park and settlements and herding were banned.

The planning and implementation of the Waza National Park is an example of an almost completely centralistic environmental project. The existing villages were disbanded, it is said, as a retaliatory measure against the inhabitants, who had voted against the incumbent president during the preceding elections. The people were not allowed to return to their villages and founded new settlements along the borders of the Park. One village still exists in the Park; its inhabitants had voted for the president. The Waza National Park service comprises about thirty guards who report directly to the Park manager who in turn reports to the Cameroonian Service for Tourism, which is represented in the regions by a Provincial Delegation. The guards live in surrounding villages around the Park but originate from other regions and often do not speak the local language (pers. com. Noordzij). They control hunting and prevent poaching, illegal herding, wood collection, etc. The penalty for poaching is a fine (equivalent to approximately 3 months' salary) or jail sentences from 3 months to 5 years (Steehouwer 1988). Tourism is also developing with a luxurious hotel managed by a semi-governmental organization. Visitors often hire guides selected by the Park manager from surrounding villages (Noordzij (forthcoming)).

The Park is the only area on the southern fringe of the West African Sahel with numerous species of wildlife in large numbers. Some species populations seem to survive reasonably, but maintenance of larger ungulate species is more difficult – the waterbuck has been exterminated, the reedbuck is rare, and the number of cob antelopes has drastically fallen from 25,000 in 1968 to about 1,700 in 1988, the latter being also threatened with extermination (Korthof 1988). Nevertheless, the establishment of the Park has significantly conserved a rich variety of wildlife. Several changes outside the Park, however, raise the question of whether this is sustainable, namely, lack of inundation (Chambers 1987). Between 1979 and 1988 the floodplain pastures largely dried up during the dry season over an area of about 1,500 sq km, of which 600 sq km lies in the Waza Park. Lack of inundation is partly caused by the construction of dykes and a reservoir about 40 km upstream for an irrigated rice culture and is to some extent permanent (Anonymous 1988).

A second major threat is poaching. Two types may be distinguished. First, local inhabitants hunt using traditional methods for their own consumption. Second, whole groups of animals are shot with modern weapons and transported for sale in Nigeria. Cameroonians say that this is mainly undertaken by Nigerians, but it is understood that local residents are hired by these poachers to act as guides or informants. The residents around the Park generally live in very poor socio-economic conditions (Noordzij (forthcoming)). The problems include the lack of reliable drinking water, unreliable and insufficient rainfall, poor soils, scarce vegetation, few market opportunities and the lack of infrastructure and governmental services, all resulting in insufficient stocks of low-quality food, lack of cash and a great number of health problems. The establishment of the Park, rather than improving prospects of most of the population, have made them even worse. They have lost the right to pastures, fields and forests, and their present fields are exposed to the detrimental impact of weaver birds and elephants that are based in the Park but leave it regularly to look for food (Steehouwer 1988). Even worse, lions and jackals also kill the odd cow, sheep or goat. Also, villages bordering the Park, a sensitive location, have little chance of ever being able to profit from development programmes. The advantages of the Park only benefit a small number of people – guides, craftsmen, waiters or those in charge of park management or tourism (Noordzij (forthcoming)).

In consequence, most people will use the scarce opportunities for personal gain, such as by assisting poachers, and feel little motivation to actively promote the survival of the Park and its wildlife; the Park is seen as an extra burden on their lives. Probably large- and small-scale attacks on the wildlife population will continue and in the long run the Park will not succeed in preserving its natural heritage. Its problems not only illustrate the ecological impacts of large-scale interventions in the environment, but emphasize that such centralistic nature conservation projects that ignore the socio-economic conditions of the local people may lead to the detriment of the very environment they are designed to protect or conserve.

AMBOSELI NATIONAL PARK IN KENYA

In 1977 a programme was launched to reduce conflict between the interests of the local people and nature conservation practices in and around Amboseli National Park. Its explicit aim was to incorporate the socio-economic interests of the surrounding population in the new management of the Park (Lindsay 1987). For centuries the land had been used by the Maasai to graze their cattle (Tapilit de Saitoti 1980) and partly due to the low population density, there have always been sufficient resources for the support and survival of wildlife. In the first 10 years following independence (1963), the new government encouraged the expansion of cattle by implementing a programme for waterhole construction. The resulting increases in cattle and the Maasai population led to some competition for the available space resulting in overgrazing and a decrease in wildlife for hunting. An alliance developed between the government, nature conservationists and representatives of the tourist industry in favour of the establishment of four National Reserves and the Amboseli National Park. This Park comprised the central part of the Amboseli Basin (about 1,000 sq km) and during dry periods is the main area with water and green pastures. However, the Maasai lost their grazing rights and access to a critically important area in their herding system and most financial benefits from tourism went to the central government in Nairobi, although to promote the Maasai's acceptance of the reserves a small sum of money was given to a district council with African members. Although the council was regarded as an indigenous, representative body, the Maasai around Amboseli Park did not benefit as the council was in Kajiado city, more than 100 km away, and represented just another bureaucratic level of interference. Conflict arose, which included the killing of animals by the Maasai as a form of protest.

In 1977 a programme aimed at directly increasing potential benefits for the Maasai was set up in which they would become joint landowners around the Park and would organize themselves in communal cattle ranches (group ranches). In return, the Maasai would assist in wildlife conservation by combating poaching and tolerating wildlife on their ranches. Prolonged negotiations between central government, the ranch owners and the district council finally resulted in an advantageous agreement. It guaranteed a water supply by the construction of boreholes outside the Park, to be managed by the park services. There was to be financial compensation for those on whose group ranches fewer cattle could graze due to the fact that wildlife also used these pastures. The Maasai would share in the financial benefits from tourism and hunting on the group ranches, and schools, health services and a community centre were to be constructed.

The first 3 years were promising. Poaching was largely controlled by the positive co-operation and influence of the Maasai elders and the number of rhinos and elephants increased. There was wildlife outside the Park and in return the Maasai got financial compensation. Boreholes were constructed on the ranches and the Maasai no longer needed to enter the Park during dry periods. For the same reason a pipeline was constructed to transport water from the central wet part of the Park to the outer zones. A new school and a medical post were built. However, from 1980 onwards problems arose. Several components of the programme depended on the bureaucratic machinery of the national government, for example a delay occurred in the payment of financial compensation due to the Maasai because the money had to come from the capital Nairobi and cash income from tourism went to Nairobi first. It became apparent that the programme was too heavily based on financial advantages, without sufficient attempts to also gain the co-operation of the Maasai on the basis of cultural and social values. The role of water, cattle, wildlife, money and responsiblity in the social and cultural life style of the Maasai was not identified, analysed or understood. Although the government did not meet its financial obligations to the Maasai, initially, violations of the agreement by the Maasai did not occur. When, however, the boreholes failed due to inadequate maintenance (again because the expertise and money from Nairobi failed to arrive), the Maasai stopped respecting the agreement and in the dry season of 1982 entered the Park and brought their herds to the wet pastures of the Amboseli basin. Access to water became more important to them than the financial compensations. Poaching recurred and in 1983 the agreed financial compensation was withdrawn. The environment project eventually failed in its objectives (see Lindsay 1987). The main reasons for its failure included the overreliance on financial compensation compared to other non-material factors and the insufficient attention to resource management and local interests and culture of the participants on whose goodwill the success of the project rested.

THE GUESSELIBODI EXPERIMENT

The Guesselibodi experiment is an environmental project that the local population participated in, managed and shaped (Heermans 1987a; 1987b, and van Dijk and de Bruijn 1989). The location is a 5,000 ha. savannah woodland, about 25 km from Niame, capital of Niger, West Africa. During the last 30 years the woodland has been drastically downgraded due to drought, over-exploitation and lack of management. The vegetation cover in 1979 was 50 per cent of what it had been in 1950; a number of important tree species had disappeared, soil erosion was a serious problem and soil fertility had decreased. In 1981 there were areas where reforestation might be possible, but if environmental degradation were to continue, within 20 to 30 years it would be irreversible. In 1981 a research programme, financed by USAID, focused on the sustainable use of the forest areas of Niger. Guesselibodi is one of sixty-six forests controlled by the Niger National Forest Service and because of its proximity to the capital and the fact that the Forest Service has been previously involved in research, it was selected as a demonstration project.

The technical aim of the project was to halt degradation and regenerate the woodland to produce timber and wood for local consumption and sale in the capital; the socio-economic aim was the development of a cost-effective management plan that could run in the long term without foreign support, in which the local people could participate from the beginning and from which they could also benefit. Finally, the entire management plan was to be co-ordinated, controlled and implemented by the local people themselves. During the first 2 years of the project, research was carried out on the technical and socio-economic aspects. The results of these studies were used to design a management plan in which the area was divided into sections in order to establish a rotation of management practices. For a period of 3 years all cattle were to be excluded from the area after which measures to control grazing were to be instituted. To make better use of the existing rainfall, contour bands and micro-basins were to be constructed and the sowing and cutting of grasses were introduced; indigenous trees and shrubs were planted between the existing vegetation and a wood-cutting scheme was introduced. Wood was sold in the city and smaller branches were to be used as mulching material to stimulate the activities of termites resulting in better soil and better growth of grasses.

Only the sedentary population of surrounding villages participated. Sedentary women were not explicitly involved nor were the nomadic people, who used the area as a grazing resource for part of the year within their seasonal movements. Thus, the social reach of the participation has been limited. Male villagers only commented on and gave opinions about the management plan and the project staff decided whether they responded or not. They followed one proposal from the villagers to add a further 30 ha for agricultural purposes and to use villagers as paid labourers for the implementation of the ecological rehabilitation activities. Agricultural development and opportunities to earn a cash income appeared to be two priorities for the males. Furthermore, measures were taken to give the (male) villagers some decision powers by instituting a co-operative represent-ing nine villages. After intensive negotiations a unique agreement (for that time) was made between the co-operative and the Forest Service of the Government of Niger: it was agreed that the exploitation rights of the 5,000 ha forest area would be given to the co-operative on condition that the latter would ensure that the management plan would be implemented and respected. The organization of selective wood cutting as a rotation scheme and the regulation of grazing activities were thus placed in the co-operative control.

In this project, then, the aim to increase participation was not realized in each phase. During the identification period it was very limited because the idea of an ecological rehabilitation project already existed and experts were looking for a suitable area to put it into practice. During the design phase, participation became increasingly important, and during the implementation and management phase, it was a major issue (van Dijk and de Bruijn 1989). In conclusion, the decision power of participants was reasonable, but the social and functional reach of this participation was limited. However, it is against the background of the many failed projects on the African continent (see Timberlake 1986) that its achievements must be con-sidered. The regeneration of the forest is already occurring and the wood-cutting scheme is successful. Experiments are under way con-cerning the cutting and drying of grass and it may be possible to sell the hay too. The project may turn out to be financially independent. Environmental management measures by the local people combined with economic advantages seem to have been potentially successful, but some serious questions need to be considered for the future. Possibly, the reforestation may not be sufficient to ensure the necessary income. Continuing support by a donor organization will be necessary for at least 5 years and these financial commitments had not yet been made at the time of writing. One question is whether an area with better soil conditions than Guesselibodi might have been selected so that regeneration would take less time. Second, given that the proximity of the capital of Niame with its market opportunities for wood products is of prime importance, this model may not be applicable in the remote rural areas in Niger. Third, do women and children share enough in the economic benefits and has the situation for the nomadic groups improved? Finally, where does the real decision-making power lie? In the event of conflict, the Forest Service retains the power to withdraw the agreement and to once again take over the management of the forest area from the co-operatives (van Dijk and de Bruijn 1989).

THE SUKHOMAJRI PROJECT

The Sukhomajri project in India has been selected largely because problems caused by unequal resource distribution and uncertainty about sustainability of the success of the project had been overcome. Sukhomajri is a village at the foot of the Himalayas where deforestation and erosion are common problems. The government has attempted to regulate such problems by restricting land use. Herding and wood cutting are allowed close to villages, but more remote areas are set aside, sometimes by fencing them off. Implementation is not very successful. The local population disagrees with the regulations and continuous control by Forest Service officers (Anonymous 1985). The project was initiated when the city council of Chandigarh asked the Indian National Research Institute for assistance with soil and water conservation (Mishra and Madhu Sarin 1987). A nearby reservoir appeared to receive a high silt load causing poor quality water and limited future storage capacity. The researchers were asked to investigate the upstream catchment area of the lake. It was found that maximum erosion occurred near Sukhomajri, a village at the edge of the plateau and the frontier of the catchment area of the lake. The village's 400 inhabitants practised rainfed agriculture, kept a few hundred head of cattle and a large number of goats that grazed on the already heavily eroded hill pastures. Periodically, sowing and harvesting were impossible through lack of rainfall and the unpredictable rainfall pattern. During the rainy season much soil was eroded, especially from the sparse hillside along various channels. Where low shrubs had been sown, the surrounding soil was washed downhill silting up the reservoir.

When a small dam was constructed in one of the erosion channels, both sediment and water were retained, and in the dry season the surrounding vegetation remained fresh and green. The villagers expressed interest and requested a second, larger dam. The assignment given to the investigators had been to control erosion not to initiate irrigation; moreover, the village fields were not in their project area. However, they also understood that participation of the villagers would be indispensable when they began to attempt to stop the overgrazing and erosion of the hillside. After long discussions a contract was negotiated between the research institute, the supervising representative of the city council and the people of Sukhomajri. A dam would be constructed to facilitate irrigated agriculture and in turn the goats and cows would be removed from the hill. Within 2 years the irrigation programme was started, but goats and cows, albeit fewer in number, could still be seen on the hills. There was some conflict, but it became apparent that the cattle on the hills were owned by people who did not benefit from the irrigation. Either their fields were too far away or they had hardly any agricultural land at all. Thus the unequal distribution of access to land and water formed an obstacle. After negotiation it was agreed that the project would redistribute the agricultural fields in such a way that every household would get a sufficiently sized irrigable plot. Further, a Water Users' Association would be founded to organize water distribution. One representative of each household would become a member and each member would get a water share with the household losing its water rights should its cattle be found grazing on the hill.

After 2 years the villagers' living conditions had improved, goats were increasingly replaced by cows (kept in stables), the hills gradually regenerated and grass production also increased. Up to that time the right to cut and harvest the grass was leased to a private enterprise, that in turn leased the rights back to villagers. Since the productivity of the hills was increasing due to the villagers' better management, the Forest Service decided to lease the exploitation rights directly to them. The village took care of collecting the licence fees, the fees were reduced and a portion of the collected fees remained at the disposal of the villagers. They decided to reinvest this in the management of the hill including the buying of seeds and seedlings. Within the village it was the Waters Users' Association which, in organizing all this, adopted the new and more appropriate title: the Hill Resource Management Society. Other villages followed suit, eighteen of them by 1987. The government was satisfied as it no longer had to build fences to keep out goats and cattle. Now that there was social control through the Hill Resource Management Societies, the initiators of the project coined the term 'social fencing' (Mishra and Madhu Sarin 1987).

The Sukhomajri project suggests that social control by local communities may be a mechanism to encourage local people to respect the restrictions of a package deal and thus avoid the over-exploitation of natural resources. However, 'social fencing' only works if the distribution of rights and advantages are accepted by all the participants. Often this involves reallocation of people's existing rights over the use of natural resources. The project must aim at full participation of all the people (social reach of participation) in sufficient phases of the project (functional reach of participation) and structural or fundamental decision-making power is given to the participants. Successful participatory environmental projects are flexible and the schedules for allocation of funds, definitions of project areas, target sectors of action and groups to be involved, can be adjusted frequently and attuned to the local needs and chances of achieving success. The case studies suggest that the projects require appropriate political objectives, skills and will on the part of all the agents from the sponsor and designers to the participants and beneficiaries.

REFERENCES

Anonymous (1985a) *Directory of Rural Development Projects*, Istedn, Brussels: Institute of Cultural Affairs (International).

Anonymous (1985b) 'The state of India's Environment 1984–85: the second citizen's report', New Delhi, India: Centre for Science and Environment.

Anonymous (1988) *Conservation and Development in the Waza Logone Region*, Republic of Cameroon Project Document, Centre for Environmental Studies. RUL; Institute of Animal Research of Min. of Higher Education, Computer Services and Scientific Research, Cameroon.

Chambers, R. (1987) 'Sustainable rural livelihoods: a key strategy for people, environment and development', papers IIED-conference *Only One Earth*, London: IIED.

de Groot, W. T. (1989) 'Participatie en milieubeheer: een begripsmatige systematiek en een inhoudelijke verkenning', in *Participatie en Milieubeheer*, Leiden: CML-mededelingen nr. 41.

Drijver, C. A. and Schrader, T. H. (1988) 'Armoede en milieudegradatie in de Logonevlakte in Noord Kameroen: naar een milieukundige benadering', *Mens en Milieu, Antropologische Verkenningen* 7/4: 50–64.

Harrison, P. (1987) *The Greening of Africa*, London: International Institute for Environment and Development.

Heermans, I. G. a. e. (1987a) *Guide to Forest Restoration and Management in the Sahel*. Based on case studies at the National Forests of Guesselbodi and Garou Bassounga, Niger. Ministry of Hydrology and the Environment Forestry Land Use and Planning Project Niamey. Niger 1987.

—— (1987b) 'The Guesselbodi experiment: Bushland Management in Niger', paper for the Conference on Sustainable Development, London: International Institute for Environment and Development.

Korthof, H. (1988) 'Les Cobs de Buffon de Waza'. *Serie Milieu en Ontwikkeling in Noord Kameroen*, Leiden: Centrum voor Milieukunde.

Lindsay, W. K. (1987) 'Integrating parks and pastoralists: some lessons from Amboseli', in *Conservation in Africa*, Cambridge: Cambridge University Press.

Mishra, P. R. and Madhu, S. (1987) 'Social security through social fencing: Sukhomaji and Nada's road to self-sustaining development', Paper for the IIED-Conference 'ONLY ONE EARTH', London.

Noordzij, J. (forthcoming), 'Mens en Nationaal Park: sociaal-ekonomische situatie van de lokale bevolking rondos het Waza Nationale Park in

Kameroen', *Serie Milieu en Ontwikkeling in Noord Kameroen*, Leiden: Centrum voor Milieukunde.

Oakley, P. (1984) *Approaches to Participation in Rural Development*, Geneva: International Labour Office.

Steehouwer, G. (1988) 'Olifanten, milieuveranderingen en gebieds inrichting', *Serie Milieu en Ontwikkeling in Noord Kameroen*, Leiden: Centrum voor Milieukunde.

Tapilit de Saitoti (1980) *Maasai*, New York: Harry N. Abrams, Inc.

Timberlake, L. (1986) *De Afrikaanse crisis: de oorzaken en de bestrijding van een failliet leefmilieu*, Haarlem: Rostrum.

van der Zee, E. (1988) *Kotoko vissers in de Logone vloedvlakte. Serie Milieu en Ontwikkeling in Noord-Kameroen*, Leiden: Centrum voor Milieukunde.

van Dijk, J. M. W. and de Bruijn, M. E. (1989) 'Participatie in mileuprojecten in West Africa', LUW (Boshuishoudkunde)/RUL (*Programme Milieu en Ontwikkeling*). Leiden: CML.

van Dijk, J. M. W. (forthcoming), *Het milieugebruik van de Mousgoum in de Logone-vlakte in Noord Kameroen, Serie Milieu en Ontwikkeling in Noord Kameroen*. Leiden: Centrum voor Milieukunde.

9 Intolerable environments
Towards a cultural reading of agrarian practice and policy in Rwanda

Johan Pottier and Augustin Nkundabashaka[1]

ABSTRACT AND INTRODUCTION

There is growing evidence, throughout Africa, that agricultural extension workers are failing to understand and communicate with food cultivators. Rwanda is no exception, but the alarm was raised only recently, by some members of the Ministry of Agriculture (Bagirameshi *et al.* 1986).

Given this concern, it is appropriate to enquire whether the physical environment has suffered damage and whether the future holds out any hope of remedy. We answer with reference to one particularly vulnerable environment: the town of Butare, Southern Rwanda. The answers expose issues of a physical nature (related to soil conditions) and reveal that much 'culture' lurks beneath the visible surface. The aim of this chapter is threefold. First, to provide a cultural reading of the Butare landscape, by concentrating on two marked aspects: the cultivation practices on hillsides (section 1) and the exploitation of marshlands (section 4). Second, hillside cultivation today (based on intercropping with bananas), is set against Government policy on agriculture (section 2); a development perspective which must be understood in terms of a cultural history (section 3). Third, we shall use our cultural reading of the Butare landscape to respond to current discussion of agricultural extension.

The context within which a better dialogue between Rwandan cultivators and extension workers (agronomists, *vulgarisateurs*) could be achieved is still a matter of speculation, since public meetings are usually too formal to be conducive to dialogue (ACORD 1987).[2] In this chapter we join the debate and focus on the organization of agricultural co-operatives (section 4). We suggest that such co-operatives, because of what they stand for in cultural terms, could become the vehicle for improving the image of extension workers. The

Ministry of Agriculture has already begun a programme aiming to reverse current attitudes in agricultural extension and aims to ensure that (male) extension personnel become willing to learn from (female) cultivators (Bagirameshi *et al.* 1986).

Despite this programme, Rwanda's policy on agrarian co-operatives is ambiguous. Enthusiastically supported only a decade ago (MRND 1985), the co-operative movement is now out of favour with the Government, and badly underfunded (*Quatrième Plan Quinquennal*, 1987–1991).

We shall extend Pottier's (1989b) suggestion that the co-operative movement in Rwanda is popular with the rank-and-file because it provides an arena for protest and challenging hierarchies, including male domination over women. From a historical perspective, it reveals some remarkable parallels with past protest movements, especially the widespread, highly challenging cult of Ryangombe. We propose that co-operatives provide a forum for questioning 'the order of things', like Ryangombe.

The legacy of Ryangombe, intimately linked to the banana grove (*bananeraie*), is relevant for understanding the debate on 'rational' farming. The banana grove, that dominates the Rwandan landscape, is the focal point of the extension workers' criticism of local farming practices. The *bananeraie* is described as *la vache du pauvre*, because it provides regular income and (though not usually implied) is a buffer against famine. We concede that the banana grove stands for much more: as an environment for intercropping, it is part of a finely tuned coping strategy; as part of a cultural patrimonium, it represents a range of strong cultural and emotional forces.

URBAN ENVIRONMENTS, WITH REFERENCE TO FOOD FARMING

First, we compare approaches to gardening in two Butare areas: a recently built housing estate (Project Rango) claiming to provide for the urban poor; and a zone of two sectors where spontaneous settlement occurred during colonization, and where land holdings are larger but subject to fragmentation under inheritance. We shall discuss the impact agrarian policy has had upon the physical landscape. The approach to gardening in Rango (see Pottier 1989a) is a 'modern' one, contrasting drastically with the traditional practices observed in the older part of the town – Tumba-Cyarwa. The latter have evolved in response to population pressure and the demand for intensive cultivation.

In Butare it *is* legitimate to talk of 'damage' caused by extension workers, but only in the sense that the model village of Rango, situated on a steep slope affected by erosion, has made almost no progress (over 8 years) in terms of land improvement. Part of the problem is that residents have other land outside the project and the project gardens are not crucial for survival.

Project Rango houses many salaried workers (often young male bachelors), and only a small group of urban poor. Being less dependent on gardening, the better-off residents readily accept the agronomist's view that Rango (where five extension workers live!) is a scientific experiment in state agriculture. Thus, gardens must look neat, plants must be spaced and lined up, crops must rotate, chemical fertilizers and pesticides must be used. The 'modern' approach opposes the complex multiple-cropping system found throughout the interlacustrine region and East Africa (Belshaw 1979) and rejects all slow-maturing crops. As such, the banana groves are absent and sorghum cultivation is prohibited. Yet the latter are buffers against famine, especially for the poor, and also provide good organic fertilizer.

The traditional farming method is found today only on family farms that sprang up two or three generations ago. These gardens have a higher humus content, as top soil is protected against run-off through multi-storey cropping and the application of plant debris (sometimes manure). Farmers in Tumba-Cyarwa retain much plant debris and use various techniques to prevent the nutrient drainage. One major farming practice today is *uninterrupted* land exploitation. As one cultivator explained:

> Here in Tumba, where people grow sorghum, they cultivate while practising fallow. Sorghum cultivation is a method of fallowing, because people use the flat top soil and do not eliminate weeds. After the sorghum is harvested they will hoe deep and make mounds (*gusekera*). Hoeing deep makes the deep soil come up (*kuzamura*). The mounds are then left for about a month, after which the garden is ready for bean planting. When a field gets older such mounds are left for longer periods.

This type of cultivation (*gutabira*) ensures that debris is dug deeply into the soil.

In Tumba-Cyarwa, a small part of the farm, near the house, is usually set aside for a dense banana grove, while elsewhere banana trees are intercropped with other plants, thus advantageously protecting associated plants against heavy rainfall or excessive heat. If enough land is available, a smaller part of the farm may also be left unshaded.

Such farming methods, sensitive to the light requirements of individual plants, are also used by rural farmers, e.g. when selecting bean mixtures for existing micro-environments. Growers in Butare often select two different mixtures: one type for growing with a relatively dense banana crop, the other where trees are more dispersed, illustrating an environment-responsive approach. Farmers experiment with new bean varieties growing them as a single crop, observing maturation time, resistance to rain, sunshine, infertile soil, and then introducing suitable varieties into one of the mixtures.

Three broad categories of banana exist: the popular wine bananas (about 85–90 per cent of total production), eating bananas and fruit bananas. There are several varieties of each category.

Tumba-Cyarwa farmers grow sorghum, but say that production has declined because of pricing policy and competition. Still, reliance on both *bananeraie* and sorghum, and soil conservation methods, e.g. *gutabira* and certain types of crop rotation, permits a relatively sustainable type of farming.

However, the soil is not good quality throughout Tumba-Cyarwa, nor is there sufficient land for every household. A further problem is firewood as cut trees are not being replaced at a sustainable rate and poorer households are now having to use organic debris for cooking fuel, e.g. banana-tree bark.

Despite the fact that 1986 was Rwanda's *Année de l'Intensification Agricole*, the agronomists and *vulgarisateurs* firmly object to integrating mixed cropping patterns and tall perennials. They advocate growing beans and maize (in rows and chemically fertilized) or soya and maize. 'All other associations,' as one agronomist said, 'amount to unintelligent gardening and are the result of ignorance. *Les associations c'est l'ignorance!* The only good gardening is one crop per *parcelle*, with rotation: tubers followed by legumes followed by cereals.'[3] Extension workers also underestimate the value of selecting bean mixtures according to soil type.

Multi-storey systems have their drawbacks, e.g. too much shading reduces yields (Steiner 1984: 47). This is not a serious problem in Tumba-Cyarwa and can hardly be the reason for the extension workers' negative attitude. Growing banana trees advantageously provides organic matter for soil fertility and helps prevent erosion (Delepierre 1970: 157; Dupriez and de Leener 1983: 45; Steiner 1984: 47). Reviewing Rwandan farming systems, Fairhead revealed the consequences of the low priority given to the *bananeraie* in the *Lutte Anti-Erosive*: 'bananas were [once] a symbol of land tenure and a means of erosion protection. Now coffee and anti-erosion protection are becoming symbols for tenure, and unhappily may further erosion' (Fairhead 1986: 50). The extension workers' negative attitude can be explained with reference to Government policy, which is categorically opposed to these banana groves. Invoking its duty to ensure the people's physical and moral health, the Government proposes:

> to rationalise the banana grove through renovation, that is to say, by growing bananas only in ecologically appropriate regions, and by reducing acreages to a maximum one-sixth of the family farm, or one-fourth in areas where bananas grow really well (e.g. Bugoyi, Gisaka, Kinyaga and along Lake Kivu). Regions where the growth of the banana tree is inappropriate [defined as being above 1.900 metres] should substitute crops such as sunflower, wheat, groundnuts, and cassava.
>
> (Nzamurambaho 1978; reprinted in *Dialogue* 1986)

The Goverment position prompted *Dialogue* writer Ntamahungiro to conclude: 'Clearly, the current exploitation of banana trees, especially those producing wine bananas, is opposed to the programme for agricultural intensification' (Ntamahungiro 1986: 105).

Recent research on agricultural intensification in Rwanda has become on-farm oriented (Nkundabashaka and Voss 1987) and first results indicate some of the complexity and ingenuity of intercropping techniques. Consequently, the Government position, unchanged since the late 1970s, may need to be revised shortly. However, certain sociopolitical hurdles must be overcome before the wisdom of indigenous knowledge will be taken seriously in Government and development circles.[4]

Extension workers still cling to textbook notions of 'modern' farming at the expense of serious enquiry into the viability of local methods. Attitudes must be reversed as suggested by Bagirameshi *et al.* 1986. Only through open dialogue involving cultivators and extension workers, on an equal footing with an emphasis on 'learning from women farmers', does Rwanda stand any chance at all of winning the *Lutte Anti-Erosive*, through which it hopes to achieve adequate food production targets by the year 2000.

In the next section we shall set Rwandan agrarian policy in its political context to give some idea of the magnitude of the task ahead.

AGRICULTURAL EXTENSION IN POLICY AND PRACTICE

Cultivator-*vulgarisateur* interactions are mostly sporadic, in Tumba-Cyarwa, and Butare generally, where *vulgarisateurs* ('who know') are not interested in wasting time on people 'who do not know'. Interaction boils down to a one-way, dogmatic delivery of textbook instructions.

One-way instructions also dominate in Rango, where contact is more frequent and varied. The complexity of producer-*vulgarisateur* interaction can be seen, for example, in the way that lessons learned from trials are not available for all. Agronomists decide on worthy recipients. What *is* available is any type of information which validates the 'modern' approach (see Pottier 1989a). In Rango, and elsewhere (see section 4), agriculture is used as an instrument for marking social distinctiveness and hierarchy. Thus, the agronomist's understanding of the potential benefits of local farming knowledge comes second to the idea that agricultural practices can be systematized and enforced via the threat of sanctions.

Sanctions are clearly linked to occupancy, as land tenure in Rwanda has become very precarious, e.g. it is now illegal to associate any crop with coffee, or uproot a coffee stand once planted. Fines and land expropriation by the state are penalties. Rwanda's *Second Five-Year Plan* anticipated legislation to enable precise use of land, to maximum advantage, and the formulation of a procedure for state recuperation of land not put to its best use (Government of Rwanda 1977: 70).

The spirit of agricultural extension in Rwanda has not changed since the days of the Conference on Agricultural Extension, held in Butare in 1977 when the Minister for Agriculture gave the following definition of Extension: 'In our opinion, Agricultural Extension means educating the rural masses; it is the transfer into the agricultural milieu of rational production techniques' (Nzamurambaho 1977: 6). With these words, the Minister confirmed what University Recteur Nsanzimana had already said on the subject:

> the agricultural programmes *set up by the political authorities* of our country must be absorbed by future cadres. Within the same mode of thought (*Dans le même ordre d'idées*), these programmes have to be disclosed to enlighten the entire population (*ouverts à tous pour être mieux orientés*).
> (Nsanzimana 1977: 3–4; my emphasis)

This confirms the very close relationship in Rwanda between power and knowledge. Peasant producers do not have power and can therefore only be the recipients of knowledge (see also Delepierre 1977: 12); the usefulness of peasant knowledge is regarded as negligible. This became evident in the early 1980s, when the Rwandan Government declared: 'exceptional population density . . . [would] render present production methods useless' (CEC 1982: 14).

A top-down approach to agricultural extension has been practised for the past 25 years, with disastrous result and can be summarized as follows: (a) *vulgarisateurs* transmit scientific ideas without understanding them; (b) they fail to comprehend *les logiques* behind local farming practices; and (c) they have no wish to learn from cultivators, whose rank is below their own (Bagirameshi *et al.* 1986: 422–3). The situation, a familiar one in Africa, is captured brilliantly with the words: 'The agronomist gives orders, and the field has to adapt' (ibid. 429).

Another characteristic of 'modern' farming is the public denial that local practice and 'modern' messages can be reconciled, if only humorously (see Pottier 1989a). Another, more forceful example was recently reported by Joachim Voss, a former CIAT anthropologist working in Rwanda:

> Several times during the evaluation of on-farm variety trials, it became clear that the technicians or extensionists responsible for the trials were extolling the virtues of planting the improved variety over the mixture. Care must be taken to explain to the people who provide the direct link with farmers that *the aim is to improve the composition of [existing] mixtures by adding the new varieties to them, not to replace them.*
>
> (Voss 1988: 11)

This indicates that adoption of an alien/scientific reference frame may exclude interest in understanding local production patterns and strategies. This will become clear in the next section, when the tendency to replace or integrate frames of reference will be considered not only within agriculture but also within the religious domain.[5]

This one-way communication must also be understood against the background of Rwanda's colonial past, since the colonial administration made access to 'new' agricultural knowledge the prerogative of men. These men, the first breed of extension workers, believed indigenous agriculture had nothing to offer as it was the domain of women, who officially have very low status.

Given today's call for open debate, and envisaged difficulties, it becomes imperative to search for contexts where dialogue does/did take place, and where the need for reversing *l'ordre des idées* is/was tackled head on, e.g. the co-operative movement. First, it is useful to scan Rwanda's recent history for similar signs of reversal and protest.

FERTILITY AND FREEDOM IN THE PAST: RYANGOMBE

To express the opinion that extension workers must *donner la parole aux femmes* (Bagirameshi *et al.* 1986) is to recall the Interlacustrine region's rich repertoire of women's protest movements (Berger 1976; 1981). The most recent prevalent one in Southern Rwanda has been the cult of Ryangombe. We relate the cult's emergence, popularity and decline, and examine sociological interpretations, to provide the backcloth for observations about agrarian co-operatives (see section 4).

The cult of Ryangombe is a particular instance of the *kubandwa* (spirit possession) cults that flourished especially in the late-nineteenth and first half of the twentieth centuries. It originated in ancient Bunyoro and was introduced by the Cwezi people (de Heusch 1966: 159). Unlike other *kubandwa*, it was open to both sexes, in spite of its concern with women's fecundity (Rodegem 1971: 928) and the fertility of the nation itself (Berger 1981: 85). The interest in membership for both sexes was typical of the Rwandan *kubandwa*. Referring to Arnoux (1912: 844), Berger writes: 'The Rwanda ceremony of *kubandwa* abolished sexual differences; all initiates, men and women alike, acquired a virile masculine quality, *umugabo*' (Berger 1976: 171). It would be wrong, Berger says, to accept the so-called 'sex war' hypothesis and classify Ryangombe as a feminist subculture through which women gained advantages over their menfolk.[6]

Initiation into Ryangombe offered protection against harmful ancestral spirits (*abazimu*) and against powerful local sorcerers (de Heusch 1966: 167). In Rwanda's traditional magico-religious system, ancestors were often intent on making life on earth intolerable, and had to be dealt with. But being out of touch with his people, *Imana* (usually translated as God) provided no protection against this rift between living and dead. Through initiation, adepts entered the privileged world of their Saviour King and his priests (*Imandwa*), where they became members of a *new family* (de Heusch 1966: 167).

Although the cult mixed alien concepts with prevailing religious ideas its dominant feature was a *new perception of deity*. The cult substituted an accessible mythical hero, Ryangombe, for the distant Imana, who was *'l'image même du roi sacré, bon et magnifique, mais inaccessible'* (de Heusch 1966: 168). Ryangombe was different:

enthusiastic mediator, accessible through initiation, and optimistic; the perfect antidote to the prevailing religious pessimism.

There were two levels of initiation: the vast majority were initiated through *kwatura* (the one-night test that culminated in mystic communion with Ryangombe); the few who could afford it then proceeded to Level II (Berger 1976: 173).

From de Heusch's reconstruction of *kwatura*, based on Arnoux' ethnography (1912), we learn that the banana grove was an important ritual space for the purpose of initiation,[7] although the erythrine tree was the most central 'natural' element. During *kwatura* the novice was taken into the grove, where he/she was: 'covered in filth (Arnoux), "soiled" by the initiated (de Lacger), and covered in excrement (Bourgeois)' (de Heusch 1966: 188). De Heusch comments: 'It has been confirmed that the initiant was urinated upon' (1966: 188). The neophyte was then left alone in the darkness of the *bananeraie* while the *Imandwa* (i.e. the Level II adepts representing Ryangombe priests) returned to the sacred erythrine tree to carry on drinking banana wine.

At dawn, the *Imandwa* brought the neophyte back to the erythrine tree. Here the initiant was invited:

> to speak words 'that caused shame': to reveal his sexual life or that of his parents or, in the case of a woman, to pronounce the name of her father-in-law, which is normally forbidden. According to de Lacger, the initiant utters incestuous vows, after which he receives a new name and is introduced to the members of his new family.
>
> (de Heusch 1966: 188-9)

De Heusch (1966: 188) interprets the defilement and humiliation as expressing symbolically how Ryangombe 'saves' the neophyte from the profane condition (*kumukiz' ubuzigo*).[8]

In the second initiation, reserved for the select few, further tests were carried out in the *bananeraie*. Upon receiving a new name, the neophyte would:

> make for the paternal house to snatch provisions and various objects. The spoils were then offered to the *Imandwa* who personified Ryangombe. The neophyte also offered him a cluster of bananas which he had cut from a neighbour's banana grove [which is an intrusion into a very private space]. Ryangombe then became ecstatic about the new audacity of the *uruzingo* [the Level I adept], who had been likened to a child but had now proved that he had grown up.
>
> (de Heusch 1966: 192)

The theft from the paternal home signified strongly the symbolic rupture of the dependence upon the profane family, a poignant gesture given the strength of paternal authority in Rwanda (de Heusch 1966: 193; Gahigi 1976); the second, from the neighbour's *bananeraie*, was a more generalized expression of anti-establishment feeling.

Mediator Ryangombe intervened not only between the living and the dead, but also among the living themselves. The two dimensions of salvation – spiritual and social – are well expressed in the following passage: 'The success of the cult reflects the enormous anguish produced by the rigidity of the social structure and by the pessimism inherent in traditional religious thinking, both of which had trapped the entire Hutu population and many Tutsi' (de Heusch 1966: 168). Ryangombe attempted first to integrate members through opposition to key features of the Rwandan *ordre des idées* providing adepts with a new type of family. Despite the two-level hierarchy it imposed, the cult provided a welcome space for radical thought and social harmony.

Enthusiasm was particularly marked in central and southern Rwanda (de Heusch 1966: 172), with many adepts coming from the politically dominated Hutu. De Heusch and others firmly believe that '*un grand nombre de Rwandais des trois castes ont adopté ce culte étranger*' (ibid.: 168; also Gahigi 1976).

The conceptual challenges were pervasive as Ryangombe aimed not only to break the power of malevolent spirits and sorcerers and to break down ethnic barriers, but also constituted '*une rupture de l'ordre familial*' (de Heusch 1966: 172). Ryangombe, the androgynous mythical hero, who accidentally impaled/killed himself on the erythrine tree when trying to seduce a married woman (de Heusch 1966: 143), longed for a society in which there would be '*ni riches, ni pauvres, ni races, ni classes sociales*' (Ruhuna 1972: 158). It is this break with '*l'ordre familial*' with which recent interpreters of Ryangombe have been most impressed (Berger 1976, 1981; Gahigi 1976).

To understand the focus on '*l'ordre familial*', the status of women must be appreciated. Based on anthropological research in the Interlacustrine region (i.e. Burundi), Albert has written: 'Unlike a man, a Rundi woman in public does not speak. . . . She is the modest and obedient wife of her husband, the mother of her children, the conscientious mistress of her house, who is always working' (Albert 1963: 180–1). This is similar to terms of reference found in the contemporary stereotype of Rwandan women, which holds that a woman's power is limited, particularly in the public sphere. Current writings on Rwanda uphold this view, e.g. ACORD, the London-based consortium of NGOs, is concerned that women find it difficult to respond to avenues opened up by its programme for rural development. The reason, allegedly, is women's low status: 'Women carry out 70–80% of agricultural work . . . [but] hold no right to land or to property. It is not usual for them to attend public meetings of the sort organized throught the programme.'[9]

Iris Berger writes:

> Throughout her life, a woman was subject to her father's will, despite the fact that after marriage she also had to obey her husband. . . . Only over her younger sisters, her children, and her husband's subordinates did she possess any authority.
> (Berger 1976: 160–1; see also Mbilinyi 1988: 569, on single women and authority in Tanzania)

The notion of 'limited power' can be placed within the debate on 'who controls sexuality?', as Gahigi has done. Gahigi makes an explicit connection between the popularity of Ryangombe and the rigidity of Rwandan sexual codes. He does not restrict his comments on sexual frustration to women alone, but indicates that the frustration affected everyone. He writes (freely translated):

> Rwandan society wishes all sexual relations to be permanent, and to make them permanent marriage needs to take place. Sexual activity is therefore defined as exclusively between spouses. It follows that sexuality is repressed. . . . The Ryangombe cult, in contrast, opposes this too severe and too ordered sexuality. Its objective is to liberate those who must live with this repression.
> (Gahigi 1976: 118–19)

Gahigi supports the structuralist interpretation by de Heusch, who conceptualizes Ryangombe as anti-structure; an arena for breaking down established patterns and hierarchies. Gahigi, Berger and de Heusch agree that the cult was a platform for dissidents opposed to the reigning socioreligious order (Gahigi 1976: 119). Or, as Berger concluded, it was a fairly successful attempt 'to master an intolerable environment' (Berger 1976: 169).

Interpreters of Ryangombe should also be aware of a conceptual link between the cult and the banana grove seen as a cultural construct, because the grove (like the cult itself) introduces a contradiction, being simultaneously a male domain (in terms of food production) and a female domain (in terms of the high soil fertility).

Like Ryangombe, who is female but becomes male once enthroned, the banana grove too is female in its physical setting but becomes male as a result of the manner in which food production and distribution is organized. Whether this parallel resulted from the cult or preceded it, we cannot say, but a powerful anomaly remains.

Also, the fact that the *bananeraie* is a burial place is important. *Abazimu* (spirits) are said to live either at the top of the active Nyiragongo volcano (when uninitiated and hostile) or on the slopes of the Karisimbi (when initiated), yet they are thought to return regularly to the *bananeraie* from where they originated.[10]

The banana grove thus is a space which sometimes integrates the sexes, sometimes divides them, an anomaly which blurs the separation between structure and anti-structure.

In spite of widespread support for its message of anarchy, the Ryangombe cult did not lead to revolution, but remained '*un processus de fuite de la réalité*' (de Heusch 1966: 172) and seems to have declined rather rapidly. Berger states two main reasons: first, its divinity became too closely associated with centralized government (Berger 1981: 89); second, it proved inflexible in assimilating the foreign elements introduced during the era of intense Christianization (Berger 1981: 86).

When confronted with external ways of thinking, old ideas tend to be replaced with new ones, and this led to the rapid acceptance of Ryangombe and the cult's rapid decline in the face of intense Christianization. Although the tendency did not preclude the possibility that foreign and local elements became integrated, as indeed happened in Ryangombe, we think it correct to emphasize the strong attractiveness asserted by external frames of reference.

By extension, we suggest that the readiness to substitute foreign (religious) ideas for local ones may well explain why the adoption of scientific state agriculture has occurred *at the expense of developing an interest in understanding local practices*. The history of agricultural extension in Rwanda (section 2) seems to indicate that salvation must come from outside. What is indigenous is rejected by potential leaders. (This does not mean that food producers will invariably perceive the new techniques as superior, but protest may not be tolerated.) Voss's illustration of bean production supports such a thesis at the local level. The attitude, however, is understandable, because agronomists have a niche within the 'modern' sociocultural hierarchy that they risk losing should they be overenthusiastic for truly local forms of agricultural innovation (Pottier 1989a).

These features of household farming (banana grove, intercropping, extension advice) have so far been presented in terms of cultural distances and hierarchy, even in terms of structure and antistructure. Another aspect of the Butare landscape, the collectively exploited marshlands, *when read culturally*, will yield a practical clue for redirecting Rwanda's extension services.

FERTILITY AND FREEDOM TODAY: AGRICULTURAL CO-OPERATIVES[11]

As a newly independent state, Rwanda's legacy was marked by ethnic domination and severe social inequality. Some progress has been made: domination by one ethnic group is abolished, at least in official rhetoric, while steps to incorporate women in the development process have been taken by the *Ministère de la Jeunesse et du Mouvement Coopératif*. However, many obstacles remain (ACORD 1987).

Observers sympathetic to 'official' development thinking will summarize the key issue in Rwanda in terms of the rational exploitation of arable land, with a view to maximizing field fertility. Others will single out population pressure as the major problem. The Government acknowledges that it must curb population growth, but stresses that this in itself will fail to bring about the desired higher living standards if there is stagnation in the food sector. It argues that Rwanda will be heavily populated by the turn of the century, even when the size of families reduces, and regards improvements in food production, through regional specialization and the intensive exploitation of marshlands, to be on a par with the concern about population (CEC 1982).

In its search for methods to improve land use, the Government declared during the mid-1970s that all marshland was to become state property. Most cultivators believed that access to such valuable land would now depend on their becoming members of agricultural co-operatives (MRND 1985), the mushrooming of which changed the landscape almost overnight.

The 'culture' of one such co-operative – CoopaduPeuple (pseudonym) – is described to reflect on a particular aspect of organization, i.e. the interaction with government representatives, to (a) expose parallels with the Rwandan movement and (b) return to the opening theme of an alternative agrarian policy.

CoopaduPeuple began in 1983, when six smaller units merged. The town authorities believed this would be more productive and enable producers better to reach Butare's central market. CoopaduPeuple, which also ran a bread project, did not have any serious production problems in 1986, but its members (totalling some 75) invested a huge amount of their time and energy, while still awaiting the first-ever cash rewards! The problem of how members could be rewarded, an issue bound up with a complex network of credits and debts, was the subject of many a debate, both in committee meetings and in plenary sessions.

Despite the workforce being predominantly female, CoopaduPeuple's organizing committee in early 1986 consisted of four men and two women, although male domination was already being criticized, both inside the co-operative and outside. The latter challenge came from officials of the *Ministère de la Jeunesse et du Mouvement Coopératif*. During Pottier's study, this high-level bureaucratic pressure intensified and led to fairer representation of women workers on the committee. By August 1986, two women were added: one a councillor, the other as vice-president.

CoopaduPeuple also received attention from regional bureaucrats, with technical advice, clarification about how to implement directives, assistance with book-keeping, etc. Help with financial accounts came from *Butare's Ecole Sociale de Karubanda*, a local secondary school.

Through reconstructing the debates within CoopaduPeuple, Pottier (1989b) has shown that the Rwandan tradition (official discourse) which defines 'rational' thought as a male domain is being undermined in a manner which reappraises the relationship between the pursuit of knowledge – i.e. development – and what Sutton *et al.* 1975: 582 have termed 'the social authorship of ideas'. Members are successfully stepping up their claim that women's ideas matter and that women want to have a say in making decisions.

This interpretation must not, however, be divorced from the national context, important because the Ministry presence pervades throughout with *communiqués* about rules and regulations and through possibile sanctions. On the other hand, not all ideas from 'the centre' are welcomed. Some types of pressure and criticism are in fact hard to accept.[12]

The laws governing co-operatives are regularly read out during assemblies, reminding members about sanctions should land not be exploited 'rationally', but they are locally treated more like aspirations. The election of the vice-president was such a case. Of course, a vice-president had to be respected, but the question of whether a female would have authority over men was much discussed. Because there were no 'higher-status' women within this co-operative, and therefore no 'obvious' candidates, the leaders 'solved' their problem (back in 1983) by deciding not to have a vice-president.

The 1986 election of a woman vice-president will now be used to reflect on centre–periphery interaction, and on the future of CoopaduPeuple.

The 1983 'solution' became the focus of heavy criticism during the visit of *un groupe féministe de Kigali* (40 members) attached to the Ministry. The group contained women members of Kigali-based co-operatives. A letter had arrived several weeks previously. The visit was both welcomed and feared and resulted in members spending much time rehearsing. Major worries were the questions that might be asked, and who would answer them.

On the day there was a strong division between 'educated/capital' and 'ordinary' members. The visitors shunned the *coopérateurs* (well, the marshland fields were a bit muddy . . .) and declined to discuss their findings with the president. Little did the 'educated' party realize how much work had gone into preparing for the visit! Instead of interacting with the ordinary members, the touring party invited the co-operative's woman treasurer to attend a meeting later in the day.

One of the findings, not surprisingly, was that CoopaduPeuple needed to have a woman vice-president. Six weeks later, such a person was duly elected, and boosted the women's confidence, but the post was nothing much to be envious about (or so it seemed). Addressing the *coopérateurs* immediately after election, the vice-president said: 'I have a question. For instance, when I have sick children at home and there is a committee meeting, and I do not have the time to attend . . . what then shall I do?' For the first time, in Pottier's presence, co-operative women had openly referred to their workload. Pottier had tried to discuss the issue on a previous occasion, and the touring '*groupe féministe*' had also raised it when talking to the co-operative's *supérieurs*, but answers had been evasive, indicative of the slow process in gender emancipation. Rwanda still has to try to make male leaders accountable to women workers (see Mbilinyi 1988, to compare the situation in Tanzania), but the appointment of a woman vice-president *was* a step in the right direction, *and would have been impossible without the pressures from central government.*

Several men in CoopaduPeuple refused to accept the appointment and one opinion was: 'She has arrived [been voted] to instruct the women, not the men.' The president backed him: 'Hear that man? All of you, listen to how he thinks!'[13]

The visitors also criticized crop selection and irrigation practices. Some made sense (e.g. that compost pits had not yet been dug, and that production figures were not available); others were not so helpful: that sorghum was an inappropriate crop; that chemical fertilizers and insecticides should be used; that the group did not rotate its crops (how did the visitors know?); that the method of irrigation was ineffective, etc.

The visitors used agriculture to show that *they* were different, 'modern' in their approach to food-cropping and socially a class apart. The difference was also brought out in other ways. All young children of *coopérateurs* had been fed sweet potato snacks as a planned subtle gesture of parental concern. However, the visitors' children were given white bread from plastic bags.

The visit was a forceful reminder that any programme for promoting equality of opportunity and reward will need to address disparities of gender and class/poverty. It showed how outsiders see *coopérateurs* as an undifferentiated group and how they may fail to grasp the contextual rationale (*les logiques*) with which food producers operate. The 'educated' women from the capital criticized food-cropping methods without ever talking to the producers. Like Rango's extension workers and elite residents, they emphasized neatness above the benefits to be gained from intercropping. The attack on sorghum cultivation was ill-founded, and rested on the idea that sorghum equalled beer. The visitors overlooked the fact that some of the sorghum would be used for the women's own bread project.

Interaction with Kigali is double-edged; the laws relating to social equality provide *coopérateurs* with a framework for action and boost their morale (without question), but will only be effective if local ideas and initiatives are respected. The visit crushed the idea of presumed (if poorly understood) central sympathetic support.

There is scope for moderate optimism, as the regular debates provide a forum for protest, for challenging seemingly established codes and instilling positive changes in the self-perception of members. Nevertheless, the question is: will the centre keep a low profile to allow sufficient local autonomy or will it put token representation above the goal of equality of opportunity and reward? The answer is difficult because future developments are hard to predict. Some Butare-based women bureaucrats, the teacher from the *Ecole Sociale* for instance, do a great but difficult job mediating between local groups and regional/national bureaucracy (Pottier 1989b). As for the maintenance and further development of local self-expression, we are less optimistic: in dealing with the centre, local co-operatives face a challenge resembling that which led to the rapid demise of the Ryangombe protest movement.

CONCLUSIONS AND PRACTICAL SUGGESTIONS

In a previous EIDOS paper (December 1986/1989a) Pottier hinted that banana groves might be unsuitable (i.e. 'feared') in the eyes of agronomists, because they are dark/shady places: darkness/shade (*igicucu*) is associated with 'fear', 'ancestral spirits', 'madness' and 'ignorance'. Linguistically, *igicucu* means any one of these four concepts. Of mental illness, for instance, it is said that 'fearful' 'ancestral spirits' use 'shade' (which ultimately translates as 'the life force') to inflict 'madness'. The banana grove would seem to encapsulate the most primordial of all existential struggles, thus becoming a physical-cum-conceptual space best left untouched, irreconcilable with notions of modernity.

In addition, two further, complementary explanations for the 'official' anti-*bananeraie* stand are suggested. The Ryangombe cult (the most secret phases of which took part in the groves) was closely associated with 'ambiguity' and 'protest'. Assuming de Heusch is correct in thinking that Ryangombe has played an extensive role '*dans les structures mentales collectives de la société rwandaises*' (1966: 167), the banana grove could be rejected by Government not only because this physical space is linked to the polyvalent concept of *igicucu*, but because it is culturally ambiguous (female yet male; male yet female) and, second, a place of political protest. In Ryangombe women/subordinates became equal to men/superiors, what Rwandan extension workers today are trying to resist. Again, the physical environment is being used to make a social statement.

A further, speculative reason may lie in the tendency that past worlds are replaced with new ones (Berger 1981). Given the previously central role of the *bananeraie* in the maintenance of fertility, it seems 'normal' that this is being discarded by those wanting another external cult: the western-styled, scientific agriculture which substitutes 'neat' laboratories/trial farms for people's 'messy' gardens.

What really matters is this: (a) that the linkages made in this chapter have unlocked a way in which natural landscapes can be read culturally; and (b) that the conceptual spaces provided by Ryangombe and today's agricultural co-operatives are alike. Regarding the latter, the parallels indicate that a range of patterns and hierarchies are being challenged and, in the case of the co-operatives, broken down with some success. This is summarized in Table 9.1.

Planners who are serious about restructuring Rwanda's agricultural extension services will need to explore and work creatively within the thought-space already provided by the co-operatives. The extension

Table 9.1 Summary of the similarities between conceptual spaces of Ryangombe and co-operatives

	Ryangombe	*Co-operatives*
origin:	alien/Ugandan	alien/international
focus:	fertility of women and the nation	fertility of crops and food security
membership:	both sexes	both sexes
aims:	to challenge social divisions	to challenge social divisions
threat:	ambiguous link with central government	ambiguous link with central government

workers' participation in co-operative debate and action will need to transcend the idea that developments in the movement are a matter of letting off steam with no further consequences; *'un processus de fuite'* (de Heusch) which merely reveals *'une crise dans la société'* (Gahigi).

The potential for restructuring must not get lost this time. It may well be 'hijacked' by a handful of elite representatives (including women) of the state. The co-operative movement would then have its own powerful 'chief priestesses' (cf. Berger 1976: 179), but this would result in the same social relations and no reversal of official attitudes towards local farming practices.

Some practical suggestions to improve communication between food producers and extension workers can be made. The conceptual space offered by agricultural co-operatives *is* conducive to a dialogue between producers and *vulgarisateurs*, because the latter do not have to lose their identity when they become 'learners', i.e. intensive exploitation of marshland is a relatively new phenomenon, using new techniques, including crop rotations and experiments with new vegetable crops. Within this context all 'learners' can also act as innovating 'instructors'.

Rwanda's *vulgarisateurs* need to become learners and should join the co-operative movement full-time, or better, the next generation of *vulgarisateurs* should be recruited from within the ranks of existing co-operatives, and on the basis of gender-related representation, an appropriate strategy if *vulgarisateurs* are to become specialists who can accept that ordinary food producers make rational decisions.

To create learner–specialists the co-operative movement must strengthen its capacity to integrate (a weakness in the religious cult). It must forget the historical idea that openness to the outside means replacing old worlds with new ones.

The marshes may not be suitable for practising a *bananeraie*-centred agriculture, but their exploitation has produced a community which, more than any other organization today, has acquired the right social conditions to successfully negotiate the new approach to agricultural extension. If the latter achieves the recognition it deserves, then the *bananeraie*, as a physical micro-environment, is certain to become reinstated as a valuable asset in the quest for food security.

The recommendations stem directly from a cultural reading of Butare's physical landscape. What goes on in Rwandan fields is not just a battle against the natural elements; it is a cultural struggle as well. The former will not be won if the latter is lost.

NOTES

1 Pottier carried out anthropological fieldwork in Butare between November 1985 and September 1986. He alone is responsible for the accuracy of the data on Rango and CoopaduPeuple (pseudonym). Nkundabashaka teaches sociology at the UNR, Butare, and lives in Cyarwa.

2 Extension workers fall into one of the following categories: 'Ingénieurs Agronomes et Docteurs Vétérinaires; les Techniciens Agricoles A2 et les Techniciens Vétérinaires A2; les Vulgarisateurs A3 et enfin; les Moniteurs Agricoles et Infirmiers Vétérinaires' (Nzamurambaho 1977). In this chapter the terms *vulgarisateur* and agronomist are used interchangeably.

3 The statement simply reiterates Government policy.

4 There is also concern that the 'modern' method of simple rotations, advocated by agronomists, will bring its own problems. Rotations ensure better yields in the short term, since successive crops exploit soil fertility in different ways, yet the technique is known to exhaust fields in a matter of years. To reconstitute fertility, intercropping and growing e.g. banana trees or sorghum to increase organic material must be carried out.

5 The themes of 'replacement' and 'integration' also run through the literature on Central African psychotherapy (Pottier 1985).

6 The emphasis on gender equality seems suspect in some French texts, because the quest for equality is expressed in a way which appears to reinforce male dominance, i.e. terms such as *virile* and *virilité* are regularly used in relation to *umugabo*, which is mostly translated as 'man' or 'husband'. Berger, too, uses these terms in English, and agrees that the 'virile masculine quality' acquired by all initiants (whether women or politically weak men) was evidence that the cult had abolished sexual differences. Our understanding of the texts published in French and English is that it would be misleading to assume that virile/virility implies

male virility. Rather, the terms are used in a wider sense to denote assertiveness, audacity, rebelliousness.

7 The secret phases of initiation, especially those in the banana grove, have never been observed directly by ethnographers. De Heusch attended some public sessions in 1949, but all ethnographic documentation of the more secret aspects is based solely on testimonies of Christian converts (e.g. Arnoux 1912; de Lacger 1961).

8 There could be parallels here with W. de Mahieu's account of male circumcision rites among the Komo of Zaire (de Mahieu 1986). Of interest too is the Komo view of the forest, which has similarities to the banana grove in Rwanda, where forests are now virtually a thing of the past. De Mahieu refers to the Komo forest as representing '*le lieu de l'obscurité, du désordre, de la dissolution des liens sociaux et de la suppression des normes morales, en un mot de l'anti-structure*' (de Mahieu 1986: 125).

9 Women cannot inherit land, but a woman, married or not, may receive land as a gift (*urwibutso*) from her elderly father. The gesture is denoted by the verb *kuraga*. This kind of land (*ingaligali*) is usually set aside for emergencies, at the time a family farm is divided up among the male children. A troubled daughter (*indushyi*) will be given such land and will have access to it for as long as she is deemed in need, if necessary for life. After her death, however, the land will be reclaimed by her late husband's nearest patrikin.

10 Both types of *abazimu* are believed capable of inflicting mental illness upon uninitiated people.

11 This is based almost exclusively on data collected during Pottier's 1985–86 fieldwork.

12 There are several reasons why *coopérateurs* put up with the absence of financial reward. First, produce is occasionally shared out among members, e.g. after meetings or special events. Second, members are entitled to one plot of marshland, which they work on an individual basis. Given the scarcity of arable land, this is most welcome and may be the overriding reason for battling on against the odds. Plots can be registered in the name of a man or a woman. Third, state patronage is valued. Members are convinced that the day will come when Government 'will do something big' for CoopaduPeuple. Aid previously received for the bread project, the supervision by students and staff from the *Ecole Sociale*, the prospect of fish farming, the interest shown by visitors (Pottier included), all social indicators, are readily interpreted as signs of a better future. Fourth, selling produce locally, on credit, puts sellers in a superior position *vis-à-vis* their customers. Sellers can then use the debt relationship later on, for example, when their own families need extra food. Credit sales (an unintended outcome of co-operative agriculture) are a coping mechanism through which members spread risk and ensure a steady, year-round food supply. The central market does not suffer any real supply problems. However, there is overproduction of certain marsh crops, especially cabbage.

13 In fairness to the president, his 'good' qualities should be stressed also, e.g.

when asked why chemicals and pesticides were not being used, he defended the local practice with alacrity.

ACKNOWLEDGEMENTS

Nkundabashaka thanks SOAS for enabling him to attend the conference. Pottier thanks the Economic and Social Research Council (ESRC, England) and the Overseas Development Administration (ODA) for sponsoring the fieldwork in Butare. The authors are grateful to James Fairhead for comments on an earlier draft of the chapter.

REFERENCES

ACORD (1987) *Rwanda's Solution: The Search for Rural Employment*, London: Acord.

Albert, E. (1963) 'Women of Burundi: a study of social values', in D. Paulme (ed.) *Women of Tropical Africa*, Berkeley and Los Angeles: University of California Press.

Arnoux, A. (1912/1913) 'Le culte de la société secrète des Imandwa au Rwanda', *Anthropos* 7: 273–95, 529–58, 840–75; 8: 110–34, 754–74.

Bagirameshi, J., Bazihizina, C. and Barnaud, M. (1986) 'Pour une Nouvelle Pratique de la Vulgarisation Agricole au Rwanda', *Revue Tiers Monde* XXVII (106): 419–37.

Belshaw, D. (1979) 'Taking indigenous knowledge seriously: the case of intercropping techniques in East Africa', *IDS (Sussex) Bulletin* 10 (2): 24–7.

Berger, I. (1976) 'Rebels or status-seekers? Women as spirit mediums in East Africa', in N. J. Hafkin and E. G. Bay (eds) *Women in Africa: Studies in Social and Economic Change*, Stanford, Cal.: Stanford University Press.

—— (1981) *Religion and Resistance: East African Kingdoms in the Precolonial Period*, Butare: Institut National de Recherche Scientifique, no. 20.

Commission of the European Community (CEC) (1982) 'Food strategies: a new form of cooperation between Europe and the countries of the Third World', *Publication DE40*.

de Heusch, L. (1966) *Le Rwanda et la civilisation interlacustre*, Bruxelles: Université Libre de Bruxelles, Institut de Sociologie.

de Lacger, L. (1961) *Ruanda*, Kabgayi: Imprimeries de Kabgayi (first edn 1939).

Delepierre, G. (1970) 'Le bananier', *Bulletin Agricole du Rwanda*, no. 4: 155–62.

—— (1977) 'Recherche Agronomique et Vulgarisation', *Etudes Rwandaises* X (Numéro Spécial 1).

de Mahieu, W. (1986) *Qui A Obstrué La Cascade? Analyse Sémantique du Rituel de la Circoncision chez les Komo*, Cambridge: Cambridge University Press.

Dupriez, H. and de Leener, P. (1983) *Agriculture Tropicale en Milieu Paysan Africain*, Paris: L'Harmattan.

Fairhead, J. (1986) 'Agriculture and nutrition in a Rwandan community', SOAS Research Report, June.

Gahigi, G. (1976) 'Lyangombe et la Société', in UNAZA/ISP (eds) *Lyangombe: Mythe et Rites*, Actes du Deuxième Colloque du CERUKI, Bukavu, 10–14 Mai.

Government of Rwanda (1977) *Deuxième Plan Quinquennal de Développement Economique, Social et Culturel 1977–1981*, Kigali: Ministère du Plan.

—— (1987) *Quatrième Plan Quinquennal de Développement Economique, Social et Culturel 1987–1991*, Kigali: Ministère du Plan.

Mbilinyi, M. (1988) 'Agribusiness and women peasants in Tanzania', *Development and Change* 19: 549–83.

Mouvement Révolutionnaire National pour le Développement/MRND (1985) *Imyaka cumi ya MRND: Dix Ans du MRND*, Kigali: Présidence du MRND.

Nkundabashaka, A. and Voss, J. (1987) *Les Projets de Développement Rural: Réussites, Echecs et Stratégies Nouvelles*, Butare: Seminaire UNR/CIAT, 4–6 Mai.

Nsanzimana, S. (1977) 'Allocution de Bienvenue', in La Vulgarisation Agricole au Rwanda, *Etudes Rwandaises* X (Numéro Spécial 1): 3–5.

Ntamahungiro, J. (1986) 'Bananier: le pour et le contre', *Dialogue* (Kigali) 117: 102–9 (special issue on 'Intensification Agricole').

Nzamurambaho, F. (1977) 'Discours d'ouverture', in La Vulgarisation Agricole au Rwanda, *Etudes Rwandaises* X (Numéro Spécial 1): 5–10.

—— (1978) 'Instruction relative à la culture du bananier', *Bulletin Agricole du Rwanda* 3: 201–4.

Pottier, J. (1985) 'Identity on trial: self and other in Central African psychotherapy', *Ethnos* 50 (1/2): 60–87.

—— (1989a) 'Three is a crowd: knowledge, ignorance and power in urban agriculture in Rwanda', Paper presented at the EIDOS conference on 'Local Knowledge and Systems of Ignorance', SOAS, December. Published in *Africa* 54 (4).

—— (1989b) 'Debating styles in a Rwandan cooperative: reflections on language, politics and gender', in R. D. Grillo (ed.) *Social Anthropology and the Politics of Language*, Sociological Review monograph 34, London: Routledge.

Rodegem, F. (1971) 'La fête des prémices au Burundi', *Africa Linguistica* V, Annales, Série in 8ᵉ, Sciences humaines no. 72: 205–54 (published by Musée Royal de l'Afrique Centrale).

Ruhuna, J. (1972) 'Quelques éléments sur l'origine des mystères de Kiranga-Lyangombe', in *Que Vous Semble?* no. 17.

Steiner, K. (1984) *Intercropping in Tropical Smallholder Agriculture, with special reference to West Africa*, Eschborn: Deutsche Gesellschaft für Technische Zusammenarbeit.

Sutton, C., Makiesky, S., Dwyer, D. and Klein, L. (1975) 'Women, knowledge and power', in R. Rohrlich-Leavitt (ed.) *Women Cross-Culturally: Challenge and Change*, The Hague: Mouton.

Voss, J. (1988) 'Farmer management of varietal bean mixtures in Central Africa: implications for a technology development strategy', paper presented to the CIP/Rockefeller Conference on 'Farmers and Food Systems', Lima, Peru, September.

10 Cows eat grass don't they?

Evaluating conflict over pastoral management in Zimbabwe[1]

Michael Drinkwater

This chapter investigates how competing analyses of environmental change might be evaluated, specifically by exploring pastoral land management in Zimbabwe's communal areas. In these areas peasant farmers keep too many animals on too little land, thus overgrazing the pasture lands resulting in land degradation. This has been a government dilemma since the 1940s, when the first stock-control and grazing schemes were introduced.

Most strategies since then have been aimed at persuading farmers that rotating their animals in turn through four or five fenced paddocks is the best way to keep cattle, particularly beef cattle, generally considered to be of the most economic use. Even if cattle are kept for other purposes, they still require proper management to ensure the land is protected.

Such a dominant theory is difficult to reject *in toto* and objections subsumed within it. For a wholly alternative theory to gain wider social credence a major campaign is required.[2] The struggle to counteract the use of power to push forward new perspectives is a tougher practical task for social scientists. To promote the peasant world view as being not only a credible but perhaps a more 'correct' version of reality, necessitates comparison and evaluation of dominant and subordinate perspectives.

The highly political evaluation process is divided into three stages. First, the nature of the competing perspectives must be understood and may entail teasing out the official perspective as much as understanding that of the less powerful. Obviously, the dominant view is usually more accessible in written and oral form. Therefore in the Zimbabwean case, I focus on understanding the perspective of the less articulate groups. Nevertheless the danger of oversimplifying and setting up a dominant position as an easy target is clear – the response of those threatened will be to belittle the account as the construction of those who are both emotional and uninformed.

To understand the viewpoints of social groups foreign to us, we must attempt to interpret action from within the 'universe of discourse' of those with whom we are interacting.[3] As we cannot shed our own histories, this does not mean negating or suspending our own perspective; it means deliberately attempting to shift and alter our perspective until we comprehend the world from another's position. By definition, because we are not the other, such understanding can never be absolute.

However, more difficult still is that we have to present the alternative perspective in a way that may be credible to those who do not hold such views. Consequently, we have to follow tenets of logical consistency and rationality which are meaningful to others and grounded in claims of truth, normative rightness and sincerity.[4]

Even if we can persuade others that their perhaps unchallenged view of the world is not the only tenable one, we still have to confront the problem of comparative evaluation. Might one perspective not be a better interpretation than the other, or might elements of each not improve the other?

The comparative moment has two levels of difficulty: undertaking the evaluation is one thing, convincing doubting others, another. As individuals we cannot do both. We lack sufficient power and, in the eyes of others, sufficient objectivity, even if we wish to declaim having left a personal imprint on our work. We will be accused of manipulation – of seeing what we want to see and persuading (or misinterpreting) others to say what we want to hear.

Comparative evaluation is thus best seen as a collective procedure, carried out over time by all who review the issues, singly or in organized forums. The three moments of the evaluative task – understanding, presentation and comparative evaluation – whilst analytically distinct, may or may not be separable in time. They involve uncovering a counterstance to what is dominant, marshalling or simply stumbling upon allies, and if there is potential victory, seeking the measurable claims that might secure the necessary recognition. Success is finally measured in terms of the ability to persuade those who have held the dominant view to reanalyse their position. A valid evaluation is not necessarily a successful one, for even if proved wrong people may refuse to acknowledge the findings because of what is at stake.

I shall now return to the case study. The communal area in Zimbabwe is Chirumhanzu in the Midlands Province. In 1986/87, there was a severe drought. As the province's veld[5] management specialist put it, the grazing area consisted primarily of stones. It seemed that little forage was available and that the animals would fail to survive to the next harvest. They in fact did die, although primarily because the 1987/88 rains were over a month late. The questions are how people manage their livestock and how might such deaths be prevented. The official response is that this will be achieved through the establishment of paddocked grazing schemes; that there is acute land shortage is treated as a subsidiary issue. It is thought that whatever the population and livestock density, grazing schemes will alleviate the problem. Land-use planning is undertaken on the basis of a capability classification, described in Agritex's handbook as:

> the systematic arrangement and grouping of different kinds of land to show their most intensive safe use and indicate their management requirements and to show the permanent hazards attached to the use of the land, in terms of increasing degree of limitation of use.
>
> (Ivy 1981: 1)

This classification system has been in use since the 1930s. Of eight land classes, the first four are deemed suitable for arable production, classes VI and VII are generally for 'grazing areas' and class VIII is sheet rock. Class V land is most controversial in terms by definition and use. It is defined as 'vleis and watercourses subject to severe wetness not usually corrected and best left under permanent vegetation' (Ivy 1981: 2).[6] Cultivation in these areas has been banned since the 1930s and cattle are kept out if the authorities have their way. To outsiders, farmers' use of these sensitive areas indicates both their ignorance of environmental processes and lack of respect for the environment. It reinforces the belief that outside intervention is required to prevent further destruction.

Farmers do not see themselves as being quite so ignorant. The following comments are taken from interviews about land issues conducted with community leaders (party, local government and lineage) in the Maware area of southern Chirumhanzu. The responses refer to the question of what had happened when government officials had visited the area to talk about the introduction of grazing schemes. I knew the response had been extremely negative and was seeking to understand precisely why; my interpretation follows accordingly.

V/H[7] Mawindi:
It has been at least a year since they talked about paddocks, but people are still not interested. When we look at it we can see it would not be possible. It will be killing the cattle. Because there would not be enough grass to eat. . . . People in the community are

very much crowded. If they introduced paddocks, some of our people would have no place to stay. . . . Destocking is something else which would make people very much angry all over.

(Interview 14/4/87)

Mawindi identifies three reasons why people oppose the introduction of grazing schemes: they fear the grazing area will be reduced, the destocking of the 1940s and 1950s will be repeated; and that some will be made homeless.

VIDCO[8] Chairman Mkata:
There is no co-operation amongst people on this issue [of paddocks]. The reason is that the place is very small and the people are crowded and the grass is not growing. I cannot understand what can be done. We really need land because there are some people who don't even have enough land for fields.

(Interview 15/4/87)

Mkata makes one additional point: 'the grass is not growing'. This is not only a reference to the drought then being experienced, but also a belief that there is now insufficient grazing area for owners to be able to leave land long enough for the grass to grow. This is also expressed by Mutumiri:

H/man Mutumiri:
Wherever there is grass people will now take their cattle there for grazing. . . . In the past when we were planting we would take the cattle with us and leave the grass to grow. Then after planting was finished, we would take them back to where the grass was growing. We would still like to do it, but the problem is that the rainfall is very low.

[On paddocks] We once tried that idea (during Smith's government); Chief Hama accepted the idea, but we later discovered the animals were dying. There was not enough grass. . . . By that time there were enough paddocks for the cattle, but what happens is that when the cattle have finished the grass in one area, it will be difficult for them to feed. There is no possibility of keeping the cattle in one place because they are used to just roaming around.

(Interview 15/4/87)

Mutumiri's point about cattle 'just roaming around' implies the animals know where to find the best forage. The belief he expresses about rainfall decline is commonly held but is not borne out by an analysis of rainfall records in the region.[9]

VIDCO Chairman Mugarisi:
If you start talking about it [paddocks] at a meeting people will start leaving. It could be that the area does not have enough grass. Personally I don't see many advantages. It could be done but people are very much crowded and to find a place for that is impossible. The only means for cattle to have enough grazing is to take them to the edges of your field and have them grazing there.

(Interview 14/4/87)

Mugarisi provides a further account of how stock owners are being forced to modify their preferred grazing system.

V/H Mazhlatini:
The previous government did not allow people to herd their animals in the *vleis*. Now they can take their animals wherever they can find grazing.

(Interview, 14/4/87)

Vleis are one of the few other areas where cattle find forage, but are normally excluded from grazing schemes. In short:

VIDCO Chairman Gova:
As you can see there is not enough grass here. How do you think we can introduce paddocks?

(Interview 16/4/87)

The Maware community leaders thus believe that restricting livestock to a paddocked grazing scheme reduces available forage, conflicting directly with the conventional wisdom.

Coupling these comments with the statements of other farmers and my own observations of farmers and livestock management, a preferred, pastoral management strategy emerges. This model has three elements: livestock, forage, and labour, for each of which the following principles obtain:

Livestock (cattle) The daily movement begins and ends at kraals or pens near the home. (Animals are kraaled to collect their manure, to ensure safety at night and to feed them with supplementary stover in winter.)

Cattle must be able to obtain forage daily at least three or four times a week and obtain access to a water supply where they can drink their fill. They must at intervals (which vary according to the season) travel to the dip.

The minimum ideal herd size (farmers think 10–12 animals) is one that has at least two mature oxen for ploughing.

The critical time for animal fitness, particularly the draught stock, is when the first rains arrive, or when ploughing begins.

Labour Adult labour time on herding should be minimized.

Forage All available forage should be utilized (except the crops during the growing season).

Some cattle rotation should occur to 'let the grass regrow'.

By linking together these principles, the basic strategic features can be understood. Forage availability determines where cattle will go if left to 'just roam around'. Thus the extent to which livestock are directed to specific areas depends on the labour input. Livestock owners have four choices when considering the allocation of labour to herding.

(a) Animals graze unattended.
(b) Animals graze near one or more household members who are engaged in other activities.
(c) One or more household members can be specifically allocated the task of herding.
(d) An agreement can be reached with other owners to group the animals and rotate herding duties.

Option (a) may be used in winter when there are no vulnerable crops and the grass does not grow. Option (c) is only desirable if children are available in the school holidays. Option (d) is unlikely to work when labour demand is highest.

One can begin to see the rationality behind the types of strategies farmers employ. Why should they feel any obligation to revise their position?

But social scientists face a choice. Do we wish to enter into dialogue with people not only from other disciplines, but also from government and other political institutions? Here is a moral–practical dilemma: do we believe in engagement on behalf of those we work with, or do we prefer to remain solely with the already difficult task of seeking to understand social others? If our choice lies with the former, we must make our work accessible outside our specialization, so others may oppose, remain indifferent or collaborate with us.

To achieve accessibility and make evaluation possible Robin Horton's argument of uncovering and explaining the theoretical bases of the competing perspectives can be used. His argument, supported by other authors, is that communication can always occur between different cultures because, at the minimum, there exists a 'bridgehead' consisting of a common core of rationality (Horton 1982: 14–20). The latter has two central features. First is 'the use of theory in the explanation, prediction and control of events'; second is 'the use of analogical, deductive and inductive inference in the development and application of theory' (ibid.: 256).

When interpretations conflict, the boundaries between cultures or perspectives can become very deep. Moreover, accepting that people are not always able to explicate why they do what they do (see Giddens' distinction between practical and discursive consciousness[10]) then the theories and assumptions drawn upon in particular strategies might be very implicit. Nevertheless, I suggest that Horton's concept is credible and can be applied in the Zimbabwean dispute.

A key point of conflict is the belief by farmers that a paddocked grazing scheme will reduce the quality and quantity of available forage. There are two issues upon which to theorize and take a stance: economic efficiency and environmental impact. Within this context, the four main possible subsetted responses to the farmers' belief are:

1 Their belief is mistaken because they are unaware of the advantages of systematically rotating animals throught paddocks.
   (a) And if they used the land adequately they would not need more land.
   (b) However, because many families have no cattle, the people need more land if they are to implement fenced grazing schemes.
2 By not confining livestock, animals are better able to use all forage available.
   (a) However, allowing animals access to even ecologically sensitive areas leads to degradation and it would be better for people to have more land and use conventional grazing management systems.
   (b) This system is not only more efficient but also ecologically sustainable, as long as people are not so constrained that they are forced into environmental abuse.

The first two responses have received the most powerful support this century. The colonial government, striving to maintain a land-apportionment policy, clung to option 1(a). Since 1980, despite implementation of a land reform policy, the current government has not altered this stance; its shift has only been to option 1(b). Thus the state still pursues vigorously the same strategy introduced in the 1940s.[11]

Most outsiders do not doubt that improved land use practices are a vital ingredient in improving the environment in communal areas, and that most peasant farmers lack the knowledge of what is required. For example in a meeting with Agritex staff, a provincial land-management specialist asked:

> How about general impressions in the grazing area; you know general conditions of erosion. Is it severely overgrazed; don't they appreciate the conditions in talking to them, you know the need to kind of embark in better land use practices?
>
> (Gweru, 13/4/87)

All the old assumptions are here: that the sense data of an (educated) outsider are sufficient to tell the extent of overgrazing and erosion and also the degree of perception by the farmers themselves. There is no consideration that perhaps the judging should be the other way round; at the local and district levels, extension staff hold to response 2(a), that, if livestock are not confined, available forage is increased – an economically more efficient grazing strategy. Yet almost universally the case held against farmers is that without controlled rotational grazing their animals degrade the landscape. Usually this attitude is implicitly or explicitly based on Hardin's 'Tragedy of the Commons' model – that communal land functions as a free-for-all no-man's land because the grazing areas have no fixed boundaries, and individuals merely attempt to draw short-term advantage at the cost of reducing longer-term community benefit (e.g. Campbell *et al.* 1986: 28).

Evidence of 'no fixed boundaries' is usually drawn from citation of disputes arising when there is an attempt to draw boundaries – for instance in the 1984/85 VIDCO delineation exercise. Cousins has argued recently that grazing schemes 'offered the possibility of taking CL grazing land out of a virtual "open access" situation to a common property situation with communal management' (Cousins *et al.* 1988: 53). Yet whilst making this statement about 'open access', Cousins noted that 77 per cent of schemes in the communal area had external conflicts, primarily over boundaries. This suggests that the opposite is true – access is fiercely contested between communities. The logic of this suggests that a government proposal to introduce such schemes could well incite a political struggle for control of land. So when Cousins argues that: 'Grazing schemes are at present a focus for an emerging redefinition of communal identity in the Communal Lands' (Cousins *et al.* 1988: 54), there are different interpretations. Does this mean that the communities concerned believe that a paddocked grazing scheme is the best remedy for the environment? Or is this the victors' response in a contest for a critically scarce resource.

Conflict over land is an interrelated but diversionary phenomenon to the primary issues – economic efficiency and environmental impact.

If we dwell too long on this we will become entangled in outsider arguments about the social nature of the insiders – with the insiders' views becoming increasingly lost.

If as social scientists we are to seek means of evaluating the competing claims of insiders and extra-local authorities, we must confine the debate to the key issues – and prevent the more powerful from drawing the debate onto their own territory and away from the core of the dispute. As the debate on pastoral management deepens, it becomes clear that evaluation of conflicting theories is likely to become increasingly complex. It is not going to be possible to remain neutral either; evaluation will mean supporting a theory and therefore taking sides. At this juncture it is probably clear that my own aim is to nudge towards response 2(b) and seek some mandate for declaring that farmers have some knowledge of economics and ecology. Also I need an ally to assist in the delineation of the detailed terrain of farmers' (not wholly consciously held) theory about pastoral management.

The ally was Ian Scoones, an ecologist and one of two other researchers working in the Midlands province who focused on ecological aspects of livestock management. Scoones' claims from his work – which included the following of cattle – overturn the formal land-use classification of the class V wet land: 'subject to severe wetness not usually corrected and best left under permanent vegetation' (Ivy 1981: 2). However, Scoones argues that land in this category – *vleis*, river banks, drainage lines, contours – has a far greater significance than is officially realized.

> Much of communal area cattles' feeding time, especially in the critical end of dry season period, is spent in small areas (perhaps 5 per cent of the total grazing area); the rest of the grazing area is simply unused for most of the year. These small areas I shall call key resources. A key resource is a patch that offsets critical constraints either of forage quality or quantity.
>
> (Scoones 1987: 22)

These 'key resources' are the areas of greatest forage availability.

Moreover, Ken Wilson, Scoones' co-researcher, has shown that the importance of this wetland is historically grounded. From oral history and the records of nineteenth-century travellers, he constructs a hypothesis that nineteenth-century production systems in the granite country of south-central Zimbabwe were centred on these wetland areas.[12]

With this information I can return to earlier elements and associated principles of farmers' pastoral management strategy, and weld them together into an outline of the normative model that farmers attempt to pursue.

In spring, before the first rains, animals graze the early flush of grass in *vlei* areas or along drainage lines, to gain strength for the planting season. At planting, animals accompany owners to the fields and graze nearby, allowing the first grass to come through in the extensive grazing areas. During the growing season animals are herded either by children or, during term-time, under co-operative herding arrangements in the main grazing areas. Some form of rotation may be used. After harvest, the animals are returned to the fields to eat crop residues and grass along the contours. Late season grazing is also provided along watercourses, and during winter, stover (predominantly maize but also crops, e.g. groundnuts) may be used for supplementary feed.

In practice, however, the ability of stock owners to do this, whatever degree of social organization exists, is usually highly constrained. Each household struggles to acquire and maintain a cattle herd large enough to provide draught power, and in the quest to avoid abusing the environment. However, social, economic and environmental factors influence livestock management practices, creating conflicts which are aggravated by scarcity of labour, cattle and forage.

In the Maware area of southern Chirumhanzu the most heated controversy over livestock occurs at the beginning of the growing season, between the first rains (often late October), when planting begins, and the time when all farmers have started to plant, which may be over a month later. It is advantageous to plant early, but for a variety of constraints not all farmers do. In this area arable fields occur in blocks – a legacy of the 1950s Land Husbandry Act – and are mostly unfenced. Newly germinated crops are thus vulnerable to the unherded animals of the late planters.

Households ensure their animals are herded once they have commenced planting, but not before this because of labour scarcity. Once school is out (early December) children are available but when they return to school in mid-January arrangements for sharing herding duties may then come into effect. These groups are now comparatively small. One of the Maware farmers explained that in his group, one of the largest, seven families now rotated herding duties, whereas before the war years of the 1970s the whole 'line' had participated – 'so someone ended up herding 200 animals or so'. Now there is no longer sufficient land and forage for so many animals to be grouped together in one place.[13] This is why farmers argue so fervently that a paddocked pastoral management scheme would curtail available forage.

Another example is that of the non-sharing household of the chairman of the Maware farmers' group, Silvester Mugarisi, considered to be the best farmer in the area. He had only six animals and, claiming that others looked after his animals inadequately, operated his own intensive, mini pastoral system. Mugarisi's farm is a 2.2 ha fenced smallholding area (including home and homefield), unlike the more general local pattern. At the lower end of the smallholding was a stream with a small dam, on the other side of which was a grassed area, the lowest end of a drainage basin which extended up the gentle slope of the land for about a kilometre. Mugarisi's cattle foraged in this area or inside the smallholding or were fed stover.

Behind his home was a rock-strewn slope which was part of the official grazing area. However, in the poor 1986–87 season only leaf browse was obtainable. Thus, the grassed area was being heavily grazed by livestock. It had a 3–4 m deep gully down one side and in a dry year the soil was friable and vulnerable to cattle hooves. As I watched during the season, parts (1–2 m wide) of the gully sides caved in. Mugarisi was worried about his cattle being able to survive the dry winter of 1987 and consequently exchanged his two large oxen for two smaller ones 'because they eat less' (Fieldnotes, 7/8/87).

Apart from his concern about forage availability, Mugarisi's strategy is satisfactory because, even during the grazing season, their animals do not need close herding, remaining near the stream and can be observed from the homefield area. The labour spent on herding is minimized. This is, though, exactly the type of strategy the grazing scheme concept is designed to prevent. In this account, the need for evaluating economic efficiency and environmental impact has therefore become imperative.

The economic aspect shall be dealt with first. The type of grazing strategy communal-area farmers employ has been termed by Sandford – a livestock and range management specialist – as an opportunistic livestock management strategy. Sandford (1983: 38–41) distinguishes it from a conservative one. The latter is one in which livestock stocking rates are kept down to the level which can be supported in all but the poorest seasons. This is the level which in past and present land-use policies in Zimbabwe has been reified as the carrying capacity of the land. An opportunistic strategy is based on an acceptance that in tropical savannah areas environmental conditions fluctuate. The land has a fluctuating ecological carrying capacity. In good years animal numbers may rise, but then, to avoid economic loss, must be sold or transferred elsewhere when forage availability decreases. Thus, 'In more variable environments the costs of underutilization under the conservative strategy rise and an opportunistic strategy is increasingly favourable' (Scoones 1987: 21).

So far as economic efficiency is concerned the suggestion is that by *de facto* pursuing an opportunistic livestock management strategy, the returns to farmers are greater than if they adhered to the government recommendations on carrying capacity.[14] If all economic uses of communal area cattle are considered, it seems incontestable. Mature oxen perform ploughing, harrowing and cultivating work; travel extensive distances annually drawing manure, crops and firewood in scotch carts; produce manure; and at the end of their working lives can still be sold for beef. Cows also do this work and produce milk, calves and manure; and again may eventually be sold. Using a rough replacement cost method, Scoones (1987: 8–9) argues that the annual economic output of a communal area animal in the dry area in which he worked, is much higher than that of commerical beef cattle in the same district.

Another indicator is that of livestock productivity per unit area and here, too, communal-area pastoral strategies are likely to win out. In 1973, Kelly showed that the quantity and quality of biomass consumed by livestock was higher on communal grazing land than on commercial ranchland (Sandford 1982: 46–7). Blaikie and Abel (1988, in Blaikie 1990) conclude that, 'both primary production (grass) and secondary production (livestock) have never been higher on the grazing lands of the communal areas' (p. 33). However, Kelly also showed that communal-area production was much more volatile within and between years (in Sandford 1982: 47). As Sandford (1983: 40) stresses, if an opportunistic strategy is to cope successfully with the variability of biomass production, stockowners must be able to reduce (without incurring deaths) and increase livestock numbers, as conditions alter. Owners thus require 'leeway' strategies. But here communal area farmers are not only more reluctant than previously to part with animals, because draught power is at such a premium, but movement is also becoming increasingly difficult. New veterinary regulations are one obstacle, and high levies by people with land available where cattle might be moved, is another.

Round one is therefore to the farmers. Despite constraints and the consequent deteriorating efficacy of local norms (as seen in the conflict over herding), their rough adherence to a socially constructed normative model allows them to derive economic benefit from livestock under conditions where the official grazing scheme strategy would not work.

It is possible, then, to make a good case for supporting response

2(a). To advance to 2(b) requires addressing environmental impact. Here, especially when the caveat is introduced – stockowners being forced against their will into environmental abuse – a strong argument can be presented that farmers' management strategies are ecologically sustainable. And even if the present constraint level is accepted, ecologists suggest that the conventional theorists are over-hasty in their conclusions about environmental degradation.

Tropical savannah is subject to extremely wide-ranging and irregular rainfall and hence biological constitution. Walker and Noy-Meir describe it as 'amongst the most variable of terrestrial ecosystems' (1982: 556) and also highly resilient. By resilience they mean 'the capacity of a system to absorb disturbance (change) without qualitatively changing its behaviour' (ibid.). Quite how resilient different types of savannah environment are is an issue of much current debate. Abel (1985: pers. comm.) suggests that, 'Resilience must be looked for in terms of the ability of the soil to carry a variety of successional stages of vegetation without losing its potential productivity, and there must be physical bases for resilience'. Walker and Noy-Meir suggest that a contributory factor to the resilience of savannah ecosystems is that they have multiple equilibria. An equilibrium condition is defined in terms of a particular balance between herbaceous and woody vegetation. An example of two equilibria possibilities in an environment would be a higher and lower successional state, each with its own 'domain of attraction' and with an intermediary, unstable equilibrium condition (Walker and Noy-Meir 1982: 557). But what is most vital about savannah environments, Walker and Noy-Meir emphasize, is that 'in all probability they require temporal variablity in order to maintain their resilience' (ibid.: 585).

In communal areas, therefore, it might be said that the use of an opportunistic strategy, even under constrained circumstances, may result in the productivity of an ecosystem declining to a lower successional state but no further (see Sandford 1982 on Zimbabwe). Within the conventional perspective there is a common confusion that signs of erosion – the gully below Mugarisi's farm – are direct measures of ongoing land degradation and productivity decline. This is not necessarily so. Sandford states unequivocally that suppositions of grazing land degradation through overgrazing are not supportable on present evidence. Defining environmental degradation as 'an irreversible (except at prohibitive cost) decline in the productivity of land and water resources' (p. 45), he argues:

No long term direct measurement of the productivity of natural grazing in the communal lands of Zimbabwe has been carried out, and the only direct measurement (Kelly 1973) which has been carried out does not support the thesis that degradation has occurred.

(Sandford 1982: 3)

Nevertheless Sandford is careful to point out that a counter-argument developed from the multiple equilibria or resilience thesis, also lacks a firm empirical support:

What we do not know is whether the communal area grazing system has now been stabilized under heavy stocking, at a low level of primary production (which can go on being consumed at a high rate) or whether, due to soil erosion and eradication of palatable species through overgrazing, production will continue to decline.

(ibid.: 17)

In the Zimbabwean debate, Sandford's views have not been particularly well received for reasons which should now be clear. One instance of theoretical defence of the more conventional position is provided by Campbell *et al.* (1986) based on an environmental survey carried out in the particularly erosion-prone area of the Save river basin.

Sandford regards the rate of soil erosion as being an indicator rather than a measure of environmental degradation. This is a matter of semantics in the case of Chiweshe; the erosion need not be quantified for its severity to be appreciated, and even if this degree of erosion only indicates environmental degradation then there is nonetheless cause for grave concern over future productivity of the grazing land.

(Campbell *et al.* 1986: 27)

In the Chiweshe area, which has particularly vulnerable sodic soils, this may be, but it is insufficient reason for not regarding erosion and declining environmental productivity as distinct, even if interrelated, phenomena.

Indicators other than erosion require even more careful scrutiny. Scoones (1987) notes that: 'With the possible exception of erosion assessments the present veld condition measures are inadequate: It is not clear that the presence of "sub climax" grassland or a high density woodland are indicators of permanent degradation' (p. 14). As Scoones and Wilson have noted elsewhere: 'the lack of standing grass biomass, by itself, should not be an indicator of erosion' (1988: 17). A closely cropped grassland, for instance, in terms of grass density and the nutritional value of the dominant species, may well be more productive than tall moribund strands (ibid.). The lack of definite indicators supporting the conventional position leads these two authors to conclude that land-use management and conservation could best proceed through supporting the farmers' initiatives and understanding. This way the key environmental resources and processes for pastoral management could also be framed in new ways for hypothesis formulation and research (Scoones and Wilson 1988: 111).

At a workshop in Zimbabwe this proposal was made and the predictable response of other ecologists was to question the high significance Scoones places on the concept of key resources (Cousins *et al.* 1988: 56); if this core element is not accepted then the proposal based upon it is likely to suffer severe mutation, even if it remains on the agenda. Sandford recommends more research involving farmers, within a broad framework of further primary research.

> Such research in other countries has often substantially contradicted previously widely held opinions. I do not believe that further refinement of estimates of stocking rates in relation to carrying capacities . . . is, at this point, a high priority. I think we need more detailed knowledge gathered within a communal area under the local livestock management system, of the relationship between stocking rates, primary productivity and soil erosion. 'Catchment level' studies are the most appropriate, with a mixed disciplinary team (including social scientists and historians).
>
> (Sandford 1982: 62)

This returns us to the starting point – the role of social scientists in interpretive and evaluative investigations. My purpose thus far has been to show how, as one digs into such an arena of conflict, the issues involved proliferate in number and complexity. The evaluation of conflicting perspectives becomes both political and technical because of the extent to which existing theories are underpinned by social contextualization rather than by undisputed empirical evidence. Social scientists continually have to distinguish between the two by peeling away obfuscating layers of socially constructed side issues and uncovering the basis upon which the conflicting perspectives are founded. Evaluation needs to be focused on these core elements if resolution is ever to occur.

Farmers' knowledge should receive serious consideration because of their lengthier, more intimate experience of the problem. In practice this rarely happens for a clear reason. In this debate it is not so much the occurrence of degradation that farmers dispute, but the nature of the processes involved and whose strategies are most to blame for aggravating these. This is what makes evaluation so sensitive. Rulings in the farmers' favour have potentially far-reaching political implications. For they switch the emphasis to the factors constraining farmers' preferred strategy, and hence bring into consideration the way the state regulates access to and influences land management. Defenders of the official version almost inevitably perceive an evaluation that finds fault with their view as an attack and will seek to neutralize it to protect their own claims, for example by attempting to keep the debate within the arena defined by the dominant theory itself. Thus, the reason why for 45 years the official Rhodesian/Zimbabwean debate has remained fixated on fixed carrying capacities, stocking and offtake rates, grazing schemes, destocking, and grazing schemes committees is intimately connected with maintenance of state control over the peasantry (Drinkwater, forthcoming). Nearly a decade after independence, change (initiated by Sandford's work as much as anything) is beginning. The growing counter-evidence is forcing certain justifications of the old policies to be declared the shibboleths they are. Thus, even deeply entrenched perspectives can be shifted, but for the evaluators, who are key players, to reach in practical instances some form of turning point, requires enormous stamina – and many allies who will continue to carry the baton. It is a long *durée*.

NOTES

1 Much of the ethnographic material presented in this chapter is taken from Drinkwater (forthcoming), Chapter 4. The remainder is from original fieldnotes.
2 For a lively account of some campaigns of this nature see B. Latour (1987) *Science in Action*, Milton Keynes: Open University Press.
3 A term taken from Jürgen Habermas (1984) *The Theory of Communicative Action*, Vol. 1, Cambridge: Polity Press.
4 Claims of meaningfulness, truth, normative rightness and sincerity are the four major claims that speech acts may entail according to Habermas (1984) in his *Theory of Communicative Action*.
5 'Veld' means 'range'. The specialist worked for Agritex, the country's agricultural extension agency. The remark was made at a provincial conference of the agency in November 1986.
6 A *vlei* is alternatively known as a *dambo*.
7 Village head.
8 Village development committee – a new local government unit established in 1984/85. In southern Chirumhanzu a VIDCO area usually incorporates the areas of five to six village heads.

9 K. B. Wilson (1986) 'The human ecology of Zvishane district: a preliminary account of rainfall and people's perception of it', unpublished paper.

10 Giddens defines 'practical consciousness' as: 'What actors know (believe) about social conditions, including especially the conditions of their own action, but cannot express discursively' (1984: 375). 'Discursive consciousness', to the contrary, is: 'What actors are able to say, or to give verbal expression to, about social conditions, including especially the conditions of their own action' (p. 374).

11 Cousins (1987: 32–4) lists as operating in the communal areas: 36 unfenced grazing schemes and 14 fenced schemes, with at the time a further 56 schemes planned. The peak period for grazing schemes was in the early 1970s – in the south-eastern Masvingo province alone there were about 315 schemes (p. 15).

12 Appendix of forthcoming PhD thesis.

13 A. K. H. Weinrich (1964) ('The social background of agriculture in Chilimanzi Reserve', *Rhodes Livingstone Institute Journal* 36: 31) corroborated this. Weinrich states that in the 1960s all the cattle in a village were herded together, each family taking a turn in herding sometimes over one hundred animals.

14 This point was made in the 1970s by Dankwerts who thoroughly reviewed the then *veld* management schemes in Masvingo province. See Dankwerts, J. P. (1975) *A Socio-economic Study of Veld Management in the Tribal Areas of the Victoria Province*, Salisbury Tribal Areas Research Foundation.

REFERENCES

Blaikie, P. M. (1990) *Comments on Pastoral Development Network Papers*, Pastoral Development Network, London: ODI (Overseas Development Institute).

Campbell, B. M., du Toit, R. F. and Attwell, C. A. M. (eds) (1986) 'Relationship between the environment and basic needs satisfaction in the Sabi catchment, Zimbabwe', University of Zimbabwe.

Cousins, B. (1987) 'A survey of current grazing schemes in the communal lands of Zimbabwe', University of Zimbabwe.

Cousins, B., Jackson, C. and Scoones, I. (eds) (1988) *Socio-economic Dimensions of Livestock Production in the Communal Lands of Zimbabwe*, Report and recommendations of a workshop at Masvingo: University of Zimbabwe/GTZ.

Drinkwater, M. J. (forthcoming) *The State and Agrarian Change in Zimbabwe's Communal Areas: an Application of Critical Theory*, London: Macmillan.

Giddens, A. (1984) *The Consititution of Society*, Cambridge: Polity Press.

Horton, R. (1982) 'Tradition and modernity revisited', in M. Hollis and S. Lukes (eds) *Rationality and Relativism*, Oxford: Basil Blackwell.

Ivy, P. (1981) *A Guide to Soil Coding and Land Capability Classification for Land Use Planners*, Harare: Agritex.

Sandford, S. (1982) *Livestock in the Communal Areas of Zimbabwe*, London: ODI.

—— (1983) *Management of Pastoral Development in the Third World*, London: John Wiley and Sons.

Scoones, I. (1987) 'Economic and ecological carrying capacity: implications for livestock development in the dryland communal areas of Zimbabwe', unpublished seminar paper, Department of Biological Sciences, University of Zimbabwe.

Scoones, I. and Wilson, K. B. (1988) 'Households, lineage groups and ecological dynamics: Issues for livestock research and development in Zimbabwe's communal areas', position paper for the workshop on *Socio-economic Dimensions of Livestock Production in the Communal Lands of Zimbabwe*, Masvingo: University of Zimbabwe/GTZ.

Walker, B. H. and Noy-Meir, I. (1982) 'Aspects of the stability and resilience of savanna eco-systems', in B. J. Huntley and B. H. Walker (eds) *Ecology of Tropical Savannas*, Berlin: Springer-Verlag.

11 From sago to rice
Changes in cultivation in Siberut, Indonesia

Gerard Persoon

Indonesia, a country with an agricultural population of over 55 per cent, became self-sufficient in rice only in 1984 due to deliberate government intervention. Increase in rice production has been made possible by the introduction of new high-yielding seed varieties, increased use of fertilizer and irrigation and annual expansion of the cultivation area. Because Indonesia has changed from a net rice importer into an exporter, the world market price has dropped. At present Indonesia is producing 'wetland rice', namely rice cultivated in swampy lowlands (Ali 1987), at a price higher than that of the world market.

This chapter focuses on the transition from sago to rice in the Mentawaian Islands off the coast of West Sumatra – one of the areas in which rice cultivation has been expanded at the cost of both natural swamp vegetation and sago stands. This complex transition in food production touches on aspects of ecology, religion, land use, exploitation of natural resources and the division and use of labour. The production of a crop not only satisfies physical needs, but also expresses power relations and social identities, including those between persons and nature and among persons themselves. Food preferences and taboos are among the least understood sociocultural phenomena, and explanations of changes in food patterns are frequently unsatisfactory in that they fail to take account of their sociopolitical and economic contexts.

THE ISLAND

Siberut, an island of about 4,460 sq km, is part of the Mentawai Archipelago about 100 km west of Sumatra. The 1986 census recorded about 21,000 people, about 90 per cent of whom are indigenous. The non-Mentawaians belong to various ethnic groups including mainly the Minangkabau (the main inhabitants of the province of West Sumatra), and also some Batak and Javanese. A few foreigners work in the missionary stations and the logging camps. Recently, the number of non-Mentawaians has increased rapidly.

Mentawaian culture differs markedly from that of the surrounding ethnic groups such as the Minangkabau, the Batak or the Nias. The Mentawaians are unfamiliar with pottery, weaving or metalwork and until recently with rice cultivation. Many mainland influences, such as Hinduism and Islam, have left the Mentawai Archipelago untouched. Older cultural traditions have either survived or have gone through processes of internal change (Schefold 1979: 17–22).

The population was spread over almost the entire island in small autonomous settlements (*uma*) along river banks, organized along patrilineal lines but with no political leaders. Hunting, fishing and gathering provided the bulk of daily food, fruit trees and cassava were cultivated and pigs and chickens were domesticated. Sago was the staple food.

There was no specialization in crafts and division of labour depended on sex and age. Each person developed many different skills and abilities and achieved a high degree of self-sufficiency. The patrilineal groups, also called *uma*, were economically independent, though limited barter with Sumatran traders had been going on for centuries in which products (mentioned in the preceding paragraph) were exchanged for ironware, textiles, and tobacco.

Traditionally, Siberut religion was based on a belief that all things had souls, including objects and even immaterial concepts. As human interference could disturb the souls, the religious aim was to restore equilibrium through an elaborate system of prescriptions and taboos and live in complete harmony with them. Disturbances were sometimes unavoidable in clearing the forest or killing an animal. Illness and death were also seen as a consequence of violations of relations with or among the souls. The medicine man (*sikerei*) restored harmony by performing healing ceremonies and also indicated which taboo should be observed in specific illnesses or misfortunes (Schefold 1979: 49–52). Taboos and rest periods (*punen*-periods) in which people must refrain from certain kinds of work or activities have been widely documented in 'classical' Mentawaian literature.

THE MICRO-ENVIRONMENTS

The Mentawaians divide the island's ecosystem into various productive micro-environments:

1 Settlement and homegarden, providing vegetables, bananas, medici-

nal plants, coconuts, fruits, flowers for decoration and herbs; also the feeding ground of pigs and chickens.

2 Taro fields: taro, tubers, frogs, small fish.
3 Sago stands: sago flour, sago grubs, pig and chicken fodder, etc.
4 Newly cleared fields (*tinunggulu*): bananas, sweet potatoes, medicinal plants.
5 Old fields: fruits, bamboo, wood for fuel, medicinal plants, ceremonial plants.
6 Rivers and swamps: frogs, fish, shrimps, worms and water.
7 Coastline and mangrove forest: shellfish, shrimps, sea turtles; durable wood for construction.
8 Primary forest: game animals such as deer, wild boar; four kinds of primates; resins, various species of rattan, wood for house construction and canoe building.

Of special interest is the newly cleared field in the forest. The men start to clear the undergrowth on the selected site. Before cutting the big trees, various kinds of bananas and tubers are planted. After felling, entire trees are left to rot. Gradually, when the leaves wither, many other species are planted and a few months later, pits or seedlings of fruit trees. Between 2 and 4 years bananas and tubers can be harvested. The trees become the dominant vegetation, another site is selected and the process repeated. In the following years, the fruit trees continue to grow along with spontaneous secondary vegetation. The forest is restored although dominated by fruit trees. This Mentawaian method of shifting cultivation is ecologically sound and sustainable and rather different from most other systems in South-east Asia. By not burning the leaves and trees and limiting field size there is almost no erosion. The topsoil is undisturbed and nutrients are released slowly because decomposition is gradual. Thus the Siberut system is a combination of hunting and gathering with agro-forestry cultivation grown with agricultural crops and animals resulting in diversified and sustainable food production and products (Wiersum 1988).

THE INTRODUCTION OF RICE

The transition from sago to rice cultivation on Siberut has a long history. In the early 1920s, the German missionary Börger believed that rice should be grown instead of sago and taro as it was more nutritious. Mentawaian men could work in fields (he thought they were lazy) and this would relieve women from their work in the taro fields. Moreover, rice cultivation would change the traditional way of life, characterized by long periods of taboos, and thus an ideal way to fight the 'persistent paganism'. It would also keep people in their villages. Thus, rice cultivation became a symbol of Christianity, progress and development.

After Indonesian independence, local authorities issued a decree that every young man wanting to get married should cultivate rice on a reasonably sized piece of land.

From the early 1970s onwards the development of the islands became the main government objective targeting larger coastal villages. Rice cultivation is a core feature, the production and consumption of which are indicators of the level of development and reflects local administrative performance. The main object of development is integration of all tribal groups in the mainstream of Indonesian cultural life.

The native Mentawaians currently live in various types of village. In the government-built resettlement villages rice cultivation is obligatory. In other villages, missionary influences are strong and religious teachers or 'enlightened' village heads encourage rice cultivation. Once this pressure is off, in certain villages and small *uma* settlements people revert, refusing to cultivate rice because it interferes with their preferred life style. The number of Mentawaians actually engaged in rice cultivation is difficult to assess as the situation changes from year to year and statistics are either unavailable or unreliable.

SAGO AND RICE CULTIVATION COMPARED

Sago and rice cultivation can be compared on Siberut with regard to: ecological and cultural contexts, labour use, yield, risks, nutritional value, additional products and functions, social status and the importance of the shift to rice cultivation on a long-term basis.

The ecological context

The sago palm or Metroxylon sagu produces far more starch than other palms. It grows to about 10–15 m, has a diameter of about 45 cm, flowers only once after 8–12 years, after which it dies. Young plants produce permanent suckers, so sago stands always contain trees of various ages. Their natural environment is fresh-water swamp where they grow in large numbers (Flach 1983). At present sago is an important food product for tribal peoples in Papua New Guinea, Indonesia and Malaysia, but other food crops (rice, maize and tubers) are heavily promoted. Early foreign observers associated sago with traditional and 'primitive' jungle life and suggested that sago growing precluded progress.

On Siberut sago palms (along with other tree species) grow along riverbanks and in the swampy lowlands. Some of the stands are natural, others have been planted. They constitute an abundant underused crop, possibly because of the changed settlement pattern (the upper reaches of the river are no longer exploited) and, in new villages, rice is cultivated instead.

Swamp rice and sago require almost identical growing conditions. In the new villages sago stands are removed to make room for rice fields. Hill rice is unknown on the island and people are unfamiliar with irrigation techniques. However, the creation of new rice fields (unlike sago stands) does impair the wild life. Moreover, the island rainfall pattern allows only one rice harvest a year.

Cultural context

Sago and rice have different cultural meanings with regard to their status as foods and as agricultural products. Sago is the traditional staple food on the island, and its cultivation and processing are fully integrated in Mentawaian culture. There are almost no associated taboos for its cultivation and sago processing is more like food gathering than food production. Neither are there cultural objections (taboos or religious sanctions) to rice.

As an agricultural product, however, rice cultivation is more complicated. Although rice is not subject to taboos either as a crop or in its use of land or water, its cultivation conflicts with traditional prohibitions on work during certain periods, the breach of which brings illness and death and affects people's attitude towards the environment. For example, there should be no work after house construction, hunting expeditions, constructing a new canoe or clearing a field in the forest. These taboo periods cannot be observed if rice is to be successfully cultivated, for it requires constant tending. Thus, its cultivation on Siberut entails a different religious attitude.

Labour

The processing of sago involves a number of clearly defined, gender-related activities (see Table 11.1). Sago processing is carried out by men but women assist in filling the sago containers. Small groups of men process one or two trees for each family at a time, working in the early morning and late afternoon but never in the middle of the day. This supplies them with enough food for a few months.

The labour requirements in rice cultivation are different. Though there is no real dry season on Siberut, the best time to plant rice is in September or October when the rainfall is heaviest. There is only one harvest a year in March or April and the field is not used for other purposes or crops. During the clearing of the fields, the weeding and the harvest, there is a labour shortage in the villages. Moreover, all activities should be carried out quickly as delay results in a reduced yield: seedlings grow too tall, weeds cause problems, the grain might start to rot or be eaten by birds, pigs or mice.

Yield

Yield can be calculated according to labour input, land input and capital input. Numbers vary depending on the quality of the harvest, and differences in calculating procedures, so the following should be taken as rough indicators. Theoretically, one hectare of sago could yield about 15 tons of starch per year if all the mature palms were used. A single trunk may contain 400–600 kg of starch. As there is an over-abundance of trees, the theoretical yield is rarely reached. Rice harvests are always maximal in the sense that people will do their utmost to harvest the entire crop. But rice yields vary due to disease and irregular rainfall. A relatively good harvest may yield about 1,500 kg/ha. One hour invested in the preparation of sago starch may yield about 2.6 kg. The nature and intensity of work are not measured in this calculation. For rice the yield is about 0.6 kg for each hour in a harvest of 1,500 kg/ha. Based on comparable calculations, sago has often been classified as a 'lazy man's food'. Apart from land and labour there are no further inputs. All tools are homemade and relatively cheap and simple. Fertilizer and pesticides are not used in rice cultivation.

Risks, diseases and pests

The sago palms are part of the natural vegetation. Locally available minerals and the quality of the soil and the water determine its growth, quality and starch content. Men simply harvest the crop. The hard bark prevents animals such as wild boars and deer from reaching the starch. Sago does not suffer from diseases or pests and the risks in keeping sago flour for future consumption are limited. The flour is kept under water in cylindrical containers made out of palm leaves that keep out mice, rats and birds.

Rice, however, is susceptible to plant diseases, irregular rainfall and plagues of mice, rats, deer or wild hog. In addition there are storage problems in the humid climate, especially in storing seed for the following year. It is difficult to calculate exactly how much of the potential harvest is lost, but clearly, additional labour is needed to avoid these risks.

Nutritional value

The idea that rice is a better food product than sago is widely believed. Analyses of nutritional values indicate a higher content of protein and fat in rice. Platt's (1977) table compares the food value of 100 g of raw sago starch with rice. Table 11.2 (based on Whitten 1985 and Platt 1977) shows the food value of sago from Siberut. The differences in value are partly attributed to the variations in moisture in Whitten's sample. What is most important, however, is the higher percentage of protein in rice.

As sago is almost pure starch it is thought to be an inferior food. However, this is not the decisive factor as it is the total composition of the diet that counts, or the quality and quantity of complementary foods. Thus, sago is a different dietary component compared to rice. Rice tastes better and is quicker to prepare so all meals contain a substantial proportion. Sago meals are served with a greater proportion of additional foodstuffs as fish, meat or vegetables and time to collect these other items is available. From an analysis of several hundred meals it became obvious that rice meals generally lack these complementary dishes, and that sago meals are more nutritious. This is the only meaningful basis of nutritional comparison.

Secondary products and functions

Apart from flour, the sago palm provides a number of other products. Harvesting sago grubs is probably one of the most efficient ways of obtaining animal protein on Siberut. The sago beetle lays its eggs at the top of the felled trunk and after a few weeks fat white larvae can be picked. Sometimes complete trees are left to the beetles by splitting the bark at various places. Cultivation of grubs is prodigious and can yield 12 kg per tree, representing about 10 hours of work (675 calories per 100 g) (Whitten 1985). Leaves of the sago palm are used for roofing and cooking, the bark is used for wall and floor construction and leaf

Table 11.1 Comparison between sago and rice on the island of Siberut

	Sago	Rice
Origin	original vegetation self-regenerating plants	needs to be planted yearly (1 harvest a year)
Habitat	natural vegetation in swamps and along river banks	cultural landscape (in swampy areas)
Ecological infrastructure	continuity in vegetation structure: no artificial obstacle for animals (no mono-crop)	discontinuity in vegetation structure: artificial obstacles for certain kinds of animals, favourable for others
Cultural adaptation (a) as a food product (b) as a crop	traditional staple food integrated part of the culture (no specific restrictions)	new but acceptable food product incompatible with traditional life style (use of labour) but no direct religious taboo connected with land use
Yield: per ha per hour per unit of capital input	*ca.* 15.000 kg per ha per year 2.6 kg per hour no additional investment	200–1.500 kg per ha per year (1 harvest) 0.6 kg per hour besides seeds no additional investment (no fertilizer or pesticides)
Use of labour	no peaks	several peaks in one season (cleaning the field, planting, weeding, harvesting)
Workforce	only men	mainly women
Risks	none	plagues diseases protection of supply

Secondary products	sago grubs material for thatching baskets walls/floors	none
Secondary functions	animal food (for pigs and chickens) exchange product in traditional relations: payments of fines and brideprices	none
Nutritional value per 100 g	water(ml) : 12° (38.8)^x calories : 352° (265)^x protein(g) : 0.5° (1.44)^x carbohydrate(g) : 88° (57.8)^x fat(g) : –° (0.48)^x	water(ml) : 12° calories : 352° protein(g) : 7.0° carbohydrate(g) : 80° fat(g) : 0.5°
Part of menu	limited part of menu	main component
Ascribed status	symbol of traditional life style and primitivity	symbol of progress and modernization but also of external influence
Long-term perpsective	no commercial value limited possibilities for mechanized processing permanent use for self-sufficiency additional products and functions will remain important	no commercial value limited possibilities for mechanization in the future less important as a crop because labour requirements: it will become import item

Notes: ° Platt 1977;
^{x} Whitten 1985.

Table 11.2 Nutritional value per 100 g of sago and rice

Sago	Platt	Whitten	Rice	Platt
water (ml)	12	(38.8)	water	12
calories	352	(256)	calories	352
protein (g)	0.5	(1.44)	protein (g)	7.0
carbohydrate (g)	88	(57.8)	carbohydrate (g)	80
fat (g)	–	(0.48)	fat (g)	0.5

Source: Platt (1977); Whitten (1985).

fronds provide good material for making baskets and hats. In comparison, rice has only one secondary product – the leftovers after threshing that could provide animal feed but the quantities are too small to be very useful.

Sago groves also fulfil certain other functions. They are important elements in brideprice along with other tree species, animals and products. They are also part of the payment of fines imposed on criminals or people who have been offensive. They are essential in the system of village justice. Sago groves are also ideal places for raising pigs and chickens. Again in comparision rice has no secondary functions. Rice fields are never included in the payment of brideprice or fines. Particularly at harvest time, there are often quarrels between owners of rice fields and owners of chickens, ducks or pigs which may cause damage to the rice. People are obliged to confine the animals, which implies additional work in providing animal feed instead of allowing them to forage freely.

Social status

The national food in Indonesia is rice. Besides being a staple food, it also fulfils important ceremonial or ritual functions on Java, Bali and various other islands. It is a symbol of fertility and welfare and important in sacrifices and ritual exchange. Filled rice barns are a symbol of wealth. Rice cultivation and consumption are preconditions of 'civilization'. People who do not (yet) eat rice are considered inferior, poor or uncivilized (Soemarwoto 1985: 208–10). Thus, it is hardly surprising that the introduction of rice is encouraged. Arguments with regard to the labour costs and the ecological consequences and losses incurred by this innovation are insignificant in this line of reasoning. Because of its ascribed superior status to sago and taro, rice represents a cultural value which cannot be reduced to economic, ecological or agricultural arguments and has partly gained ground among the Mentawaians, in that rice becomes part of a new complex of 'progressive' cultural elements. Rice offers a possibility of escaping a label of inferiority along with zinc roofs, modern education, Islam, modern clothing and the possession of radios, watches or outboard motors; it is necessary for those who want to break away from tradition. For those who wish to retain the traditional life style, it remains an incompatible element of foreign influence.

The long term

As the population is limited and the sago stands abundant, sago could easily remain a food product in the subsistence economy as its cultivation is a sustainable mode of exploitation of the natural resources. Rice was introduced on Siberut to 'raise' the population from its existing human condition under pressure from government and outsiders. Should this tendency to abandon traditional values continue, another phenomenon may appear – the increasing commercialization of the agricultural system in which other crops may become more profitable than rice. No sooner would rice eating become incorporated into society and in the market economy, then rice might lose its significance as an agricultural product as the annual labour demand becomes too heavy a burden for the farmer. They might start looking for alternatives like copra, cloves or coffee. The increasing importance of these monocultures would require more and more land with serious ecological consequences for the erosion-prone hills. Traditional varied food resources would be neglected. While some men would start to work in the logging camps, others would try to become crew members on the small trading vessels or turn to commercial fishing. People would also intensify the exploitation of rattan resulting in complete depletion of the species with commercial value. Once used to rice as a staple food, and if assured of a cash income, they would prefer to buy rice instead of cultivating it themselves, with other crops offering better returns and requiring less labour input. Moreover, arable land is not a limiting factor on Siberut. Labour is the problem. So the Mentawaians optimize their labour and not land as do the farmers on Java for instance.

The introduction of rice has led to an undesirable effect. Instead of becoming a rice-exporting island, it has through the monetization and commercialization of land and agricultural labour become a rice-importing area and will increasingly remain so. As a result, the island, traditionally covered by tropical rain forest containing a large number of endemic species of plants and animals, will lose its natural value as logging operations and cash-crop production do not allow for the continued survival of its rich natural heritage.

THE LOCAL POPULATION

All analytical criteria and aforementioned arguments are aspects of sago and rice which can be analysed and evaluated by outsiders, both planners and scientists. They attach different values to the criteria which serve as the background for their policies and recommendations. At present the authorities still favour an increase in rice production both through intensification and extending the cultivation area. The local population is also involved in the process, weighing one argument against the other. Sometimes fear of the outside world prevails, but sometimes a positive choice in a situation of relative freedom can be decisive.

A surprising item in the comparison between both products as conceived by the local population are the prices of sago and rice in the small local market. Sago costs about Rp 2,500 per *tapri* (container) which equals 50–60 kg rice requiring about 4 to 4.5 times as much labour as sago (see Table 11.1), thus the labour investment in rice is also expressed in the local price. Rice is an expensive or luxury food. The difference in nutritional value between both products and the indirect consequences for the composition of their diet are barely known to the people.

The burden of producing for consumption, in particular that of women, is accepted by various groups because the men are seen to be more occupied with wage labour or the cultivation of cash crops. It is the price paid in the name of progress (*kemajuan*). I believe that the burden is only temporary until rice can be eaten without having to produce it oneself. Other groups act out of fear of the local authorities, the result of perceived power relations and future expectations; their choice between sago or rice is not based on their appraisal of the characteristics of both products, but on the power relations that have particularly determined the history of rice production on Siberut.

REFERENCES

Ali, I. (1987) 'Rice in Indonesia: rice policy and comparative advantage', *Bulletin of Indonesian Economic Studies* XXIII (3): 80–100.

Ave, J. B. (1977) 'Sago in insular Southeast Asia', in K. Tan (ed.) *Sago-76*, Kuala Lumpur: Kemajuan Kanji, pp. 21–30.

Börger, F. (1920) 'Wie man sich freuet in der Ernte', *Das Missionsblatt*, pp. 71–3.

Flach, M. (1983) *The Sagopalm: Domestication, Exploitation and Products*, Rome: FAO.

Harris, M. (1985) *Good to Eat: Riddles of Food and Culture*, New York: Simon & Schuster.

—— (1987) 'Comment on Vayda's review of "Good to eat": riddles of food and culture', *Human Ecology* 15 (4): 511–17.

Pembantu Bupati (1985) 'Monografi Wilayah Mentawai', Padang (unpublished).

Platt, B. S. (1977) *Table of representative values of foods commonly used in tropical countries*, London: Her Majesty's Stationery Office.

Schefold, R. (1979) *Speelgoed voor de zielen, kunst en cultuur van de Mentawai eilanden*, Delft: Volkenkundig Museum Nusantara.

Soemarwoto, O. (1985) 'Constancy and change in agroecosystems', in K. L. Hutterer *et al.* (eds) *Cultural Values and Human Ecology in Southeast Asia*, Michigan: University of Michigan, pp. 205–48.

Spina, B. (1981) *Mitos dan legenda suku Mentawai*, Jakarta: Balai Pustaka.

van Buuren, J. (1932) 'Memorie van overgave Mentawai Eilanden', Muara Siberut (unpublished).

van den Breemer, J. P. M. (1984) 'Onze aarde houdt niet van rijst, een cultureel antropologische studie van innovatie in de landbouw bij de Aouan van Ivoorkust', Leiden (diss.).

Vayda, A. P. (1987) 'Explaining what people eat: a review article', *Human Ecology* 15 (4): 493–510.

Whitten, T. (1985) 'Tanaman sagu dan pengolahannya di Pulau Siberut', in G. Persoon and R. Schefold (eds) *Pulau Siberut*, Jakarta: Bhrata-ra, pp. 30–6.

Wiersum, K. F. (ed.) (1988) *Viewpoints on Agroforestry*, 2nd edn, Wageningen: Agricultural University.

12 'Nature', 'culture' and disasters

Floods and gender in Bangladesh

Rosalind Shaw

In September 1988, three-quarters of Bangladesh was submerged in the most devastating flood in living memory. This and other recent disasters have generated worldwide concern about the human impact on the environment which, in relation to Bangladesh, has been focused overwhelmingly upon the theory that recent damaging floods are the direct outcome of deforestation in the Himalayas. While deforestation is clearly of crucial importance in relation to such other issues as global warming, its applicability as a unilinear explanation of particular floods is highly questionable (e.g. Currey 1984; Park 1981). More seriously, the most popular solutions generated by this explanation (popular with national governments and international aid organizations), namely large-scale afforestation projects upstream and large-scale construction of embankments downstream in Bangladesh, rely upon one-dimensional conceptions of the interaction between people and the environment. In the case of Bangladesh, such narrowly defined understandings obscure the relationships between floods and those who live with them. It is with these relationships, in particular how they vary for men, women and others with differential access to material and symbolic resources and consequently different 'environments', that this chapter is concerned.

A fundamental aspect of the people–environment relationship is emphasized by geographers researching natural hazards. Thus 'Floods', wrote Gilbert White, 'would not be a hazard were not man tempted to occupy the floodplain' (1974: 3). Such writings commonly begin in this way. Part of a reaction against environmental determinism, geographers were careful to incorporate human agency into the definition of 'hazards', raising a quite different issue from the adverse environmental impact of, e.g., pollution or deforestation. The question here is not what *causes* events but their *conceptualization*.

Yet such research has all too often failed to live up to the promise of its humanized definitions of hazards, since in actual usage in the same writings the term often becomes interchangeable with geophysical events themselves – floods, droughts or earthquakes (see Torry's criticism of this semantic slippage (Torry 1979a: 370)). Indeed, this primacy given to an apparently autonomous physical environment is embedded within the term 'natural hazards' itself, in which such hazards are attributed to nature. Although the delineation of 'natural' and 'man-made' events is highly problematic (see Turton 1979), a view polarizing 'nature' and 'culture' is characteristic of thought patterns concerning hazards in many western institutional contexts – international-aid agencies, the environmental movement, natural hazards research and even anthropology.

This polarization has apparently marginalized research on hazards within anthropology since they are ascribed to nature. Anthropologists recognize that the 'nature' versus 'culture' dichotomy is socially constructed and of restricted cultural provenance, so it is ironic that the definition and practice of 'cultural anthropology' reifies it. Our conceptions of disciplinary boundaries appear to be protected from those insights about the 'nature–culture' opposition which our own discipline has developed. Even cultural ecology and ecological anthropology, explicitly concerned with the environment, have themselves been pervaded by this polarity in the form of biological and cybernetic models of culture's 'interaction' with or 'adaptation' to a distinctly conceived 'natural environment' (e.g. Bateson 1972; Rappaport 1979). A recent exception, however, is Ingold's critique from within ecological anthropology of the latter's tenet of cultural 'adaptation' to the environment (Ingold 1986; Chapter 3, this volume). Prior to this, the major alternative to such neo-functionalist models within anthropology has been the work of the French Marxist school of economic anthropology, in which drought and famine in the Sahel are situated both ecologically and historically, in terms of the history of colonialism, cash-cropping and the creation of dependency as well as the climate (e.g. Meillassoux 1974; Copans 1975; 1983).

Apart from this, the nature–culture distinction has been used to define disciplinary boundaries, confining hazards to the 'proper' domain of geography. Hazards research has usually, until recently, been approached within geography in such a way as to eclipse the social and cultural nature of hazards by the 'natural' nature of hazards. In such research, investigations of human involvement have usually been limited to such questions as how accurately people appraise risks, how they cope with and adapt to 'the hazard' (the cyclone or the earthquake, in the definition contours of which people are now excluded), and/or how personality factors influence both of these. Causal priority is given to nature. People merely respond and adjust on the basis of 'subjective' knowledge. Attention has been given to people not as social actors but as bearers of idiosyncratic qualities such as 'personality differences'. Khan (1974), for example, relates responses to cyclones in Bangladesh to such constructs as 'optimism and pessimism' and to 'superstitious' beliefs.

In their 'adaptationist' assumptions, these approaches run parallel to ecological anthropology (Watts 1983: 235). The dominant perspective which they represent, however, has been challenged by radical critiques within geography which both parallel and draw from the analyses of the French neo-Marxist anthropologists (see esp. Hewitt 1983). Watts (1983) argues that the escalation of disasters over the past 50 years, and their increasingly 'Third World' locations, can be much more clearly attributed to domination and dependency than to climatic change. Similarly, Susman *et al.* (1983) formulate a theory linking disasters to the process of underdevelopment, in which marginalized people are forced into 'marginal', often hazard-prone areas. Slum-dwellers of Guatemala City, well aware of this, referred to the 1976 earthquake as a 'classquake' (ibid.: 277). Since 'natural hazards', then, are as much products of human agency and power as of geophysical events, 'we would be right to replace the term *natural* with the more appropriate term *social* or *political* disaster' (Richards 1975).

Such approaches entail the dissolution of two polarities implicit in most natural hazards research. The first is that of the natural and human worlds: instead of discrete entities in interaction, they are a people/environment mutuality in an '*inner*action' which is internally differentiated according to social relations and inequalities (Watts 1983: 234, following Sayer 1980). The second polarity is that of 'normal' versus 'abnormal' events, which misrepresents the precariousness and instability of everyday life for those whose marginality makes them vulnerable to hazards. As Hewitt (1983) has observed, the 'forces of nature' which furnish the basis of explanation in such studies of natural hazards are typically represented as discrete, sharp discontinuities, distanced from everyday life by their 'un'-ness as *un*predictable, *un*precedented, *un*certain, *un*managed situations. In our mental maps, a 'disaster archipelago' is drawn:

> In the technocratic style of work there is a structure of assumptions, and a use of science and management that always situates natural calamity beyond an assumed order of definite knowledge, and of reasonable expectation. More importantly it places disaster outside

the realm of everyday responsibility both of society and individual. More important still, it makes assumptions about everyday life – about its being 'normal', 'stable', 'predictable' – that are in turn debatable.

(Hewitt 1983: 16)

Although hazards are thus viewed as largely removed from 'ordinary' human action, they are represented as potentially amenable (to some degree) to prediction and control by specialists: planners, managers, scientists and engineers. We thus have a hierarchy of agency, under-pinned by a conception of hazards as 'nature' which favours the authority of (usually western expatriate) experts and institutions and their scientific and technical knowledge, and which tends to discount the 'culture' of those who live with hazards.

FLOODS AND BANGLADESH

To those in Bangladesh the 1988 flood was clearly a hazard. But far from being distanced from everyday life, many of its features (under-stood as a people/environment 'inneraction') were constituted by social processes and structures. In Bangladesh, highly variable floods are a regular feature, and experiencing some as 'hazards' does not depend merely upon the presence of people who live in the floodplain, but upon how those who do so *utilize* floods and, must importantly, who has access to such use. Thus, the 'hazardous' nature of the 1988 flood was differently constituted for men and women, for urban and rural dwellers and for poor and wealthy.

Being on the delta of three major rivers, Bangladesh is flooded annually, no more than a third of the country being submerged at any one time. Because of its fertile alluvial deposits, floods are resources, enabling three harvests per year. The cropping pattern spreads the risk of flood or drought by the cultivation of different rice varieties on different elevations of land at different times of year (Ralph 1975: 46–50). The rice variety *aus*, which cannot survive flooding, is planted in the dry season in February/March and harvested in June, while the flood-tolerant *aman* variety is also planted during February/March, grows in the monsoon floods from June to late September and is harvested in October. Sometimes both are sown together in the same field: *aus* will survive if the water level is low, *aman* if flooding is greater. Since the *aman* harvest is the main one, it might be said that an adjustment has been turned to an advantage so that farmers have become dependent on floods.

Other crucial resources provided by rivers and floods (the few available to the poor landless) include fish, shellfish, snails and turtles, the major (and often only) source of animal protein available to poor families (Bangladesh Agricultural Research Council 1989: 4–5). While not everyone in rural areas has access to land, the surface floodwater is a common property resource to which the poor have equal access, the reduction of which would itself constitute a hazard for the landless.

The construction of villages and houses are part of everyday 'flood-practices'. Villages are built on mounds (*bhiti*) whose heights indicate the usual levels of flooding, and houses are further raised on mud plinths, which are renewed after every flood, if possible, although this is a very labour-intensive task. Some houses also have a 'false roof' (*kar*), where goods can be stored and people can inhabit if necessary. If water enters the house, the bed (*choki*) becomes the living area: households live, cook and store belongings on it, raising it on bricks. Food, clothes and even chickens are hung from the roof in jute nets (*shika*). Cattle and goats are placed on bamboo platforms (*machan*) or taken to a road upon an embankment.

These are just a few examples of the varied (and differential) ways in which people live with and use floods. This is not to suggest a 'traditional' perfect environmental homeostasis, a long coexistence in a benign equilibrium. Damaging floods have characterized this delta for centuries. An account of a flood in 1787–88 could describe the 1988 flood: the rivers rose to such a height that they flooded the country 'to an extent never remembered by the oldest inhabitant', boats sailed through the flooded streets of Dhaka, and those in rural areas took refuge on rafts and bamboo platforms (Taylor 1840: 301, cited in Ralph 1975: 10). Sixty thousand people were estimated to have died, either in the flood itself or in the resulting famine (ibid.).

Most floods are not so extreme but are still very variable in timing, duration and magnitude. They also effect changes in parts of the river system from year to year: different areas are flooded, and rivers change their course. Flooded land is resurrected in the form of highly-fertile new islands (*char*), and form the basis of fresh settlement. So farmers are continually adjusting cropping strategies as floods vary, perhaps losing their land through erosion, migrating to new areas and exploiting new islands (immediately colonized and controlled by the most wealthy landowners). Farmers also negotiate ritually with powers behind the river, praying in the mosque and sometimes throwing offerings into the water.

There are two related points here: first, the duality of floods as resources and hazards – even the 1988 flood resulted in excellent harvests in some areas, although taking the country as a whole, a third of the *aman* harvest was estimated to have been lost. Second, given this duality of floods (and countless other contingencies), 'everyday life' for most Bangladeshi farmers is unstable, unrepetitive, but characterized by a series of calculated risks and strategies.

The duality of floods finds expression in Bengali terminology. Whereas the English term 'flood' connotes an abnormal phenomenon, in Bengali there are different terms, which vary from region to region, with different connotations. Around Dhaka, *borsha* and *bonna* are used. *Borsha* is used generally for the monsoon season, and specifically for rain and the annual inundation of the river, thus associating flooding with a certain degree of regularity and seasonality. *Bonna*, like 'flood', implies extremity, but refers to a different range of contexts from the English term. Instead of a sharp dichotomy between a predictable 'normality' and an unpredictable 'hazard', the distinction between the Bengali terms suggests the crossing of a line on a continuous scale beyond which the damage of the 'flood-as-hazard' outweighs the benefits of the 'flood-as-resource'. The line will not be the same throughout society: the asymmetries of power and interests between men and women, landlords and the landless, rural and urban dwellers will mean differentiated environmental 'inneractions' and very different experiences. When these asymmetries change through time, the distinction between *bonna* and *borsha* changes with it. Although it is questionable whether extreme floods have increased in the recent past, it is certain that people have become more flood-vulnerable, largely due to processes set in motion during the colonial era.

Prior to British colonialism, Bengal was a prosperous province of the Mughal Empire, famous for its cotton industry and agriculture. In the mid-eighteenth century, the British East India Company established control and acquired through coercion and violence large quantities of cotton cloth at minimal cost from Bengali weavers, which they sold at considerable profit. Subsequently, the cotton industry was eliminated to create a monopoly for imported cotton from Manchester. Towards the end of the eighteenth century, under British colonial rule, agriculture suffered due to changes in land tenure. Formerly, the Mughal rulers had collected land tax from Bengali farmers via an elite known as *zamindars*. Under British rule, the *zamindars* were made the owners of the land from which they collected taxes, as part of the common British strategy of creating a loyal elite. The *zamindars* (mostly Hindu) then moved from predominatly Muslim East Bengal to Calcutta in West Bengal, becoming absentee landlords who used the rents from their tenant farmers (inflated via intermediaries who subleased the land) to invest in Calcutta. Thus agriculture stagnated and the tenant farmers, forced to become indebted to moneylenders in order to pay their rents, grew increasingly poor. Jute cultivation was encouraged as a cash crop, but its processing took place outside East Bengal. There was a second era of colonialism in 1947 when East Bengal became East Pakistan. While Bengalis formed the majority in Pakistan, they were greatly under-represented in the government, the civil service and the military, and their jute exports were controlled by and invested in West Pakistan. When Bangladesh became independent in 1971, it had a colonial legacy of over two hundred years in which its surplus had been channelled out to finance development elsewhere. Today, a third of rural households are landless, rising to 48 per cent if those households owning less than half an acre are included, the latter considered functionally landless (Chen 1986: 60).

Landless households do not, then, have the same access to the flood-as-resource as landowners. For poor households (unable to maintain the *bhiti* of their house, unable to afford a bed, without reserves of rice and/or having been forced to move into more marginal and flood-prone areas), the flood becomes disastrous considerably earlier than for resource-rich households, whose flood practices have not been undermined.

Gender, danger and floods

For men with land in rural areas, cultivation focuses not only one's relationship with the physical environment, but with the sprirtual world. 'A good Muslim is a good farmer' is a common Bengali expression. The origins of agriculture, Islam and flooded rivers in the region are linked historically. The shift of the Ganges delta from West to East Bengal was accompanied by the extension of Mughal rule and economic exploitation of the area, leading both to intensive rice cultivation, and to large-scale conversion to Islam (Eaton 1985).

Bonna, accordingly, is perceived by farmers in terms of disruption to cultivation. According to Ralph's study of floods in Char Bhaba-nathpur village, southeast of Dhaka:

> The villagers describe abnormal flood to be those times when the water rises one and a half to two times the normal height on the fields (fifteen–twenty feet on *aman*, as opposed to the normal eight–

nine feet). A few call abnormal those floods when water comes on
the *bhiti* and into the homestead area.

(Ralph 1975: 71)

Since the focus of Ralph's study was primarily agriculture, the
respondents to the questionnaire were male (ibid.: 61–5). Whereas
only a few men in Ralph's sample defined *bonna* in terms of disruption
to the homestead (*bari*), this disruption is much more central to
women's perceptions: a flood is *bonna* when it enters the home.

For most Bangladeshi women, the experience of the environment is
centred upon purdah, as well as concepts of pollution which have
become incorporated into Bengali Islam. Purdah ranges from
women's seclusion in the home (except when wearing the *burqa*, a long
black garment completely covering head and body) to simply placing
the end of the sari over the hair and avoiding eye contact with male
affines and strangers. These observances are stricter among Muslims
than among Christians, among young brides than older women, and
may vary for the same person in different circumstances (Ahmed and
Shamsun Naher 1987: 53–60).

Many scholars have also observed the status associations of purdah
practices, particularly their more complete observation among the
wealthy. Deserted or poor women in landless families are forced to
face the shame (*lojja*) of working outside the home to survive. Elite
women, however, are often able, by for example having had a western
education or a professional occupation, either to abandon purdah
practices or to redefine them as the 'inner' observance of modesty
(ibid.: 55, 57). For women in between, work is usually confined within
the homestead.[1] However, such women are responsible for storing and
germinating the seed rice and threshing, winnowing, parboiling and
husking the paddy after the harvest. They also grow vegetables in
small plots near the home, while men tend larger plots further away in
lowland fields (ibid.: 67–8). However, such work is not considered to
be 'work' by men, and is undervalued and discounted (see Chen 1986;
Hartmann and Boyce 1983).

Purdah is underscored not only by status considerations, but also by
concepts of pollution. Purity and pollution have, as Blanchet (1984: 30–
50) has argued, become transformed in the Muslim Bengali context into
auspiciousness and misfortune. Women are defined as more subject to
pollution than men, particularly with regard to childbirth and menstruation, and this pollution is construed as potentially dangerous for
crops, cows, the river and the granary – all of which as Blanchet (1984:
48) observes, form the basis of the rural economy. At the same time

'the perfect wife' (defined in terms of thrift, modesty, cleanliness and a disinclination to quarrel) is linked with fertility and prosperity. Thus, auspiciousness is maintained and pollution guarded against by purdah observances restricting women's contact with the environment.

The latter relationship, however, is more complex that such restrictions might suggest. According to Blanchet, 'Women have more to do than men with . . . spirits of the land, for women are associated with fertility' (1984: 14). Moreover, Blanchet argues that by performing rituals involving local spirits who may either disturb or protect them when menstruating, pregnant or giving birth, and as mothers, 'women have maintained separate pre-Islamic and pre-Brahmanistic traditions which give meaning and value to their specific roles and functions in society' (Blanchet 1984: 16).

This argument appears, however, to overstate the positive aspects of women's relationships with land and river spirits. Purdah restriction is central to such relationships. In Blanchet's research area in the northeast of Bangladesh, considerable ambivalence is apparent in the relationship between women and Kwaz, an Islamicized guardian spirit of the river (ibid.: 44–8). Kwaz is honoured at marriages, during pregnancy and protects children from attack by ghosts (*bhut*) during their first 5 or 6 years. Sometimes Kwaz is attracted to women and their sexuality, sometimes pulling a woman bathing naked into the depths of the river; conversely menstruating women are forbidden to bathe in the river because he is angered by female pollution which brings calamity. Kwaz's anger manifests itself by river erosion, in which he 'eats' the river bank, aided by invisible manual workers.

The relationship between women and another group of beings is, however, unambiguous. River banks, bamboo groves and road junctions are inhabited by *bhut*, ghosts of those who have not died peaceful deaths: suicides, murder victims, stillborn children and women who died in childbirth. Blanchet has also collected traditions which claim that *bhut* were once masters of the land prior to the 'great religions' (1984: 54). Everyone is vulnerable to possession or illness from *bhut*, especially women and children. *Bhut* are especially attracted to women when they are at their most polluting, and to foetuses and young children. When *bhut* are most active (usually dawn, sunset, midday and midnight), and during menstruation, pregnancy, and up to seven days after giving birth, women should stay indoors. The best protection is afforded by purdah practices; non-observance endangers a woman and makes her children more vulnerable. There is considerable overlap between *bhut* and the specifically Islamic *jinn* and *pori* ('fairies'), as well as a more impersonal and indistinct category known as 'bad wind' (*batash*), protection from all of which is secured by remaining inside the home and by wearing Islamic amulets (*tabiz*). Since, then, *bhut* attack both sexes, but are particularly feared and avoided by women, can women really be said to be their custodians?

Blanchet argues that the ambivalence of women's sexuality in relationships with these 'spirits of the land' derives from the different chronological layers of religious ideas, in which female sexuality is valued positively in relation to the original, local spirits and negatively in relation to Brahmanized deities and to Islam (1984:47–8; 61–3). However, the static spatial image of layers may obscure the extent to which originally distinct sets of ideas merge and mutate in 'inner-action' with each other. Thus 'whether women are interacting with high spirits who are repulsed by their pollution, or low *bhut* who are attracted to it, the end result is the same; a woman is always safer "inside" ' (Blanchet 1984:48). There is a contrast between harmful autochthonous spirits of the 'outside' which endanger women, and beneficent Brahmanized spirits of cultivation which are endangered by women. But in both cases, purdah practices are protective. There is overlap in the case of the river, whose power either enables or destroys cultivation, but here, too, the association of women with fertility and prosperity in relation to the river depends upon its insulation from direct contact with female sexuality. The interfusion of earlier traditions with ideas from Brahmanical religion and Islam has given rise to contradictions in women's relationships with the spirits, sometimes being custodians, sometimes victims. (See Blanchet 1984:69–123 for an account of birth rituals.)

Women's experience of floods, then, is shaped by the necessity to maintain purdah and pollution-removal practices. Floods may cause women to temporarily abandon purdah and pollution-removal practices, as Ahmed and Shamsun Naher relate:

I have been to the fields twice, once when flash floods suddenly hit upon us, the crops would have been ready for harvesting in two or three days, but with the flood waters rising there was no way we could wait. Kamlas [labourers] could not be found and we couldn't even wait for them to be hired, so then I accompanied my husband to the field and did the harvesting along with him. No, no one spoke bad of me because it was such an emergency situation and then, every one else was in the same boat. But villagers refer to it as the bad times (*durdin*), when *even* women had to go to the fields.

(Ahmed and Shamsun Naher 1987:68)

When not forced out by such contingencies, women tend to be confined more than usual by floods. During *borsha*, the mobility of women may be curtailed, since their visits to each other are impeded by mud or water (Sushila Zeitlyn, pers. com.). During a severe flood (*bonna*), female mobility is severely restricted, since women's work is confined to the dry space of the bed. Flooding can also reduce restrictions on women since boat transport is facilitated: this is the traditional occasion for the *naior*, a wife's visit to her natal home, where she usually has much more freedom of movement and is fed better food than she would eat in her husband's household. Thus, for women and men there is a duality to floods. A particularly damaging flood, however, has more serious consequences for women than for men. In addition to women's work being confined and undervalued by men, wives in poor homes are perceived as a burden and finally deserted by their husbands during the severe impoverishment, which is the long-term consequence of flood disasters for the very poor.[2] The downward spiral of impoverishment, then flood-vulnerability, increasingly damaging floods and further impoverishment, has thus been steeper for poor women.

THE FLOOD OF 1988

In the summer of 1988, the river Buriganga suddenly flooded alarmingly so that two-thirds of Dhaka (later three-quarters) were underwater. Relief camps for flood victims were set up by the government, wealthy businessmen and various organizations. I regularly visited a camp in Azimpur, in the southeast of the city and also visited an island on the outskirts of Dhaka (Kamranghir Char), from which most victims in the camp had come. Kamranghir Char is a settlement of landless migrants from rural areas who came to Dhaka to find work (mostly as rickshaw pullers), and who live in the Char because rents are cheap owing to the low-lying area's vulnerability to flooding.

The government-run camp was directed by a city Commissioner, and the daily organization was managed on a volunteer basis by young men (mostly relatives of the Commissioner) from two organizations whose membership overlapped: the junior branch of the ruling Jatiya party, and a cultural group which performed Bengali plays. There were over 1,200 people in the camp, divided into 260 families, using six bathrooms into which the water flowed for about half an hour in the morning and an hour in the evening. Each adult received a half kilogram of uncooked rice (almost) every day. Food was cooked by individual households on their own stoves (*chula*) (see Shaw 1989).

Most people in the camp had already passed through two major stages: living on a raised bed in a flooded house followed by living on the roof. Once outside on the roof, people extended their usual flood strategies: bamboo platforms were built, and some people lived on top of their bed raised by bricks on the submerged roof itself. They carried as many possessions as possible on to the roof with them, and built shelters out of anything they could find. In one case two households had a jute sack stretched over a couple of square yards of roof space, which provided some privacy for women. Rickshaw pullers, all men, could still work as rickshaws and boats were the only viable forms of transport in much of the city. They worked in Dhaka, bought food and went back at night to their families on the roof.

For most families, considerable pressure was required before they left their homes for the relief camp. The risk of having their possessions stolen or squatters in their houses was thought to be worse than staying on the roof. Staying put meant not having a secure food supply or clean water, becoming ill without access to medicines, being bitten by the snakes which competed with people for shelter, and the attentions of 'muscle men' (pirates, *mastans*). Moreover, the reduced privacy, and thus purdah for women, would be completely lacking in the camp, compared with the shelters, a situation both wives and husbands were reluctant to have. Since Kamranghir Char is a community of migrant workers with kin and affines in different parts of the country, only very few women were able to make the *naior* to their natal home (which probably would also have been flooded). For many families it was the illness or near-accident of a child (usually falling in the water) which precipitated the move to the camp, as Muhammad, a rickshaw puller, recounts:

As we were living in an open space my children became very sick. Then I asked other people about a better shelter. They told me about this camp. We stayed on the roof for two days. Living on the roof is very dangerous. I couldn't go to work, leaving my children on the roof. I was worried about their health, problems with washing; and of course there's always a chance the children may fall in the water.

In the camp at Azimpur, households occupied a single mat each in the rooms and corridors of the school, their stove in front of them and their salvaged possessions (cooking pots, knife, a change of clothes and a couple of quilts) demarcating them from neighbouring house-holds. Most men worked pulling rickshaws during the day, often while weak and ill. The women mostly stayed in the camp, queuing for rice and medicines, cooking, caring for their children and visiting each other, the worst aspect being the difficulty in maintaining purdah. To be seen by strangers while washing, sleeping and especially eating (since a wife is defined as a provider, not a consumer, of food) caused them great shame. The latter was perceived by all as the cost of physical survival, but with far-reaching consequences extending beyond shame.

For instance, living in the camp (or on the roof of a submerged house) entailed exposure to the 'invisible hazards' of *bhut* and *batash*. All of the households in the camp had had at least one sick child, whose illness was usually attributed both to the camp's dirty conditions and to attack by a *bhut* or *batash*. Also, the camp was situated next to a graveyard, a favourite habitat of these entities.

The predicament of women who gave birth during the flood, and were unable to perform rituals to remove pollution and thereby protect themselves and the babies from *bhut* and *batash*, was perceived as particularly serious. A young mother in the camp, Halina, had given birth in her flooded house, and remained there with her husband for 3 days while her mother-in-law searched for a camp. Her mother-in-law, Momataz, was a midwife (*dai*), and described her problems in not being able to carry out birth rituals after the birth of Halina's baby:

It was in the morning when my grandchild was born. I was standing in knee-deep water in the room during his birth. As soon as it was over I came to Dhaka to look for shelter. After three days, when I went back to get them, it was impossible for them to get out of the house. The roof had to be taken off. As I knew many people in this neighbourhood, they gave me shelter in this camp. . . .

There are so many people here in this camp, she can't wash herself, or eat, or take rest. A new born child is not to be taken outside the house for the first seven days, but we had to bring the child out. Then the child is vulnerable to a *batash*. If a child is possessed by a *bhut* or *batash* he will stop taking any food and will be very irritated all the time. . . . Usually, we bury the placenta and the umbilical cord in the earth so that no *jinn, bhut* or *batash* can put their eye on it. When my daughter-in-law had the child I tied his placenta to a rock so that it wouldn't come up to the surface. After seven days the child's hair is shaved off. This hair too, we bury it. I have kept the child's hair. When we go home I will bury it in the ground. If this is not done, the child will get a very severe cold which will last a long time. If the mother doesn't follow the customs (*achan*) properly and does things which she is not supposed to do, this harms the child. The child becomes sick, and it may even cause the child's death. A new baby and the mother are not allowed to go out of the house for the first seven days, except for going to a doctor or a *fakir*. Because at this time they are unclean (*napak*): this will harm cattle, crops and other things.

Thus the flood was far more dangerous for Halina and her baby than for other women and children. Purdah and pollution beliefs transform the whole character of floods as 'hazards' for women, and this varies in degree not only between different women (poor or wealthy), but for the same woman at different times. This gendered nature of hazards also intersects with rural and urban contrasts.

For both men and women in the urban environment of Kamranghir Char, the duality of floods as both resource and hazard has disappeared: the men are not farmers who depend upon certain levels of flooding, while the women, usually far from their natal homes, cannot visit during a flood. A further contrast lies in men's perceptions of *bonna*, which rickshaw pullers in Dhaka do not, of course, define in terms of disruption to rice cultivation but, like women, in terms of water entering the house. Additionally, since the river, crops and cattle are no longer central to the economy of the residents of Kamranghir Char, women's 'ideal' behaviour and ritual observance no longer enhances fertility. It is interesting, however, that this relationship between women, cattle and crops was drawn upon by Momataz in explaining the negative consequences of the flood's disruption of women's birth rituals. But even this underscores the fact that for women, the negative consequences of uncontrolled contact with spirits of the land are a feature of urban as well as rural life, while the positive aspects of their relationships with certain of these spirits are not.

CONCLUSIONS

The deforestation theory of disastrous floods presumes a balanced 'natural' environment which does not include human culture and which is upset by (in this case local) human agency. Both of the favoured solutions – large-scale afforestation and embankment-building – imply that the forces of nature thus unleashed can only be returned to their presumed former equilibrium by applying specialized ecological and technical knowledge by western-trained experts. Such one-dimensional explanatory schemes, single-tracked upon a straight path, are based upon a perception of 'nature' and 'culture' as dichotomized entities which have 'an impact' on each other in mechanical Newtonian cause-and-effect sequences without being *instantiated* in each other. Thus the social and cultural nature (and consequently the heterogeneous, differentiated nature) of 'natural hazards' is disregarded. This chapter shows that floods not only have varying consequences for rich and poor, men and women, and rural and urban dwellers, but that their very nature as hazards is *constituted* by these and other forms of human social difference.

By overlooking this heterogeneity, large-scale afforestation projects and high-tech embankment projects fail to take account of their own differential consequences, in which they may themselves present hazards for the most vulnerable people. Certain afforestation projects, for example, have benefited industry rather than the rural poor (see Shiva *et al.* 1982) and, by failing to alleviate poverty, may in fact be contributing to further deforestation. As Currey observes, it is because the poor urgently need resources that the tree resource is being reduced, yet '[t]he same fences which keep the goats and cattle from reafforestation projects may also be the boundary lines for poor farmers who formerly grazed their goats on the scrubland' (Currey 1984:10). Similarly, the construction of embankments can reduce the soil moisture and fertility (Hossain *et al.* 1987:36; Rasid and Paul 1987:164), leading to deteriorating rice harvests for those farmers who cannot afford irrigation. Embankments can also reduce surface water and the latter's resources, upon which, as already seen, the poor particularly rely. Also, because husbands desert their wives and children during extreme hardship, any further impoverishment generated by such projects has more serious consequences for women and children than for men.

Setting aside such considerations, in a river system as vast, complex and shifting as that of Bangladesh, the practical problems of flood control by large-scale building of embankments are immense, and perhaps insuperable. In the end the vast sums of money may be 'poured into the water', a high-tech equivalent of the ritual offerings traditionally thrown into rivers. For Bangladeshi farmers, rickshaw pullers and most women the powers behind the rivers are considerably easier to negotiate with than the powers behind the World Bank, which are unamenable to local knowledge and established strategies. For many western aid organizations, however, disasters such as the 1988 flood are important resources ('We'll get three more jobs out of this flood', crowed an official from one such organization in Dhaka), as large-scale projects ('offerings') maximize the flow of money ('fertility'). This might be described as a new duality of floods, in which the agency of those in charge of mega-projects is augmented while the agency of the majority of Bangladeshis in their relationship to floods is impaired.

The perceived remedies are, to say the least, uncertain. Many geographers in Bangladesh are advocating alternatives to embank-ment-construction, for example, the development of local warning schemes, zoning and the support of indigenous strategies towards floods at village level (e.g. Islam 1986; Rasid and Paul 1987). It is even more important to recognize that since floods are constituted as environmental disasters by poverty and, additionally for women, by ideas of female pollution, they can be radically ameliorated by attacking poverty and empowering women.[3]

ACKNOWLEDGEMENTS

Fieldwork in Bangladesh in 1988 was financed by the Carnegie Trust for the Universities of Scotland and Edinburgh University. The Bangladesh Centre for Advanced Studies kindly allowed me to use their facilities in Dhaka. Thanks to: Atiq Rahman for encouraging my interest in Bangladesh, for exchanges of ideas and logistical help throughout my research; Sushila Zeitlyn and Rahnuma Ahmed who were also invaluable; former colleagues in the Department of Social Anthropology, Edinburgh University for their comments on an earlier paper presented in November 1988 at a meeting of the Scottish Branch of the Royal Anthropological Institute; the participants in the VIth EIDOS workshop on 'Cultural understandings of the environment' in June 1989 at SOAS for their discussion of an earlier draft; my greatest debt is to those in the Azimpur relief camp and in Kamranghir Char for their extraordinary patience and kindness during this research.

NOTES

1 This is less true of Christian women. Ahmed and Shamsun-Naher observed Christian women – especially older ones – working in the fields beside their husbands (1987:61–2).
2 The Association of Development Agencies in Bangladesh's Flood Disaster Report (1984) states: '[o]ne striking phenomenon is that no less than eleven organisations have reported increased instances of abandonment of wives and children by menfolk' (1984:2).
3 Female empowerment is likely to be, if anything, undermined by patroniz-ing attempts to 're-educate' women about purdah and pollution. Develop-ment programmes which increase poor women's access to economic and

social resources, on the other hand, can sometimes transform women's attitudes and relationships along with their economic security and opportunities (Chen 1986).

REFERENCES

Ahmed, R. and Shamsun Naher, M. (1987) *Brides and the Demand System in Bangladesh*, Dhaka: Centre for Social Studies, Dhaka University.

Association of Development Agencies in Bangladesh (ADAB) (1984) 'ADAB's Flood Disaster Report', *ADAB News* XI (6): 2–3, 6.

Bangladesh Agricultural Research Council (1989) Report on 'Floodplain Agriculture', Dhaka.

Bateson, G. (1972) *Steps to an Ecology of Mind*, New York: Ballantine.

Blanchet, T. (1984) *Meanings and Rituals of Birth in Rural Bangladesh*, Dhaka: University Press Limited.

Chen, M. A. (1986) *A Quiet Revolution. Women in Transition in Rural Bangladesh*, Dhaka: BRAC Prokashana; Cambridge, MA: Schenkman Publishing Co.

Copans, J. (ed.) (1975) *Secheresses et famines du Sahel*, Paris: Maspero.

—— (1983) 'The Sahelian drought: social sciences and the political economy of underdevelopment', in K. Hewitt (ed.) *Interpretations of Calamity*, London: Allen & Unwin.

Currey, B. (1984) 'Fragile mountain or fragile theory?', *ADAB News* XI (6): 7–13.

Eaton, R. (1985) 'Approaches to the study of conversion to Islam in India', in R. C. Martin (ed.) *Approaches to Islam in Religious Studies*, Phoenix: University of Arizona Press.

Hartmann, B. and Boyce, J. (1983) *A Quiet Violence. View from a Bangladesh Village*, London: Zed Press.

Hewitt, K. (ed.) (1983) *Interpretations of Calamity*, London: Allen & Unwin.

Hossain, M. A. T. M., Islam, A. T. M. A. and Saha, S. K. (1987) *Floods in Bangladesh. Recurrent Disasters and People's Survival*, Dhaka: Universities Research Centre.

Ingold, T. (1986) *The Appropriation of Nature: Essays on Human Ecology and Social Relations*, Manchester: Manchester University Press.

Islam, M. A. (1986) 'Alternative adjustments to natural hazards; implications for Bangladesh', Presidential Address, 11th Annual Bangladesh Science Conference, Rajshahi University, March 2–6, Section V: Geology and Geography.

Khan, A. A. (1974) 'Perception of cyclone hazard and community response in the Chittagong coastal area', *The Oriental Geographer* XVIII: 1–25.

Meillassoux, C. (1974) 'Development or exploitation: is the Sahel famine good business?', *Rev Afr Polit Econ* 1.

Park, C. C. (1981) 'Man, river systems and environmental impacts', *Progress in Physical Geography* 5: 1–31.

Ralph, K. A. (1975) 'Perception and adjustment to flood in the Meghna flood plain', MA thesis, Department of Geography, University of Hawaii.

Rappaport, R. (1979) *Ecology, Meaning and Religion*, Richmond: North Atlantic Books.

Rasid, H. and Paul, B. K. (1987) 'Flood problems in Bangladesh: is there an indigenous solution?', *Environmental Management* 11: 155–73.

Richards, P. (ed.) (1975) *African Environment: Problems and Perspectives*, London: International African Institute.

Sayer, A. (1980) *Epistemology and Regional Science*, Falmer, Sussex: School of Social Science, University of Sussex.

Shaw, R. (1989) 'Living with floods in Bangladesh', *Anthropology Today* 5 (1): 11–13.

Shiva, V., Sharatchandra, H. C. and Bandyopadhyay, J. (1982) 'Social forestry: no solutions within the market', *The Ecologist* 12 (4): 158–63.

Susman, P., O'Keefe, P. and Wisner, B. (1983) 'Global disasters: a radical interpretation', in K. Hewitt (ed.) *Interpretations of Calamity*, London: Allen & Unwin.

Torry, W. I. (1979a) 'Anthropological studies in hazardous environments: past trends and new horizons', *Current Anthropology* 20: 517–31.

—— (1979b) 'Hazards, hazes and holes: a critique of *The Environment as Hazard* and general reflections on disaster research', *Canadian Geographer* XXIII: 368–83.

Turton, D. (1979) ' "Comment" on W.I. Torry, "Anthropological studies in hazardous environments: past trends and new horizons" ', *Current Anthropology* 20: 532–3.

Watts, M. (1983) 'On the poverty of theory: natural hazards research in context', in K. Hewitt (ed.) *Interpretations of Calamity*, London: Allen & Unwin.

White, G. F. (ed.) (1974) *Natural Hazards: Local, National, Global*, Oxford: Oxford University Press.

13 'Arctic ethno-ecology'
Environmentalist debates in the Soviet North[1]

Igor Krupnik

For many years, I have been working on questions of demography and ecology among the Eskimo of the northeastern tip of Siberia facing Alaska, whose livelihood depends on hunting whales and other sea mammals; this in turn implies a very elaborate and subtle understanding of their environment and its capabilities. In this respect, the Siberian Eskimo are similar to other so-called 'small peoples of the North' in the Soviet Union, who all particularly depend on the resources of their natural environment.

Despite this dependence it is only very recently that the phrase 'traditional resource use among the peoples of the North' has begun to be heard more and more frequently in speeches, discussions and pamphlets about the Soviet North. It began with the first specialist conference on the subject held in Leningrad in March 1988, entitled 'The rational utilization and conservation of natural systems in the islands and coastal regions of the Arctic Ocean'. This was rapidly followed by articles and reports of 'round-table' discussions published in the official press. In a country where the development of the North was associated with large-scale industrial complexes in which highly paid immigrant whites extracted oil, gas, gold, diamonds and timber, the concept of 'traditional resource use' was, it seemed, no longer novel.

Simultaneously, three very important shifts in public perceptions of the Far North occurred. Firstly, it was recognized that the unbridled industrial expansion of the past had already ruined the ecological balance in many Soviet Arctic regions and that continuation would lead to an ecological catastrophe, especially for the native population. Two gigantic industrial projects became especially symbolic of this trend: the exploitation of the gas deposits in the central Yamal Peninsula (see Vitebsky 1990) and the construction of the Turukhansk hydro-electric dam in Evenk territory (Savoskul and Karlov 1988).

Both developments were officially halted as they threatened the culture of the indigenous population and their use of the environment.

Secondly, the press began to write openly about the alarming situation of the 'small peoples of the North' and the critical state of their economy, cultures and systems of resource use (Pika and Prokhorov 1988; *Sovetskaya Kul'tura* 1989). Thirdly and most importantly, in the opening of the Soviet Union's Far North there were numerous contradictory opinions on the peoples' future. Experts had never been unanimous, but the variety of opinions had never before appeared in the press. Indeed, some of these opinions have only taken shape in recent months during the course of new, more open discussions. All these viewpoints are directly related to Arctic ethno-ecology, since they tie the northerners' future either to preserving or to radically transforming traditional systems of natural resource use.

The first conception is that the basis for the existence of the northern peoples in the modern, changing world can only be their own native culture. Most anthropologists and 'old northern hands' agree on this (Institut Etnografii 1988). Accordingly, culture is understood as a broad complex of elements: occupation, productive skills, material culture, native language and intellectual heritage. Only the support, development, and often, revitalization or rebirth of native cultures, can preserve these small populations during intensive industrial development. Native tradition in this scheme remains in the rural population – the medium-sized and small settlements and the occupations such as reindeer herding, fishing and hunting. All need maximum support, especially reindeer herding, which is the only profitable way of life for the indigenous population and the most viable culturally.

Another argument is that the industrial opening of the north is progressive and inevitable and that, consequently, the small peoples will have to enter the 'big wide world'. This means maximum effort to include the northerners in industrial labour and contemporary city life, and to change their social structure radically, a position maintained by the Novosibirsk sociologists (e.g. Boiko *et al.* 1987). They believe that to support traditional cultures and forms of resource use and to preserve their environment is artificial, leading to archaization or to the 'establishment of reservations'.

However, there is a compromise: that the traditional branches of the economy must be stimulated by the maximum use of modern techniques and equipment, that is, they must be converted into a semi-industrialized form of resource use, including: construction of gigantic fences around reindeer pastures; making permanent shelters in the field with all modern conveniences; having a shift system for reindeer herding and hunting; and modern types of portable dwelling. Thus, 'a new life' will unfold in the forest and tundra, with a modern life style in well-equipped villages constructed by the generous hand of the state.

Another suggestion is that the people's future must be sought by economic and social restructuring in the spirit of the contemporary reforms occurring in society at large, which include cost-accounting (*khozraschet*) and flexibile development planning, brigade contract and family contract, co-operative principles and individual initiative (see Humphrey 1989; Vitebsky 1989), and consequently, inevitably there will be some production expansion with conservation, tourism and commercial land use becoming economic. Thus, the worst problems of the past will disappear giving way to good sense, economic initiative and popular policies, arguably the most propitious formula for the northern peoples.

Finally, more researchers, practical workers and the northerners themselves now perceive the future to lie in the development of a genuine native autonomy, based on maximum growth of local self-government and economic and legal independence of each community – a route that is the most difficult. Autonomy in the realm of economic and social policy means that any minority must evolve a new relationship with the state, with other peoples, with researchers and especially with their own land – the setting of their lives and source of their livelihood. It is argued that a concern for the future evolves from responsibility, with the possibility of taking independent decisions. Pika and Prokhorov (1988) argue: 'Let people decide for themselves what is best for them: traditionalism or industrial development, reindeer or oil, ethnic subsidies from the state or economistic approach.'

Experience in the non-Soviet Arctic shows that reforms, choices and debates stimulate interest in national traditions of resource use, cultural values and the experience of subsistence activities, resulting in new ecological perceptions. While it is recognized that most north-erners can no longer live exclusively on hunting and fishing, reindeer herding or hunting sea mammals, it is also acknowledged that these activities must be an option available to all – as permanent employ-ment, a source of additional income or, ultimately, as a way of preserving cultural traditions and a native way of life.

The possibility of returning to their native land must be available both for today's inhabitants of the Arctic and for their descendants. Popular ecological movements march under the banner of 'for ourselves and for our grandchildren'. People fight for the present to save the future for all and this has been written into the first ecological manifestos of the Soviet northern peoples, which have recently appeared in the press (e.g. Aipin 1989).

Popular ecology movements also seem to have their own logic of development: starting from separate appeals, manifestos and petitions, growing into mass protests against specific technical projects and then arriving at the concept of the rational long-term use of resources combined with mandated popular representation. The fight for clean land and water and for preservation of hunting grounds and pasture thus becomes indistinguishable from cultural, ethnic and even sociopolitical demands. This was certainly the pattern followed by the Canadian and Alaskan Eskimos, American Indians and Scandinavian Saami and is likely to characterize the course of development for the Soviet northern peoples. This was evident by summer 1988 when the need was expressed for a new organization – the Association of the Peoples of the North – which would represent the indigenous cultures of the twenty-six small peoples of the Soviet North. The Association was finally established in spring 1990. Local cultural clubs and societies were formed in the main towns of autonomous provinces and regional centres. Simultaneously, increasing criticism of paternalistic attitudes embraced the plundering of resources and the bureaucratic mismanagement by which government agencies deprived northerners of any present or potential, intelligent long-term utilization of the riches of their land. Hence, ecology, cultural tradition and ethnic politics become indivisible.

Researchers, practical workers and representatives of the northern peoples for the first time planned a meeting to evaluate the native experience of resource use across the entire Soviet Far North – to take place at an all-union scientific and practical meeting entitled 'Traditional forms of natural resource utilisation among the population of the north', organized by the Soviet Committee of the UNESCO programmes on 'Man and the biosphere' and the Soviet Cultural Foundation. The subjects on the agenda include: contemporary legal, economic and social problems in the use of the environment by the native and the long-standing Russian populations, i.e. the earlier peasant settlers rather than the more recently settled industrial workers and managers; the conditions of northern ecosystems and their safeguards; the delineation of ecological and ethnic boundaries; the preservation of native traditions and the contribution of local experience to contemporary systems of rational resource use; and finally the role of traditional uses of resources in preserving the languages and cultures of northern peoples. All these are critical issues which are of urgent interest to applied anthropologists in the new field of Arctic ethno-ecology, a field whose development nobody could have foreseen even 15 years ago when I began my field work in the Far North.

NOTES

1 A longer version of this paper was translated by Piers Vitebsky.

REFERENCES

Aipin, Y. (1989) 'Not by oil alone', *Moscow News* 2: 9–10; English version reprinted in *IWGIA (International Work Group for Indigenous Affairs) newsletter* 57 (1989): 136–43.

Boiko, V. I., Nikitin, Y. P. and Solomakha, A. I. (eds) (1987) *Problemy sovremennogo sotsial'nogo razvitiya narodnostey severa* [Problems of the contemporary social development of the nationalities of the North], Novosibirsk.

Humphrey, C. (1989) 'Perestroika and the pastoralists', *Anthropology Today* 5:3, 6–10.

Institut Etnografii (1988) *Etnokul'turnoye razvitiye narodnostey Severa v usloviyakh nauchno-teknicheskogo progressa na perspektivu do 2005 g* [A perspective to the year 2005 on the ethno-cultural development of the nationalities of the North under conditions of scientific and technical progress], Moscow: Institut Etnografii.

Krupnik, I. I. and Chlenov, M. A. (1988) *Budushcheye korennogo naseleniya Sovetskoy Arktiki: kontseptsii razvitiya i rol' gosudarstva* [The future of the indigenous population of the Soviet Arctic: conceptions of development and the role of the state], Leningrad.

Oborotova, Y. A. (1988) 'Narody severa v sovremennom mire: vzglyady i pozitsii' [The peoples of the North in the contemporary world: views and positions], *Sovetskaya Etnografiya* [Soviet Anthropology] 5: 146–51.

Pika, A. and Prokhorov, B. (1988) 'Bol'shiye problemy malykh narodov' [The big problems of small peoples], *Kommunist* [The Communist] 16: 76–83, translated in *IWGIA Newsletter* 57 (1989): 122–35.

Savoskul, S. S. and Karlov, V. V. (1988) 'Turukhanskaya GES i sud'ba Evenkii' [The Turukhansk hydroelectric scheme and the fate of Evenkland], *Sovetskaya Etnografiya* [Soviet Anthropology] 5: 166–8.

Sovetskaya Kul'tura [Soviet Culture] (1989) 'Na perelome' [At the turning point] (transcript of a round-table discussion between specialists), 11 February.

Vitebsky, P. (1989) 'Reindeer herders of northern Yakutiya: a report from the field', *Polar Record* 25 (154): 213–18.

—— (1990) 'Gas, environmentalism and native anxieties in the Soviet Arctic: the case of Yamal Peninsula', *Polar Record* 26 (156): 19–26.

14 Landscape and self-determination among the Eveny

The political environment of Siberian reindeer herders today

Piers Vitebsky

INTRODUCTION

I shall discuss the role of landscape in the former Soviet Union, among two neighbouring groups of Eveny (pronounced Evény, singular Evén), native reindeer herders who straddle the Arctic Circle in Siberia.[1] In talking of 'cultural understandings of the environment', the environment need not be envisaged as something given, onto which human consciousness in any form (such as culture) imprints itself. Children's books are illustrated by landscapes where volcanos belch flames over lush forests alive with dinosaurs, busily eating the trees and one another. What fascinates the viewer is that although the artist appears to have been an eye witness, and although the landscape could hardly be called deserted, it remains terrifyingly lonely. The worst thing that could befall a time traveller would be to become marooned in such a place, for this landscape pre-exists all human consciousness.

As we can now witness it, however, there can be no landscape which is not already moulded by human consciousness and does not in turn form part of it. Anthropologists have explored the use of landscape as a map of society which functions as a map of morality and of the sense of personhood, e.g. Basso 1984; Vitebsky (in press). I shall take this for granted in order to focus on how this landscape is defined and used as part of a wider 'environment', one that is as much political as literal. In this sense, the political aspect of environment is not limited to 'environmentalism', though this is now a powerful force in Soviet politics. The Eveny are a community whose basic economic activity, reindeer herding, keeps them in close contact with the landscape. At the same time, they are a sophisticated people, fully integrated into a large and complex bureaucratic state. The major local political development among the Eveny from 1988 onwards has been their demand for an administratively 'autonomous *rayon* (district)' of their own.[2] This had existed in the past but was abolished in 1962, when each of the two settlements was allotted to a different neighbouring *rayon*. In September 1988, the demand seemed far-fetched to senior officials in Yakutsk, the regional capital, but by mid-1989 it had been granted. This chapter will explore, not so much how they achieved their demand so quickly, as the strands of meaning which this has had for the Eveny themselves in relation to their 'natural', social and political environment.

Like the rest of the country, the native reindeer herders of the Soviet North are undergoing a period of intense change. Perestroika (reconstruction) is envisaged simultaneously as a political, economic and social process (cf. Zaslavskaya 1987) and a process of moral cleansing (Gellner 1990). Above all, it is ideological, involving a fundamental reassessment of the relationship of the state to its citizens and of their mutual obligations. At the heart of this lie democratization and decentralization. Ethnic groups, and indeed all Soviet citizens, have thus been presented with a situation which arises in history only rarely: they are poised at a decisive moment in the development of the encapsulating state which gives them the possibility of renegotiating their own position in the overall picture.

Yet, as Humphrey put it in her study of the Buryat some 1,300 miles to the south, 'Soviet culture . . . repeats itself but does not reflect on its own nature' (1983: 375), leading to the problem of deciding 'what it is to live to good purpose in Soviet society' (ibid.). Looking back at the Buryat in the 1960s and 1970s, Humphrey now writes:

> It is not easy to discover the political attitudes of minority peoples of the USSR in the pre-glasnost' period. Any such idea . . . exists in a context consisting of the domain of possible concepts. 'Possible concepts' include memories, ideas expressed in dialects or the vocabulary of special groups, latent and about-to-be-formulated notions, and ideas which cannot be stated in given political circumstances.
>
> (Humphrey 1989a: 145)

What light can we throw upon this problem today, one so obscure and yet so absolutely central to our understanding of the Soviet Union?

Ethnicity is a major force in Soviet society today. Lenin originally regarded 'nationality' as something which would fade away as socialism developed, in favour of class – an expectation which has not been fulfilled. Simultaneously, he established a principle of acknowledgement of ethnicity, such that many peoples received territorial autonomy in the region where they were most concentrated – at various levels, partly but not entirely reflecting the group size. Thus some peoples, like the Georgians, Armenians, Latvians and Estonians, have fully-fledged Union Republics. Descending the administrative hierarchy, many others have autonomous republics, *okrugs* and finally *rayons*. The degree of autonomy which some of these titles confer is questionable, especially since the titular people are often outnumbered by (mainly Russian) immigrants. None the less, ethnic territory remains an important constitutional principle in the Soviet Union.

The whole of Siberia is attached to the Russian Federation (RSFSR), an enormous area which is equivalent to a Union Republic except that it contains the capital, Moscow, and the heartland of the USSR's dominant people, the Russians. Apart from the larger Buryat and Yakut, Siberia (broadly defined) contains around thirty small native ethnic groups, belonging to several language families and each numbering from a few hundred to a few thousand. In most of the Soviet north, reindeer herding is the main or only viable form of native economy. Since plants here grow slowly, herds range over a vast area in complex seasonal patterns and human populations are thinly and widely scattered. In several places herding is badly affected by competition from mineral extraction, an industry which mostly employs immigrants from the European parts of the USSR, who live in large settlements and greatly outnumber natives. This is especially severe around Tyumen' in western Siberia, a region with the world's biggest reserves of oil and natural gas which has been the scene of well-publicized battles between energy ministries and a combination of native and environmentalist groups (Vitebsky 1990a).

My fieldwork was conducted in the Verkhoyansk Mountains, some two thousand miles to the east of Tyumen' and three to four hundred miles north of the regional capital, Yakutsk. Here there is no direct competition from the minerals industry. About 17,000 Eveny are scattered across northeastern Siberia in small groups hundreds or even thousands of miles apart (Levin and Vasil'yev 1964). Those in the Verkhoyansk Mountains are one of several small ethnic groups within the Yakut Autonomous Republic, an area roughly the size of India within the Russian Federation and containing one million people. Here there is extensive intermarriage between the Eveny and the regionally dominant Yakuts. Though virtually all Eveny now speak Yakut rather than Even as their main language, incoming Yakuts are still assimilated to Even identity, which is sustained by a combination of their distinctive occupation of reindeer herding and of long-established government policies granting special privileges to the smallest ethnic minorities.

In these mountains, the nomadic Even reindeer-herding clans were collectivized in the 1930s into several collective farms (*kolkhoz*) and the resulting settlements were further reorganized in 1961 as two State Farms (*sovkhoz*) centred around the villages of Sakkyryr (on maps often given as Batagay-Alyta) and Sebyan-Kyuyel', situated some 250 miles apart on either side of the Arctic Circle with an Even population of 783 and 655 respectively, plus some 3,000 Yakuts, Russians and others, mostly in Sakkyryr (see Figure 14.1) Despite these population figures, the tone of the area is definitely Even. Each farm consists of a central village of substantial wooden houses containing administrative offices, a community hall, kindergarten, school, hospital, stores, airstrip, a cattle farm, a fur farm, veterinary facilities and slaughter-house. Outside, anywhere between 50 and 200 miles away are sprinkled a dozen or so reindeer herders' camps. Each camp contains a 'brigade' of 6-7 herders. In winter they share a wooden hut, while in summer, each member lives in a canvas tent shared perhaps with a few dependent relatives and helpers.

This landscape is vast. The Verkhoyansk Mountains rise to nearly 8,000 feet and form the highest rim of the bowl which in winter encloses the deep frosts of the coldest area in the entire northern hemisphere, with temperatures often dropping to -70°C. The short summers are often hot, but since the ground below the surface never thaws, melting groundwater drains badly, mountain slopes are often boggy and the countryside then swarms with mosquitoes. Between them the two *sovkhozes* cover an area the size of most of England. Reindeer herding under these conditions (far tougher than in Scandinavia) requires 150 acres of pasture per deer. As a production system, it depends on an intimate knowledge of one's animals and of the latter's interaction with the landscape. It uses a special vocabulary and imagery of reindeer markings, behaviour and moods, with unceasing teamwork from before dawn till after dark among a handful of people who for weeks on end, year in, year out may see nobody but each other. Reindeer herding here is thus a profession in which productive work is clearly indistinguish-able from a whole way of life and its culture.

Contours are intersected by streams which flow into fast-moving rivers and brilliant blue lakes, all frozen hard in winter. Though helicopters are also used, Eveny travel mostly by pony in summer and by reindeer sledge or snow scooter in winter. From my own journeys, I remember the unending winter movement on sledges up and down the steady slopes of frozen rivers with their huge turquoise slabs of buckled ice; or the sparse larch forest turning vivid gold in autumn, throwing into relief the burnt out areas of forest fires, dated by their new growth and linked to people's own lifespans.

Across this landscape run pathways and boundaries of the mind.

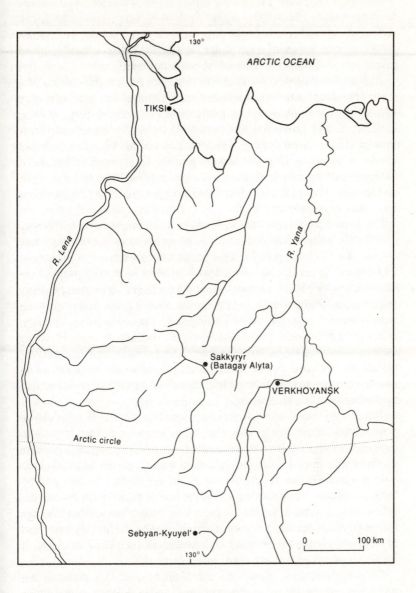

Figure 14.1 Location map of Sakkyryr and Sebyan-Kyuyel'

Those of the administration include, most importantly, the boundary between the two *rayons* which separate the two farms and their satellite herding camps. There is also a plan devised by agricultural scientists in terms of agronomy and carrying capacity, which determines the locations and dates of each stage of the brigade's annual cycle of migration. Brigades are not named but numbered.

Against this vastness, human shelters assume great significance. Away from the camps are innumerable places suitable for overnight stays containing stacks of ready-cut poles on which a canvas can be hung. Equipment and provisions are stockpiled in huts or on tree platforms (*arangas* [Even, from Yakut]). The focal point of any village or mountain shelter is the stove. Here the crackling of the fire frequently 'speaks' to humans and anyone whose attention it catches can divine by listening for its message. The spirit of the fire (*Tog* [Even]) is given the first portion of any meal, especially any alcohol, before humans can eat or drink, and will not allow a newcomer to sleep easily until it has been fed in this way.

Though shelters outside the village now consist of canvas ridge tents over a frame of larch poles, people retain a strong memory of the tepee-like conical *ilumo* (Even) covered with reindeer hide. Any point on the landscape which has been humanized with a lingering human presence, may be signified by a replica of the *ilumo*: burials in the wild are marked with a shelter of three poles leaning together, containing sacrificed reindeer remains and various deliberately broken household effects such as a sledge, a tin bath or, for a child, toys. Until recently, a person's afterbirth was also buried under a miniature *ilumo* in a site called *golomo* (Even), so that older people know and visit the sites of their own and other people's afterbirths.

These and other sites containing spirits embody suggestions or possibilities about what one should or might do: they crystallize moments of choice. It is inadvisable to sleep with your head pointing downstream, in case your soul is carried away with the flow; you must always leave a cigarette, coin or sweet on any grave you pass and not look backwards when moving away, for fear of enticing the deceased to follow you. Shamans' graves are especially dangerous and best avoided unless you have special protection. In addition to the fire, the behaviour of animals, plants, the weather and dreams all furnish clues about the future to which people are constantly alert.

People often work alone and travel alone over this immense and dangerous landscape in an atmosphere of independence, sound judgement – and fear. They huddle round the stove, with their backs to the wilderness, scaring themselves with an exchange of true-life ghost stories, many set in lonely night halts.

THE PETITION FOR THE RESTORATION OF THE EVEN *RAYON*

During my fieldwork, there was another constant topic of conversation: the need for the restoration of an 'autonomous' Even national *rayon*. The Eveny are particularly concentrated in this corner of Siberia and during a liberal moment in 1930 they were given their own *rayon* – the Sakkyryrskiy *rayon*, which somehow survived the abolition of many similar *rayons* in the less liberal later 1930s. However, in 1962, under a sweeping policy of 'amalgamation' or 'enlargement' (*ukrupneniye*) of *rayons*, it was broken up. Sakkyryr village was given to Verkhoyanskiy *rayon* and instead of being a *rayon* centre itself, became an outlying upland outpost in another *rayon* whose centre was the town of Batagay. The smaller village of Sebyan-Kyuyel' was assigned to Kobyayskiy *rayon* with its capital at Sangar, a coal port on the river Lena and virtually inaccessible across the Verkhoyansk Range. Both these *rayons* are more populous and are dominated by Yakuts or Russians.

Some large-scale amalgamations were seen as a mistake and in 1965 certain abolished *rayons* were reinstated. Sakkyryrskiy *rayon*, however, was not restored because of its small population and economy and its abolition remains a source of bitterness to this day. At the time any protests were in vain and no public moves for reinstatement were made until early 1988 when, after developments in the Baltic and the Caucasus, the Central Committee of the Communist Party of the Soviet Union was planning to hold a Plenum on 'the Party's nationality policy under contemporary conditions'.[3]

In anticipation, some Eveny in both villages began openly to discuss the question of restoration (*vosstanovleniye*) of their former *rayon* and by August–September 1988, the 'rayon question' (*vopros rayona*) had become one of the main topics of conversation, rivalling even ghosts and omens. I was briefed on it several times a day in both official and private conversations. The management of one *sovkhoz* even asked me to appear on television in Yakutsk advocating their cause (an invitation which I declined).

Each village had held meetings and reformist factions had drafted a letter addressed in Russian directly to Mr Gorbachev and the members of the Central Committee of the Party. Copies of these were shown to me and later published in the local press.

The letter from Sakkyryr starts 'We, Veterans of War and of Labour [titles awarded by the state], Even by nationality . . .' and declares the support of the signatories for a declaration by the Central Committee regarding the 'right of a people to self-determination (*samoopredele-*

niye)'. Summarizing the history of the area since 1930, the letter continues by saying that under the enlightened national policies of Lenin the *rayon* and its inhabitants became independent, happy and successful and there developed both a Soviet way of life and the culture of a small people (the contradictory ideal of Soviet nationality policy). All this was changed in 1962 when without apparent reason the *rayon* was split 'forcibly' and the link between Sakkyryr and Sebyan-Kyuyel' sundered. The request for its restoration along with certain others which had been restored in 1965, was refused. Since then, the letter declares, life has been difficult. These difficulties are then itemized as follows:

1 Because of their small numbers, the Even population are forgetting their own language and culture. In Sakkyryr (the village with a large population of non-Even), the language is not taught in any school.
2 Because the *rayon* administrative centre is so far away, the local population lags behind in ideological work, aesthetic and spiritual (*dukhovnyy*) education, the preparation of national cadres, and educational facilities.
3 Though it was recognized 4 years ago the gene bank (*genofond*) of cattle (a special hardy local kind) is not being developed.
4 Transport has deteriorated since there are no direct services between the two villages, which can now communicate with each other only through Yakutsk. There are now no direct flights to Yakutsk from Sakkyryr, the former *rayon* capital, either. Passengers often have to wait days in Batagay (the new *rayon* centre) for a connection. The people of Sakkyryr have enlarged the airstrip themselves to take larger aircraft direct from Yakutsk but the aviation authorities refuse to send them.
5 Construction of housing, etc. is delayed by the inadequate transport facilities, since all outside materials must be flown by this long route.
6 Transport of freight connected with the national economy is difficult, for the same reason.

The letter ends by saying that conditions are even tougher in Sebyan-Kyuyel' and then by giving the combined vital statistics of the two *sovkhozes* which would make up the new *rayon*: a population of 4,500 with 1,000 children in three middle schools, inhabiting five village *sovets* (councils) and farming 36,000 reindeer, 1,255 cattle and 2,450 horses. The income from furs is 215,000 rubles and the annual turnover of the two village stores is over 4 million rubles. Finally, the writers state that the Eveny and the Yakut are 'kinsfolk by their origin and historical development' (this is to avoid the charge of 'nationalism') and the letter is signed by '15 Eveny' (named separately) 'and many others'.

The letter from Sebyan-Kyuyel' opens by calling on the spirits of glasnost', perestroika and democratization in order to undo the effects of the 'stagnation' (*zastoy*, the official term for the Brezhnev era, as opposed to today's 'reconstruction', *perestroyka*), then points out that of the 17,000 Eveny scattered across eastern Siberia, the Sakkyryrskiy *rayon* before it was split was their only administrative unit. All sorts of otherwise apparently unrelated problems are ascribed to this abolition:

> The Eveny of Verkhoyaniya have lost their national autonomous status, which has given rise to negative tendencies in our lives. For example, in recent years the provision of fuel and electricity has become a serious social problem. At present more than 65% of homes are heated by iron stoves. A stove's average annual consumption of firewood is over 40 cubic metres. Around 70% of our motor transport capacity is tied up just with fetching firewood. . . .
>
> The loss of our national status has been the main reason for the loss by us, and especially by our children, of our national culture, our language and our national distinctiveness (*samobytnost'*) . . . There are many similar examples of unresolved problems. One of the most burdensome is the absence of regularly functioning transport and postal links with the *rayon* centre and the capital of the republic. Delays in air services, our only link with the outside world, can last up to 20 days or more. . . .
>
> We hope that the former Sakkyryrskiy *rayon*, as a national focus for the worthwhile development of the culture, economy and national characteristics of the Even population of Eveniya, will be restored. The path of genuine international development [i.e. multi-ethnic within the Soviet context] is opening up in front of our children.

The *rayon* status was granted in summer 1989, just under a year after these letters were written.[4] This came about partly as a local concession related to the Yakuts' own demand, now under negotiation with Moscow, for upgrading from an Autonomous to a Union Republic (Vitebsky 1990b). But above all, the demand fitted in perfectly with the nationwide move towards decentralization. To understand the local implications of this, it is necessary to examine the effects of the centralizing programmes of the past 50 years.

Collectivization began in the late 1920s and early 1930s and aimed to bring about the socialist transformation of the agrarian society of the

European part of the USSR. On ideological grounds it was applied without appropriate adjustments to nomadic herders (who, like the peasants, often resisted fiercely). Here, it had at least two aims. The first was to 'rationalize' herding by subordinating herders' practice to expert advice. The second was to 'civilize' the herders by settling them in central villages. The results were only partial and the 1950s to 1960s saw a further large-scale transition to a 'sedentary' (*osedlyy*) way of life throughout the native Soviet north. The abolition of the Even *rayon* at this time was linked to a parallel process of 'enlargement' (*ukrupneniye*) on a more intimate domestic scale across the Soviet north. Small settlements were combined so that instead of 5,000 deer a farm might have 15,000; instead of 400,000 or 500,000 hectares it might have 1,200,000 or 1,500,000 hectares (Lashov 1973: 97). A large proportion of the population deserted the reindeer-herding camps and moved into the central villages where schooling and medical facilities were provided. Indeed most such villages were formed only at this time.

Yet the reindeer still needed to remain out in the forest, moving around an extensive annual cycle, attended by herders living in tents. The result was an administrative distinction between the earlier 'nomadism as a way of life' (*bytovoye kochevaniye*) and a newly introduced 'production nomadism' (*proizvodstvennoye kochevaniye*). In the former, the entire family lived and moved together: this was eroded in the 1930s and eliminated in the 1960s, when all children of school age were removed to the village for education, usually followed by their mothers. In the latter, the care of reindeer is isolated from its social base and reduced to a worker's job like any other – herders working together are supposedly no more than workmates as in a factory.

Though the intention was also to intensify the attack on the patrilineal clan as the basis of social organization, the removal of women and their children to the villages was justified by economic rationality. 'Production nomadism' was to include only 'the able-bodied population directly concerned with reindeer herding – the members of the herding brigades (herders, tentkeepers), for whom in a given system of carrying out their work nomadism is essential', as Lashov (1973:94) put it. It was not going to include, as way-of-life-nomadism had done, those 'not directly involved in reindeer herding, i.e. those for whom nomadism is not essential for production' (ibid.). Lashov spells out who these are: 'hunters, fishermen, craftsmen, whose activity is possible even without any connection with reindeer herding, and their families, and also strictly speaking the members of reindeer herders' families' (ibid.).

Those 'not directly involved' in reindeer herding outnumbered the herders by about 5 or 6 (ibid). They consisted of wives and any other adults not formally employed as herders. Such people were considered to be 'unutilized labour resources' (ibid.: 96, 107–8), and the problem was to ensure 'the development . . . of occupations for *kolkhozniks* [or *sovkhozniks*] previously not occupied in the common economy (*obshchestvennoye khozyaystvo*)' (ibid.: 99). According to this policy, the 'full use' of female labour depended on the development of settled occupations quite distinct from reindeer herding (ibid.: 111–12). To this end, secondary occupations were introduced, especially the rearing in cages of fur-bearing arctic foxes – though today women are tied to the village not so much by these as by the proliferation of 'clean' jobs like administrator, accountant and teacher.

The official attitude to the landscape is significantly revealed by the criteria for choosing sites for the central settlements of these enlarged farms. These should be chosen with an eye to the development of the new branches of the economy, with ease of import and export of materials (ibid.: 97–8). Ease of access to pastures was contra-indicated since it limited the scope of the other branches (ibid.: 98) and Lashov gives examples where sites were chosen according to the herders' needs and were therefore 'mistaken' (ibid.: 93, 97). Farms had 'failed' because of this until they were 'liquidated' and relocated in more suitable sites. Clearly, the intention was to isolate herding from the rest of life and push it outwards to the margins of a space now occupied by a new centre which to the herders was becoming largely inaccessible.

The long-term aim was to bring even the fully occupied herders into the village to live and fly them out to the pastures by helicopter in shifts (modelled on a system used elsewhere in the Soviet North for industrial workers and miners). For reindeer herders at least it has since been acknowledged as a failure, largely because with the lack of continuity herders ceased to know their own animals, pastures and landscapes. The introduction of other forms of production has proved equally unsuccessful: while reindeer herding still produces a handsome profit (despite growing social problems), all other activities run at a heavy – and by now planned – loss.

The social consequences of 'enlargement', however, were set. Placing children in central schools means that for herders the family no longer lives together. Thus in attacking the clan, the policy destroyed the nuclear family and tilted the balance between village and camp decisively in favour of the villages which it had established. The relationship of kinship to territory was also broken. Before the 1930s, the landscape was also a map of social relations in a way which is no longer possible today. Each patrilineal nomadic clan had its own territory over which their reindeer moved constantly with the seasons in search of pasture. Segments of a clan, or individual tentholds, combined and separated in a variety of ways reflecting the economics and micro-politics of the moment. Today, clans no longer regulate marriage and since the 1960s, even marriage between the two villages has fallen off owing to lack of transport across the *rayon* boundary.[5]

The camps in which I lived were typical demographically of all reindeer-herding areas of the northern USSR. One contained men of various ages while all the women except one were elderly and there was only one child, a baby. Another consisted entirely of men since the only woman, a girl of 18, had just moved to another camp to live with her boyfriend. Despite the significance of herding for the economy, only 101 out of Sebyan-Kyuyel''s population of 655 are employed as herders; out of 308 children of school age, not one lives permanently in the camps and only 30–40 spend their summer holidays out there – that is only those whose closest relatives are herders. Only 19 of the 101 herders are women (one is a brigade head) and only three of these are under 30 while eleven are pensioners (a number of other retired people choose to live in the camps and work part-time). The majority of men, especially the younger ones, are thus bachelors – either metaphorically, in that most young wives remain in the village, or else literally: 37 of these 82 male herders are unmarried. So, apart from the pensioners, each camp generally contains a salaried female 'tentkeeper' (*chumra-botnitsa*) who cooks for the working herders.

The absence of family life is very obvious in the style of a bachelor tent. Although larch fronds are carefully spread on the ground to form a dry floor on which reindeer skins are spread for sitting or sleeping, they are dirtier than women's tents. In the latter, heavy boots are left outside or else just inside the doorway, and only light indoor shoes or socks are worn inside. The bachelors, by contrast, wear their heavy, muddy boots inside the tent. The tone is generally coarser and the absence of women is a constant preoccupation.

CULTURE, LANDSCAPE AND TERRITORY

What is the connection between this kind of frustration and the demand for autonomy? The first generation reared in the boarding schools of the 1960s, with their unfulfilled domestic lives and their lack of proper training in herding, has come to maturity just in time for the opening up of discussion which has accompanied perestroika. Just as the landscape is socialized by virtue of human habitation, so it is politicized by the very need to decide how it is to be used and by whom. Indeed, because it is now permitted to talk about this, the landscape has been revitalized as a political idiom and is more laden with meaning than at any time since the 1930s.

Today's situation in the USSR raises the problem of choices, since every citizen is obliged to make weightier decisions than before, and not simply by voting at free elections. Thus, though herders welcomed the newly introduced family contract (cf. Vitebsky 1990c), which may help to keep families together, and though management assumed that every brigade would adopt this system, by late 1990 only three brigades in Sebyan-Kyuyel´ had actually done so. The reason given for this was caution about making a commitment to a scheme which would drastically alter one's life but, it was still believed, could at any moment be reversed. Thus, uncertainties at the most direct level of dealing with the landscape (storms, loss of livestock) are matched by uncertainties in the political environment: even though one must act, people fear that the latter may still retain some of its arbitrariness.

Krupnik's contribution to the present volume (Chapter 13; cf. his *Arkticheskaya Etnoekologiya* [Arctic Ethnoecology] 1989) lays out the main strands in the expanding array of political possibilities, the alternative paths of 'development', for Soviet northern people. These are common to many parts of the world and are perhaps particularly reminiscent of the native American Arctic and sub-Arctic in the early 1970s, a region about which Siberian natives are becoming increasingly aware. However, the presence until recently of the Communist Party, and the exceptional power of the ministries which extract raw materials (and which play the role of both ministries and corporations in the west), introduce complex and unpredictable elements.

The native peoples are well informed and articulate, and realize that if they do not move quickly to control this unstable situation themselves, then others will continue to do it for them. It is this, I believe, which explains the timing of the Even move to have their *rayon* restored. The uncertain combination of vehemence and pragmatism which this calls up is well conveyed in a letter written to a local newspaper by Vasiliy Pavlovich Keymetinov, a clever and eccentric old Even poet:

The Eveny received the Great October [i.e. the Revolution] like the rising of a resplendent sun. . . . The Eveny do not cease and never will cease to utter words of gratitude to Soviet power. [However, times changed since then and difficulties arose. But now] the time has come for a general regaining of sight. The right to speak openly has been given to all. Bitter thoughts have been dragged to the surface, hidden in the depths of people's souls for many, many years. [Perestroika has allowed] the righting of mistakes and injustices of the stagnation era. . . . That is why I was among those Veterans of Labour who first raised the question of the Even National Rayon.

(in *Leninets* [The *Leninist*, published in Sangar], 3/11/88, p. 3).

The sense of indignation is palpable, as old people recalled when interviewed by the newspaper:

Three representatives came, called everyone together in the club in the evening and told us: 'Till yesterday you were in Sakkyryrskiy *rayon*, from tomorrow you'll be in Kobyayskiy.'

No-o-o! There was no debate. They didn't even allow us to ask questions. They gave us to understand it has all been decided – that's that, and it's not for you to discuss it.

I was out hunting at the time. I came home and found that we already belonged to another *rayon*.

(ibid.)

Discussion and lobbying about old wrongs is a new phenomenon, and in a volatile climate the style was and is uncertain. In contrast with this 'publicist literature' (*publitsistika*), old forms and old cautions are still observed in the text of the letters to Gorbachev and the Central Committee. I shall discuss in particular how vague and underplayed the cultural arguments are, in favour of the economic and the logistical. The first letter stresses the practical impediments to development which it claims spring directly from the abolition of the *rayon* and would be put right by its restoration. Probably to emphasize this, several closely related items (e.g. nos 2, 4, 5 and 6 (p. 230)) are spread out under separate headings, where they are little more than parts of the same point, i.e. the increased difficulty of transport.

The stated or implied economic difficulties concern the import of materials and the export of produce, but do not impugn production itself in the primary secor (effectively, of course, mostly reindeer). Indeed, great emphasis is put on their productivity and consequently on the turnover of the retail stores (despite the stores' reliance on air transport to bring in goods). The meaning of the figures given at the end of the letter is spelled out in yet another letter sent independently to Gorbachev around the same time by five residents of Sakkyryr and later published in the same issue of *Leninets*:

Some people think that the quantity of gross production is too small for the restoration of the *rayon*. This is not true. One *sovkhoz*. . . yields more than some separate *rayons*. And together . . . they yield more than three *rayons*. . . . We count on your wisdom and support.

(p. 3)

This often-repeated point seems designed to counter what I found in Yakutsk to be virtually the only overt argument against the restoration of the *rayon*, that the population and economy were too small to be viable. The Even radicals' argument is that the *rayon* would be economically viable despite the small population. Indeed, this smallness is turned into a virtue since it gives an extremely high rate of productivity and per capita income. The area is already financially self-sufficient and has a strong profile in the press of the Yakut Republic for winning many productivity prizes. Thus, the 'lagging behind' (*otstavaniye*, difficulty no. 2, p. 230) is in no way admitted to lie in the economic realm.

Where, then, is 'lagging behind' acknowledged to exist? It is in the realm of culture, yet this term seems strangely rhetorical, mentioned but circumscribed and concealed in conventional, highly Soviet formulae. It is taken for granted that 'culture' refers to the kind most closely associated with political health in the orthodox sense, in the areas of ideology and education. Though the Russian phrase for this is 'spiritual' (*dukhovnaya*) culture, this has of course nothing to do with spirits (*dukhy*), but everything to do with the great Soviet value of being 'cultured' (*kul'turnyy*), a term which suggests approbation of civilized values on a much wider scale than its equivalent in English. The Eveny whom I know are not short on this kind of cosmopolitan culture. They read Russian and foreign classics and subscribe to the reformist Moscow magazine *Ogonek* in their tents, where I saw old ladies discussing the pictures of Salvador Dali among many other topics. Many people have been schooled in Yakutsk and further trained in Khabarovsk, Ulan-Ude or Leningrad (a quarter of the way round the globe); they work as sailors in the Arctic and the tropics and take their holidays in Mongolia, Prague and on the rivieras of the Crimea and Bulgaria.

What is not revealed in the petitions is their concern about another form of culture – their inner culture. This brings us to the detailed texture of ethnic consciousness. Many Eveny are or were members and officials of the centralized Communist Party (now defunct) or the civil authorities; everyone has a greater or lesser knowledge of three languages, each with quite distinct implications; and all 'Eveny' have many recent 'Yakut' ancestors and continue to intermarry with 'Yakut'. None the less, where power relations and marginalization are partly tied to ethnic boundaries, and when Even ethnic identity is being consciously strengthened (e.g. through pressure for more Even-medium schooling), we can say that however diverse or integral it may be, Even ethnic consciousness will have at the very least an outer and inner surface.

The 'outer' surface contains local elements which are also acceptable in the outside world because they correspond to supposedly universal (in Russian *obshchechelovecheskiy*, 'pan-human') and thus presumably wholesome values. For example, the view of the reindeer herder as lover of the wide open spaces strikes a chord with the European romantic tradition of nature appreciation, which is common in Soviet thought right down to illustrated magazines. Similarly, native arts, crafts and costumes are approved, especially when they are seen to use local materials. Perhaps in this category belong novels in the classic European tradition but written about native themes in the native language.

Such aspects of a culture can be commoditized and captured by visiting impresarios (including ethnographers). Novels can be translated. This is a native culture about which an outsider could theoretically know as much as a native. Exteriorizing one's inner self in this 'negotiable' way to a partner with greater power, carries the risk that one will do so at a poor rate of exchange so that the self will end up cheapened. As elsewhere, the museification and prissification of 'cultures' is widespread in the USSR (the Soviet nadir is surely the costumed folk-dance ensemble). This reification can enter one's own consciousness. I saw practical processes such as meat and fish preparation and preservation in the camps being discussed, imitated and looked up in books as ethnic delicacies by white-collar workers in the village. Such people could also be more punctilious in their observation of taboos than were full-time herders, but at the same time more bookish.

What is the inner part of Even culture, in the sense of being inalienable? This is something which is not mentioned in the letters to Gorbachev but which underlies many remarks I heard and seems to be struggling through to the surface of Vasiliy Pavlovich's letter, forming a curious blend with his otherwise elaborately diplomatic phrases. It lies in a range of realms: in kinship and its close correspondence to labour; in the way in which reindeer range across the mountains and the location of persons, events and moods in this landscape; in the conceptualization of these as spirits, with their continuing implications for the unfolding of a person's destiny. This kind of culture is generative and regenerative: it is hard to package since when put in an ethnography or a novel it dies.

It is this sense of culture which was recognized and expressed in the old shamanistic worldview, until very recently the most condemned and persecuted. Spirits and omens constitute a reservoir of meanings with scope for interpretation and potential for activation. By telling stories, one explores the rules of how these meanings work; by remembering them in context, one considers whether and how they apply to one's own life. I learned that one should not sleep with one's head downstream only after my host realized one morning that we had indeed done so. The fact that we had not lost our souls during the night did not undermine the prohibition: it was a failure of respect (*uvazheniye*) on our part towards the landscape as a whole and he would make a point of being more careful next time.

Humphrey (1983: 409) observed that rituals on a Buryat *kolkhoz* in the 1960s and 1970s were not merely survivals of a dying Buryat religiosity, but realistic responses to contemporary problems to which Soviet ideology provides no answer and which it even masks. Among the Eveny in 1988–90, such ideas and practices remained central to one's sense of self even among Party members, officials and activists. Ghosts were sometimes seen while going home from Party meetings. An unrepentant Stalinist lit his stove from scratch at great inconvenience on a hot day and tossed the first glassful of vodka into the flames. He explained that because he fed the fire regularly, he had no fear of shamans. The constant checking of minor omens everywhere among almost everyone I know suggests a moment-by-moment fine-tuning of one's sense of personal destiny and a continuing fragility of control both in trivial matters and at turning points in one's own biography – at moments of illness, exams, entry into the army or stages in one's career.

An accommodation had been reached between these beliefs and life articulated through the Communist Party, which until mid-1990 still dominated the channels for career satisfaction and counted a healthy membership among the reindeer herders. Indeed, just as elsewhere in the country, the Party's very monopoly made it inevitable that it would shelter an internal opposition under its umbrella. Many who have been active and outspoken over the '*rayon* question' have been intellectuals with roots in reindeer herding who are now office holders and white-collar workers, and were largely Party members. When signing petitions they added 'member of the Party since 19xx'. I was told both that they were fulfilling a Party member's duty to express an opinion in a time of debate, and that they felt they had a particular right to expect to be heard.

It may be that the accommodation between traditional beliefs and the Party remained fairly stable under the stagnation, but now that the Party itself was undergoing rapid disintegration, so this accommodation, and one's sense of self, had to change. Thus what has been growing is not a *sur*vival, but a *re*vival. Throughout the former USSR, this was already feeding back into the official level of high 'culture', where the encapsulation of the local has spilled beyond the bounds of official control. In much of the Soviet North the packaged, negotiable form of local culture has joined up with the Green movement to provide native writers and other intellectuals with a platform from which to fight mineral-extracting ministries. In the 1989 elections to the Moscow Chamber of People's Deputies, a number of natives stood as candidates across the North and were elected, despite the fact that in every case natives were heavily outnumbered among the electorate by Russian and other settlers. In one region near the Chinese border, a female native ethnographer defeated the Commander-in-Chief of the armed forces of the entire Soviet Far East. The day was won largely by a blend of environmentalism and an appeal to 'justice' (*spravedlivost '*) for the region's small native peoples, on the grounds that natives know best how to use the landscape in an environment-friendly way.

The tone of this kind of appeal can be seen in an article by Yeremey Aypin (English Aipin), a native Khant writer who was elected as People's Deputy for a region at the heart of the west Siberian oil industry. In a piece tantamount to an election manifesto, he recounts how his father's boots were stolen by two (Russian) oil workers on a January night so that he had to return home in his socks.

> The next winter his sledge, pulled by three dogs, was stolen from him in the logger village. The timber felling enterprise cut down all the trees on the tribal cemetery thus ruining the final resting place . . . during his 76-year lifetime . . . he had not once plucked a fir needle or a leaf, not a blade of grass unnecessarily on his land, on the land of his ancestors. He can't understand why they cut down his pine grove if the logs still lie in stacks needlessly rotting. . . . My father has been in a sort of trap. Further west down the Agan there is the town of Pokachi bossed by the Pokachi oil and gas company. In the north there is the town of Kogalym . . . bossed by another oil company. In the east up the Agan there are geologists' settlements . . . and the town of Raduzhy bossed by the Varyegan oil and gas company.
>
> 'What do you want old man?' I ask my father. 'Can I help you?'
> 'I don't want anything', he says after a long silence. 'Only my land.

Give me my land back where I can graze my reindeers, hunt game and catch fish. Give me my land where my deers are not attacked by stray dogs . . . where the rivers and lakes have no oil slicks. . . . Just a patch of my own land.'

What can I say in reply?

(Aipin 1989: 137-8)

This is a new tone in Soviet regional politics. Born of a combination of the writer's skill and the greater desperation existing in oil areas, it shows the extent to which Vasiliy Pavlovich's letter by contrast represents a new idea still couched in old language. But despite the diversity of tone in different Arctic regions, the goals are similar. Aipin goes on to call for 'sanctuaries, reservations, autonomous territories' where his people could use the land under 'self-government (*samo-upravleniye*)' and be guaranteed immunity from drilling activities and their accompanying pollution and poaching. Here the bounding of a group's own life, in the sense of exerting their own political control, is made to depend directly on the maintenance of a bounded territory.

However, this approach is not such a counsel of despair as the English word 'reservation', with its North American overtones, might suggest. The concept of the autonomous territory is a traditional Soviet one; while the sense of landscape which it can be made to protect, is the foundation of a people's 'inner culture'. Used in this way, a landscape commands a sweep of meaning which gives it a continuing power to unite a person's outer and inner life. On the one hand, it provides a map for the overlay of administrative boundaries, the sites of camps, depots, pastures; it is the object of official plans, calendars, reports on vegetation and calculations of carrying capacity, annual yield, etc. On the other hand, it encompasses the sites of animals' activities and behaviour, the graves of ordinary persons and shamans, and the burial sites of afterbirths – features which, by their contribution to one's own life story and store of memories, contribute to the sum of one's own person (and, in their various permutations, of the persons around one). The persistence of omens can be explained by their foundation on this landscape, recharged by constant contact and use. They form part of a habitus (Bourdieu 1977) or sense of aesthetics which makes the question of literal 'belief' a secondary one.

At the same time, this landscape also allows this interior culture to be exteriorized in a manner which shields it from appropriation by others. In confrontations between small, ecologically vulnerable minority cultures and a centralized state, the culture has weak bargaining power because the state sees itself as transcending any 'culture' and as representing objective reality. Thus across the Soviet North, the protest movement aims to shift the emphasis from non-renewable mineral resources worked by immigrants, to renewable resources such as reindeer and fish. In these terms, the natives become the only people competent to handle this landscape. The Russian word for 'to develop' or 'to open up' supposedly undeveloped regions is *osvoit'*, derived from the adjective *svoy*, 'one's own', meaning literally 'to make one's own'. Thus when Aipin (1989) and others call for the creation of 'reserves', this is meant not in a defensive sense, but as part of an assertive attempt to clarify whose 'own' land this is to be. This is a way of standing the gas and oil ministries' model of landscape on its head and forcing recognition that landscape does not simply exist as a given. The oil and gas ministries are dinosaurs, not simply in the obvious sense of being enormous, thick-skinned and obsolete, but also because they still graze on a supposedly pre-conscious or pre-human landscape. Ministries see only 'natural resources', which they have a brief to 'make their own'. Natives see cultural resources, threatened by the ministerial interpretation of them as merely natural. The native strategy must be to place the disputed resources in an arena where their new-found moral power (aided by a largely sympathetic press) forces the ministries to accept a compromise, elements of which include the notion of regulation by local authorities as well as of financial compensation for land used or ruined – a new concept in the Soviet Union, where land and natural resources were earlier deemed to have no price or value (Vitebsky 1990a: 23). In this way a skill like reindeer herding is presented, not as a part of a culture, but as an ecologically unchallengeable achievement of a particular group of humans in the face of nature. The soft, inner side of Even culture cannot allow itself to be exposed as culture at all, but presents itself as in the petitions to Gorbachev, as a rival objective reality cast in the idiom of a hardheaded practicality. In this form, it is negotiable, and at a high rate.

Behind this lies a layer of culture which has always resisted centralization and indeed could not survive it (hence the paradox implicit in the first petition, that centralization has diminished access to the central form of culture). For decentralization will not entail simply putting right one unfortunate mistake or injustice, as stated in Vasiliy Pavlovich's letter. Even the most practical of the petitions' concerns implies a systematic critique of every aspect of centralization. This created a contradiction between one's private, inner feelings about the landscape as a home, and an official view of it as a gigantic, open-air factory floor. In the latter view, the homogenized landscape is stripped of all meanings except the economic, which operates in a currency to which all other meanings can supposedly be reduced. One mountain, one pasture, one region is exactly like another. As Lashov (1973) showed, this inflexible approach spreads beyond land to encompass persons. It persists even under the new, enlightened 'family contract' which is now being offered, where every brigade is still allotted an identical production plan regardless of the age and strengths of the herders, or of the differences in pasture freely noted in the veterinary master plan (cf. Humphrey 1989b for a similar problem in southern Siberia). Decentralization reasserts the uniqueness of the landscape, just as of every other aspect of human life. The landscape is proving vaster than the ideology which would deny it.

The autonomous *rayon* provides a ready vehicle for this. Starting from landscape as the ground of their most intimate existence, it represents the Even consciousness of landscape writ large onto the official world of map space. Here it creates an enclave where Evenhood can be considered and discussed, and where the development of Even-language teaching programmes does not need to be justified. An autonomous *rayon* defines this landscape as an Even one. Being a classic Soviet expression of territoriality, it legitimates this definition in a (negotiable) language which is understood on both sides and where powers and rights are in principle agreed. Though those other native Siberian peoples (not all) who do have autonomous territories (including those in the western Siberian oilfields) have not yet gained the control they want over outside intervention, they do at least have an administrative framework through which to fight – as now do the Eveny.

What does this tell us about the dilemma pinpointed earlier by Humphrey, how to live to good purpose in the Soviet Union? The Eveny share with the rest of the USSR the same uncertainty in the thread which leads from one's culture as the centre of one's consciousness (or in which one shares one's consciousness with others), through the growth of the market and of ideological pluralism, to an outside world which is no longer based on a Stalinist dualism in which one is supposedly sure on which side one ought to stand. If it was not easy to discover political attitudes before glasnost', because they were heavily veiled, now it is difficult for a combination of both the old reason (which still lingers) and of its opposite, an exuberant explosion of articulate self-expression.

Now there are so many possibilities, and no proposal is ruled out. Any suppressed aspect of pasturing, family life, political representation or religion can be selected as good and campaigned for. There is a heady sense of living on a knife-edge, as writers and informal organizations in Moscow and the regions produce manifestos and lists of demands. At the same time, there are still ambiguities and uncertainties about the levels at which it is safe to commit oneself openly. 'People remain cautious about the family contract, and were careful to keep ethnic mysticism out of their letters to the Central Committee.'

Amidst all this, the Eveny have a real moment of choice, to which they have responded with brilliant opportunism. But it is difficult to predict the future. Since the 1930s, socialism has challenged shamanism in the public arena, driving it first underground and then near to extinction. Former shamans I met seemed to fall into two distinct types. Some would tell in detail about their former spirits and spells, while others were extremely reticent. The former probably had accepted their abandonment of the tradition, while for the latter it remained alive. But what has certainly disappeared from shamanism is its -ism (cf. Basilov 1984 for a distinction between shamanism as a system and 'shamanry' as an array of unsystematized survivals). It seems likely, at least among the Eveny I know, that divination has expanded to fill the vacuum left by the retreat of shamanism as organized public practice.

If the native peoples of Siberia represent a post-shamanistic society, they were also moving towards a society which would become post-socialist. I also heard of expectations of the imminent reincarnation of deceased shamans, suggesting the persistence of ideas about cyclical time. It is unclear whether these are going to become serious, but they suggest that despite the decay of the clan and the problem of transmission in an oral tradition, the move towards a post-socialist society may include an element of re-shamanizing – perhaps in a 'cultured' form based on reading ethnographic texts, combined with a rediscovery of the landscape.

NOTES

1 I carried out fieldwork in August–September 1988 and in March–April and August–December 1990. Thanks to: to the Academy of Sciences of the USSR, the University of Leningrad, the British Academy, the British Council, and the Wenner-Gren Foundation for Anthropological Research. My debts to local people are enormous and will be acknowledged in detail in a future monograph. None of these people is responsible for my interpretations here. The USSR, or Soviet Union, ceased to exist as this article was going to press. These names have been retained here since they applied to the period under discussion. The whole of Siberia and of the former Soviet North remain inside the new Russia.

2 All foreign terms used here are Russian unless otherwise stated. Transliteration of Russian follows the system used in *Soviet Geography*. The languages used locally are Even (belonging to the Tungus-Manchu family) and Yakut (generally considered to belong to the Turkic family with strong Mongol influences). I have transcribed these words as I heard them locally. The Even people were formerly known as Lamut and are not to be confused with the closely related Evenk, formerly known as Tungus.

3 This Plenum was delayed several times and finally took place only in late 1989.

4 In the event, the village of Sebyan-Kyuyel' remained outside the new *rayon*, which thus consists only of the village of Sakkyryr. Instead, Sebyan-Kyuyel' has acquired its own form of self-government through the unusual status of a 'national village council' (*narodnyy sel'sovet*), for reasons involving old clan rivalries between the two villages, so that influential groups within the smaller Sebyan-Kyuyel' were reluctant to place themselves under the dominant clans of Sakkyryr. The present status of Sebyan-Kyuyel' is lower than that of a *rayon*, but those who finally came out against joining the *rayon* controlled from Sakkyryr are now pressing for the formation of a national *okrug*. This is higher and would encompass the whole or parts of four *rayons* where there is a significant Even population. Under this arrangement, if it is achieved, the economic dominance of Sakkyryr will be diluted while the undisputed cultural purity of Sebyan-Kyuyel' will be at a premium.

5 It is significant that it was this question of territoriality which has called forth the strongest expression of clan identity in recent times (see note 4).

REFERENCES

Aipin, Y. (1989) 'Not by oil alone', *Moscow News* 2: 9–10; English version reprinted in *IWGIA* (*International Work Group for Indigenous Affairs*) *newsletter* 57 (1989): 136–43.

Basilov, V. N. (1984) *Izbranniki dukhov* [Those chosen by the spirits], Moscow: Politizdat (trans. and ed. P. Vitebsky in preparation, Oxford: Blackwell).

Basso, K. (1984) 'Stalking with stories: names, places, and moral narratives among the Western Apache', in E. Bruner (ed.) *Text, Play and Story: the Construction and Reconstruction of Self and Society*, Washington, DC: Proceedings of the American Ethnological Society.

Bourdieu, P. (1977) *Outline of a Theory of Practice*, R. Nice (trans.), Cambridge: Cambridge University Press.

Gellner, E. (1990) 'Perestroika observed', *Government and Opposition* 25:1, 3–15.

Humphrey, C. (1983) *Karl Marx Collective: Economy, Society and Religion in a Siberian Collective Farm*, Cambridge: Cambridge University Press.

—— (1989a) ' "Janus-faced signs": the political language of a Soviet minority before glasnost", in R. Grillo (ed.) *Social Anthropology and the Politics of Language*, London: Routledge.

—— (1989b) 'Perestroika and the pastoralists', *Anthropology Today* 5 (3): 6–10, June.

Krupnik, I. (1989) *Arkticheskaya etnoekologiya: modeli traditsionnogo prirodopol'zovaniya morskikh okhotnikov i olenevodov Severnoy Yevrazii* [Arctic ethnoecology: models of traditional resource use among sea hunters and reindeer herders in Northern Eurasia], Moscow: Nauka.

Lashov, B. (1973) *Nekotorye voprosy razvitiya natsional'nykh rayonov kraynego severa* [Some questions of the development of the ethnic regions of the Far North], Yakutsk.

Leninets [The *Leninist*, local newspaper published in Sangar, Yakut ASSR], 3 November 1988.

Levin, M. G. and Vasil'yev, B. A. (1964) 'The Evens', in M. G. Levin and L. P. Potapov (eds) *The Peoples of Siberia*, Chicago: Chicago University Press.

Vitebsky, P. (1989) 'Reindeer herders of northern Yakutiya: a report from the field', *Polar Record* 25 (154): 213–18.

—— (1990a) 'Gas, environmentalism and native anxieties in the Soviet Arctic: the case of Yamal Peninsula', *Polar Record* 26 (156): 19–26.

—— (1990b) 'The Yakut', in G. Smith (ed.) *The Nationalities Question in the Soviet Union*, London: Longman.

—— (1990c) 'Centralized decentralization: the ethnography of remote reindeer herders under *perestroika*', *Cahiers du monde russe et soviétique* XXXI (2–3), avril–septembre: 345–56.

—— (in press) *Dialogues with the Dead: the Discussion of Mortality, Loss and Continuity Among the Sora of Central India*, Cambridge: Cambridge University Press.

Zaslavskaya, T. I. (1987) 'Socioeconomic aspects of perestroyka', *Soviet Economy* 3 (4): 313–31.

Name index

Subject index